P. 60
P. 66 - eval. criteria

The Evaluators' Eye

"A unique and never-again-to be-repeated study. Derrick tracks the views and approaches of peer reviewers in assessing research impact, as part of the UK's 2014 Research Excellence Framework (REF) exercise. Unique as no one has looked at the peer review of impact in this detail; never-again-to be-repeated as REF is the first time that research impact was assessed on a national scale. A must read for anyone interested in the assessment of research impact. A thoughtful, salient and important book."

—Jonathan Grant, *King's College London, UK*

Gemma Derrick

The Evaluators' Eye

Impact Assessment and Academic
Peer Review

palgrave
macmillan

Gemma Derrick
Lancaster University
Lancaster, UK

ISBN 978-3-319-63626-9   ISBN 978-3-319-63627-6   (eBook)
https://doi.org/10.1007/978-3-319-63627-6

Library of Congress Control Number: 2017959337

Cover illustration: Science Photo Library - PASIEKA / Getty Images

Printed on acid-free paper

This Palgrave Macmillan imprint is published by Springer Nature
The registered company is Springer International Publishing AG
The registered company address is: Gewerbestrasse 11, 6330 Cham, Switzerland

Para Ruben and Dario—solo tengo mis ojos para vosotros

Preface

The title of this book has two connotations. The first is that it is a look at evaluative practice and peer review through the eyes of the REF2014 evaluators, and the second relates to the way in which the value of Impact is constructed within peer review panels. The apostrophe in the title is purposefully placed to acknowledge that through peer review, despite involving a number of experts and a plethora of their expert opinions, the group processes the evaluation as one, through one eye.

For Impact, it is this eye which determines its value.

This book is the evaluators' story of valuing Impact. Their interactions, debates, deliberations and struggles ultimately defined the operationalisation of the Impact criterion in the UK's 2014 Research Excellence Framework (REF2014). This perspective is different from those stemming from the numerous articles, critiques, commentaries and the inevitable politics published in the wake of the REF2014.

The UK's REF2014 represented a brave step forward in research evaluation by including a formal criterion around Impact. This brave step was made not only by HEFCE, the government department behind the implementation of REF2014, but also by the evaluators themselves. In the midst of my fieldwork behind this book, one participant told me that he hoped that my work would provide the praise and acknowledgement that the evaluators deserved. Indeed, by engaging with this group of experts, I have come to appreciate the bravery with which these evaluators approached assessing Impact, a virtually unknown concept. Sure, it is easier to champion new endeavours in academia if you have already been awarded a professorship and/or are widely acknowledged as a leading voice in your profession, but these evaluators still did it and they did it sometimes in the face of increased negativity and doubt from the mainstream press, UK HEIs, international critics and even their own peers.

There is also a contradiction implied within the title between an idealised approach to peer review, which is by definition deaf to the political, economic and social distractions beyond academia; and Impact, which by its nature values these very distractions. Yet, peer review was chosen as the very tool to evaluate the political, economic and social outcomes from research (Impact). Can it be done? Should it be done? And what exactly is the problem surrounding the use of the "gold standard" of research evaluation to assess the societal benefits of research. This book does not necessarily problematise this approach or that of the REF2014. Rather, through a methodologically rigorous design which utilises the very best that qualitative research has to offer, this book highlights that the future objective of Impact assessment should not be to get a different or better outcome, but rather should be focused on how we can get peer review panels to work smarter around this ambiguous concept. Impact is a normative and subjective concept that is sensitive to changes in its value as public perceptions and requirements from research shift, and therefore the challenges facing peer review panels when faced with Impact are also liable to change. Working smarter therefore implies an approach whereby peer review panels make not necessarily better decisions but decisions that reflect a rigorously expert-led process that maintains the integrity and legitimacy of peer review decision making. This book offers a number of ways in which this can be achieved, and therefore a number of recommendations for governments around the world looking to formally include a research evaluation criterion about societal impact.

Centre for Higher Education Research and   Gemma Derrick
Evaluation, Lancaster University, UK

Acknowledgements

This book is the result of three years of research that I conducted as part of a Future Research Leaders Fellowship awarded by the UK's Economic and Social Research Council (ESRC: Grant reference: ES/K008897/1). I am grateful to the many people, especially those involved at the pointy end of the production of this book, who supported me in this work.

I am grateful to Dr Gabby Samuel who has been my partner in crime for much of this project, as well as to a number of people who read over previous drafts of this book and/or provided comments, ideas and feedback. Their names, in no particular order, are Prof Murray Saunders, Prof Richard Sullivan, Dr Ingeborg Meijer, Dr Claire Donovan, Dr Karin Tusting, Dr Kirsty Finn, Dr Koen Jonkers, John Whitfield, Prof Jordi Molas-Gallart, Prof Phillippe Laredo and Prof Paul Ashwin. I am also grateful to a number of people in the field who have supported and fostered this work over the last 4 years. They are too numerous to list here, but we see each other regularly at conferences and exchange ideas and aid where needed. To you all I am forever grateful.

Finally, and more importantly, I would like to thank my boys Rubén and Darío, both of whom have been extremely patient while I prepared this book. I love you both.

Contents

List of Figures

List of Tables

1

Impact from the Evaluators' Eye

Critiquing peer view doesn't always win friends among academic colleagues!
Personal correspondence sent to the author, July 2016

If you read nothing else about the UK's Research Excellence Framework (REF2014) and the Impact criterion, then let it be this book.

Not because it is a critique of the REF2014, it isn't, but because this book is about the most important mechanic of the REF2014 and one that has been vastly overlooked: the evaluators. The evaluators had a mammoth task. In light of no precedent, little experience and monstrous professional and political pressure, they embarked on evaluating an object that was considered a new influence using the very traditional evaluation tool of peer review. Specifically, this book examines how evaluators navigated this object, together, and the importance of group dynamics in attributing value to ambiguous evaluation objects such as the Impact criterion.

I do not question the evaluation outcomes, but by examining how these outcomes were reached, I do question how these evaluators worked.

© The Author(s) 2018
G. Derrick, *The Evaluators' Eye*,
https://doi.org/10.1007/978-3-319-63627-6_1

To clarify, it is not just a question of whether these evaluators came up with the right answer or not, but instead to focus how they worked and in the future how they can work smarter.

So while this is not a book about the REF2014 per se, it is a book about what goes on behind the REF2014 and its evaluation processes. This is the evaluators' story.

This book is also about Impact.

When the UK government first announced its plans to not only recognise the importance of the societal impact (Impact) of research, but to award funding on the basis of its evaluation as part of the 2014 Research Excellence Framework (REF2014), there was an explosion of dissent from the academic community. Part of this discontent was based on a fear that a focus on Impact would steer research in undesirable directions, and another part stemmed from misgivings surrounding the nature of Impact, its assessment and how value can be attributed to such a broad concept. Despite numerous studies on the aspects of Impact and its evaluation, understandings of the concept and models of Impact evaluation remain merely theoretical. This book turns the focus away from Impact as the subject of an evaluation, and towards Impact as a process of valuation through the eyes and actions of REF2014 evaluators. Because for me the value of Impact cannot be made independent of the process used to assess it.

So, finally we have peer review, the domain where a value was assigned to Impact. Peer review, as with most evaluations, is a construct. It is not a naturally occurring process, but instead is constructed from the public's need for accountability and transparency, the academic community's desire for autonomy, and a political need for desirable outcomes achieved through a fair process (Chubin and Hackett 1990; Dahler-Larsen 2011). An ingrained pillar of academic life and governance, group peer review works by allowing for contesting and conflicting opinions about a concept to be played out, and negotiated in practice. All academics are conditioned towards the importance of peer review; we question its outcomes (How could I not get that grant!) but accept them because we believe that our peers and experts have valued our proposals as worthy (or not) based on a shared understanding of what is considered as excellent in research. This shared understanding is less clear for Impact, which is a new, uncertain and ambiguous evaluation object, one that as a concept is forever in flux, and one where our regular peers are not necessarily Impact experts. In theory, peer review appears the perfect tool for evaluating Impact as, during this flux, it provides an excellent forum where competing ideas can be aired in practice. However, as a construct, the practical necessities of the evaluation, where mechanics are used to frame and potentially infiltrate debate, question the purity of the process as expert-driven, as well as the suitability of peer review as a tool to value ambiguous objects.

Combining these three concepts is a difficult marriage to make, but by considering them together I bring the field out of the theoretical and hypothetical, and into an empirical world. For this book, all previous (and current) debates about Impact including how to measure it, what it is and how to capture it are put to the test within a peer review evaluation panel. Within these groups, panellists interpret and define these conceptual debates and meanings of Impact among themselves before producing evaluation outcomes. For this study, I was motivated by an overarching objective of exploring the suitability of peer review as a tool for assessing notions of Impact. Specifically, I focused on whether I could understand how the group's dominant definition influenced the strategies developed to value Impact (the evaluators' eye); the extent to which peer review as a constructed exercise helps or hinders the evaluation of ambiguous objects; and the extent to which the Impact evaluation process was at risk of the drawbacks associated with group behaviours. By considering the attribution of value about Impact as a dynamic process, rather than one that is static and dependent on the characteristics of the submissions alone, this book alters the focus to go beyond sedentary debates about the definition, nature and pathways to impact, and instead look at how notions of research excellence beyond academia are played out within groups of experts. What emerges is a totally different focus of how to understand Impact, one that considers that the real value of Impact cannot be divorced from how evaluators play out their evaluation in practice, within their groups. Viewing the challenges facing Impact evaluation on the group level, rather than solely at the individual evaluator or individual case study level, changes (for the better) the types of recommendations that are available for future assessments.

Why Study Peer Review and Impact Together?

Plenty is already known about how experts straddle the concept of excellence or scientific impact in peer review panels. Likewise, there has been a large amount of new research concerned with models of research impact assessment; however, few pieces of research bring these concepts together in order to study them empirically. As two difficult and, until now, independently considered areas of study, this book has its work cut out for itself in bringing these together. However, this book also testifies that there is no way of understanding Impact that can be separated from the practice of its evaluation and valuation by peer review panels. Within panels, concepts and meanings are assigned to submissions that demonstrate Impact, and the result of these evaluations is as much to do with the social interplay of evaluators as it is with the attributes of the submissions themselves.

Too many studies have focused too much on the attributes of the submissions (REF2014 Impact Case studies) and cross-referenced these with the results of the evaluation, labelling these as examples of Impact without understanding how such assessments were formed. This rather simplistic assumption, where too much attention is paid to a submission's attributes, overlooks the importance of the group-based dynamics around the outcomes. It is somewhat foolish and perhaps naïve to assume that the value of difference in Impacts can be determined without considering how this value is deliberated by the peer review panel. In this way, the book takes you on a journey with the REF2014 Impact evaluators as they reason among themselves about what constitutes excellent and, by proxy, valuable Impact.

This is interesting because not only are academics essentially novices when it comes to evaluating Impact, so too in essence are the "users" or the non-academic experts included in the evaluation process. In fact, previous studies have found that if the choice of evaluating Impact is made by peers, rather than by indicators, then it is difficult to find peers with "experience" of this type of evaluation. Research has shown that *"scientists generally dislike impacts considerations"* as it *"takes scientists beyond the bounds of their disciplinary expertise"* (p. 244) (Holbrook and Frodeman 2011), and, as such, many scientists and stakeholders alike struggle with evaluating the concept.

Whereas the involvement of experts and peers brings status and credibility to the process (Gallo et al. 2016), evaluation is highly subjective and even more so when dealing with a unique and problematic criterion such as Impact. The incorporation of "societal impact" as a criterion for peer review can be described as a Kuhnian revolution for research evaluation (Lee 2012). As such, in order to achieve a revolutionary change towards considerations of societal impact, the idea must be constantly debated, redefined and reformed before the new paradigm is adopted. An important implication of using peer review is therefore that during the period of time in which the paradigm shift is occurring, there are multiple scientific contenders who support highly variable viewpoints, making it challenging to achieve consensus. The dynamics of these multiple contenders is expected to be heightened in peer review panels, where the peers driving the evaluation are a subset of this community-wide tension, and are tasked with the evaluation of this unknown criterion within a specified time limit. Ironically, peer review as a system aims to protect evaluations from social, political and economic influences (i.e. non-academic), and yet evaluating Impact requires panels to consider these very social, economic and political influences. This contrast, if nothing else, makes impact assessment within peer review panels an intriguing process that relies more heavily on social interplay than expertise and experience for its valuation.

A methodological strength of this study was the inclusion of pre-evaluation interviews with the panellists. By sampling the opinions of panellists before they engaged with the evaluation, I was able to gain a raw, baseline understanding of the values around Impact, free from any follow-on constitute/perverse effects (Dahler-Larsen 2007, 2011, 2012, 2014) that may have stemmed from Impact being more institutionalised with time. Furthermore, these pre-evaluation views were free from any implicit learning that would have been gained through participating in any prior formal evaluation of ex-post Impact. The REF2014's Impact criterion presented a unique opportunity to not only gain these baseline opinions, but, through triangulation with the post-evaluation interviews, explore how views had changed as a result of the evaluation process. Gaining these views in later evaluations, REF-related or otherwise, would not have been possible as all pre-evaluation views would have been tarnished by previous association with the REF2014, or else from the tacit learning of Impact more broadly.

So, why study peer review and Impact together? To be blunt: Because it is interesting, relevant, never been done before and we will never have another opportunity to investigate it like this again.

Peer Review Groups and Ambiguous Objects

The peer review of Impact: within these five words is the potential hypocrisy that leads this book.

How can researchers, trained in research and used to evaluating research academically, put all these socialised notions of excellence aside to consider the work of their peers beyond these confines? Beyond this, how can researchers evaluate Impact using a tool that was designed to keep the world *"beyond academia"*[1] at bay? Impact, although implicitly yes, does not (yet) have a confirmed role in notions of research excellence. It is ambiguous and will remain as such until researchers gain more experience in creating it, evaluating it and being evaluated against it.

Traditional academic judgement is already steeped in various forms of cognitive and institutional bias (Bourdieu 1975; Chubin and Hackett 1990; Travis and Collins 1991; Chubin 1994; Langfeldt 2001, 2006; Hemlin and Rasmussen 2006; Lamont 2009; Taylor 2011; Huutoniemi 2012), and these effects can only be expected to be amplified in group situations for objects that exist beyond academia.

As groups, peer review panels make better decisions than individuals (Levi 2015). A decision based on the combined expertise of group members is superior and defers the responsibility of the decision away from the individual and onto the group (Kerr et al. 1996; Cooper et al. 2001; Aubé et al. 2011; Faigman et al. 2014; van Arensbergen et al. 2014). Group peer review works because it is assumed that a lack of knowledge of one evaluator will be compensated by the knowledge possessed by another. Hypothetically, this also works for normalising biases (unconscious or not), where the biases of one evaluator will be counteracted by the equal and opposite biases of another, reducing their influence on outcomes. When we consider that during the REF2014 process user-evaluators were specifically introduced to provide the panel with the necessary perspectives to evaluate Impact, we tackle a plethora of new questions regarding to what extent these outsiders added value to the decision-making process, if at all. Although this research cannot explain how or why decisions were made, it can explore how consensus within this group was reached and the way in which individual members negotiated their own standpoints in order to reach this consensus.

However, groups do not always make the best decisions (Janis 1982), especially in peer review situations (Bornmann et al. 2008). Indeed, the benefits of group decision making also come with their own risks. Risks of groupthink (Janis 1982; Esser 1998; Baron 2005) and polarisation (Baron 2005) on the group level come with equal risks of anchoring (Roumbanis 2016), unconscious bias (Bernardin et al. 1995; Viner et al. 2004; Langfeldt 2006; Lee et al. 2013) and social loafing (Latane et al. 1979; Comer 1995; Hall and Buzwell 2013; Simms and Nichols 2014) on the individual level. These risks question the authority with which these expert groups make decisions, as well as the legitimacy of the resulting outcomes and the evaluative tools used to reach them. The existence of these risks, however, does not question the importance of the Impact agenda and its formal evaluation. Furthermore, it certainly does not provide a reason to completely abandon Impact peer review or partially substitute it by a range of proxy indicators. Instead, the key for Impact evaluation is not to table all types and place a value on each, nor is it to juggle the myriad of methods of measurement and squeeze them into a neat indicator proxy assessment model. Rather, the key is to understand how the concept is mediated through traditional assessment channels such as peer review.

Underpinning this book's assertions is that impact does not become "Impact" unless someone or a group of someones recognises it as such. That is, the assessment of Impact is not independent of the judgements or the evolution of these judgements that recognise it as Impact. Here, and for the REF2014, peer review was the process for these academic and expert judgements made in isolation and behind closed doors. The key to winning in these types of assessments is for an applicant to align their conceptualisation of "excellent" with the conceptualisations of the peer review panel. Considering that different group members can, at different times during the evaluation, possess different conceptualisations of excellence, then having this level of foresight can be a difficult task. However, a successful submission is one that captures the group's conceptualisation of Impact excellence (the evaluators' eye and dominant definition) and mirrors it in their own submissions. However, for Impact, when its definition and nature is unknown, ambiguous, untested and subject to the negotiation between different evaluators, aligning perspectives of submissions with evaluation panels is difficult. We already know from studies on interdisciplinary research that peer review panels don't deal with foreign objects well, preferring to adopt a conservative approach to minimise the risk of a wrong decision, and this is reflected in the evaluation outcomes of these panels (Porter and Rossini 1985; Luukkonen 2012). This lack of foresight necessary for submissions to navigate the ambiguity of Impact can also be blamed for the extraordinary cost UK universities had to bear preparing for the REF2014 evaluation (Manville et al. 2015). Therefore, considering peer review approaches to valuation and, in particular, understanding how decisions about Impact are constructed within these panels is key to deconstructing Impact as an evaluation object and identifying examples of success.

Group Evaluation as an Object 'Tug-of-War'

It is easier to understand the dynamics at play within this book if you imagine a tug-of-war. You know, that game you used to play as a child where two teams pulled a rope in opposite directions? In every game, the winning team was collectively the strongest, whether this was because one team had more members or because their collective force was greater.

Deliberation is the hallmark of the peer review process. Through deliberation, the panel develops a consensus by mitigating adjustments in the individual perspectives of panellists. Epley et al. (2004) noted that when people are in groups, using debate, they tend to "jump" from their original egocentric "anchor" and evaluate whether this new perspective plausibly captures the perceptions of other group members (Epley et al. 2004; Epley and Gilovich 2006). These views, when adjusted during group interplay, reflect the group's dominant definition (Chaps. 2 and 6). The dominant definition is the lens through which all applications are viewed, our one evaluator's eye. The tug-of-war focuses on the way that this consensus and dominant definition is reached through in-group social interplay.

This analogy naturally takes "power" and in-group alliances into consideration. As with a real tug-of-war, the winning side is usually the side with the most members pulling in the same direction. In addition, the force with which the winning side is able to pull the equilibrium towards them is determined by the collective and individual weight of each team member. If we picture a peer review panel as, in the beginning, containing numerous different viewpoints, all represented as a tug-of-war rope pulling the equilibrium in a different direction, then notions of power between panellists becomes an important determinant of where the equilibrium will eventually fall. In this way, as discussions progress, sides are chosen and individual evaluators acquiesce their own viewpoints in preference for other, stronger viewpoints. They start to join alliances of similarly thinking or attractive individuals on their side of the rope, increasing the strength and weight behind this point of view. This collective force increases the likelihood that the group equilibrium will be pulled in this direction. When enough members adopt one conceptualisation of the object (or valuation strategy) the tug-of-war is significantly pulled in this direction, developing a consensus and becoming the dominant definition and the evaluative recipe book that determines the way in which all evaluations will be made.

All this consensus building and negotiation between points of view in practice is business as usual for peer review, but here I consider what happens when a new, untested criterion is introduced into the group's fray. Assessment of this criterion is then not business as usual, relying little on a "researcher's intuitive sensitivity" (Merton 1973) for its evaluation. Instead, it requires a new eye capable of filtering a broader range of research excellence. The level of debate, negotiation and interplay will also increase relative to the amount of intellectual and temporal space required to negotiate a consensus. For Impact, the number of pre-conceived ideas regarding value and excellence is broadened and this, using the tug-of-war analogy, increases the number of directions in which the equilibrium is being pulled. Considering that for business as usual types of peer review panels tend to be conservative and to avoid risk (Langfeldt 2006;

Luukkonen 2012), to task these panels with the assessment of highly risky and unique criteria may result in developing counter-productive group behaviours during deliberations. These risky panel deliberations, if combined with other warning signs, risk the panels adopting a group-think-based consensus, overly pragmatic shortcuts and the use of other unintentional heuristic criteria not associated with an ideal expert, robust deliberation-driven judgement of research excellence.

What Did You Find?

Evaluating Impact is less a question of providing a list of alternative tools (metrics, crowdfunding, wisdom of the crowds, etc.) and is instead more one of understanding how peer review panel groups work, and getting them to work smarter.

To evaluate Impact, peer review panels must overcome three main hurdles: (1) Navigate an ambiguous evaluation object relative to the mechanics offered to the panel; to do this they must (2) utilise all resources and voices available to them including how to consider additional, potentially dissenting voices in the decision-making process; and at all times (3) avoid overly pragmatic and simplistic approaches that echo group-think. These recommendations are based on the premise of increasing the levels of temporal and intellectual space necessary for the type of democratic deliberation between experts underpinning the strength of peer review and, by extension, the perceived legitimacy of its outcomes.

How an evaluation process is structured influences how a culture of "togetherness" and its strength influences the ease with which panels conduct an evaluation, around ambiguous objects (Impact). Indeed, this is what I was told by participants prior to the assessment, that there was a sense of unease about the task that lay ahead of them. As a result, participants planned to "wait and see" and they said that they "hoped that everything works out on the day". This strategy, or non-strategy, for want of a better word, indicated that there would be a big reliance on the group consensus or committee dynamic, in order to navigate the Impact assessment. This increased the risk of groupthink developing, and the evaluators being motivated to reach a consensus, rather than ensuring the evaluation reflected the attributes and arguments of submissions in front of them. If committee culture is an essential player in the peer review process and for developing the dominant definition and valuation strategies adopted, allowing sufficient space (temporal and intellectual) for its development through deliberation is vital. This also decreases the risk of groupthink.

By not allowing sufficient space for deliberation as a democratic process, the validity of the peer review to address notions of Impact is questioned. Michelle Lamont, in her study of peer review panel assessment of research excellence, showed that, similar to the concepts of committee culture and groupthink, panellists adopted a pragmatic approach to evaluation (Lamont 2009). This pragmatic approach sees panellists, within their group, develop a sense of shared criteria and values towards submissions. However, overly simplistic pragmatism risks conservative outcomes powered by groupthink. This is not to say that evaluators take unnecessary shortcuts or easily resort to groupthink, but instead to highlight that this evaluation was more a social process than a prescriptive one. I do question, however, the reliance evaluators had on the pre-determined evaluation mechanics. I do not blame evaluators for adopting a pragmatic approach to Impact and leaning heavily on these mechanics, but rather I question the extent to which assessment outcomes are claimed as either a product of an expert-driven peer review process or a product of the construct's pre-determined guidelines to which evaluators rigorously adhered. Indeed, if the peer review process is based on the presumption that it is the result of robust expert deliberation, acts to avoid deliberation make the outcome prone to manipulation by extraneous influences that are not "expert", thereby risking groupthink. Therefore, the integrity of the process, the criterion and the legitimacy of peer review as a tool become shadowed. Since the outcomes of peer review are accepted only if the processes are perceived as fair (Chubin 1994), then jeopardising this illusion has wide-ranging effects on the research community and the Impact agenda. I am sympathetic to the plight of the panellists rather than critical, and try not to draw any conclusion of false or inadequate evaluation on the behalf of the panellists or the REF2014. There are already a large number of studies available that adopt this stance.

Equally important was how the evaluators themselves were influenced by the evaluation process. Prior to the evaluation process, evaluators expressed a myriad of opinions on what they believed Impact to be and how it would be valued. In many cases, the passion with which these beliefs were expressed remains a result on its own; likewise, it painted an interesting predictive picture (hypotheses) about the deliberations around Impact. In particular, one trait that united all evaluators prior to engaging with the assessment process was the unease they felt towards assessing Impact. They openly admitted that they had little experience (Derrick and Samuel 2014; Samuel and Derrick 2015), but, then again, there was no one who could be described as having sufficient experience (Chap. 5). Nonetheless, the fact that all assessors were novices meant that they relied more on their own personal belief systems, as well as the opinions of other evaluators (loafing) and the mechanics (Chap. 3) provided to aid the evaluation.

In addition, I found that contrary to the debate surrounding the best model of Impact evaluation (PayBack, SIAMPI, RIF, etc.), during the evaluation process no specific model was applied. For this study where peer-review is; a social process; where the actors bring competing values, tendencies and biases to the assessment process; and where the extent to which these contribute to the panels dominant definition of Impact, it is dependent on social dynamics sensitive to issues of power, perception of expertise and other forms of social interplay. Instead, an effective model of Impact evaluation is best constructed in practice, by the evaluators during the evaluation. This dilutes the contribution of several prior models of Impact evaluation, though not their intellectual contribution. Rather, I argue that the definition, meaning and value of different types of Impact cannot be determined without an understanding of how these considerations are constructed in practice. To do so would be akin to focusing solely on the outputs of a black box, an analogy that is not foreign to studies of peer review. Instead, understanding Impact evaluation requires an acknowledgement and appreciation of how the value of Impact results from social interplay between evaluators during the peer review process and not solely characteristics of submissions.

By understanding the dynamics of its evaluation, this book reveals new strategies for Impact valuation, beyond the debate on the merits of indicator proxies and Impact evaluation models. Indeed, if the future of Impact evaluation is a question of what indicators we should use and when, rather than if we should use them, <u>understanding how social pro-</u> ✳ <u>cesses within peer review panels frame assessments is vital</u>. Through a greater, empirically informed understanding of the tensions and difficulties faced by peer review panels around Impact, we can more effectively integrate a new generation of research excellence within academic practice.

Is This Study Timely?

How to evaluate research efficiently, robustly and reflexively is a task many governments, funding agencies and research organisations currently grapple. Although this study is based on the UK's REF2014 Impact criterion, many countries are interested in implementing their own Impact agenda and moving towards incentivising societal returns from research and maximising their public investment in science and innovation. This has been viewed positively and negatively by researchers and research managers alike, and in many cases is perceived as an unnecessary financial and bureaucratic burden on universities and public research organisations. This extra burden is in need of downplaying or at least being seen to be actively relieved by using indicators and similar proxies in evaluations. Nonetheless, despite advances in metrics and an increased realisation of the drawbacks of traditional peer review, a completely indicator-driven evaluation system has been actively and sometimes passionately rejected by the research community.

A metric system is the antithesis of peer review. In this war, using peer review is sometimes seen as a compromise of a fully indicator-driven system, and its use ensures a level of self-governance and autonomy remains in the hands of the academic community. Debate has raged between the benefits of indicators and the disadvantages of peer review and vice versa, which means that <u>Impact evaluation will always remain a balancing act</u> <u>between indicators and peer review</u>. Although we can combine the strengths of each into one evaluation system, these two poles are our major options. Therefore, one can be forgiven for thinking that the only ammunition that we have to resist the political temptations of implementing a totally indicator-driven assessment of Impact is by fully understanding how peer review panels negotiate it and by making active moves to promote its advantages and correct processes that demean its credibility as an evaluation tool.

So this study is very timely. I hope that the lessons outlined in this book will be used to inform the development of better policies and procedures for the peer review of Impact. This also means embracing its shortcomings and being brave enough to not only acknowledge them, but to robustly address them within the peer review process, rather than providing a Band-Aid. It is about understanding how these academic groups work, and then getting them to work smarter, and not about changing the evaluations' outcomes. The popularity of Impact, academically, politically and publically, means that it is likely that the criterion will continue in future REFs,[2] as well as emerge in various forms in other countries and research organisations. Rather than repeat the misgivings of the last REF Impact evaluation process, I hope that these insights will be used to inform a more robust peer review evaluation process for Impact and provide empirically informed practice to act as a shield against the desire to resort to a solely indicator-driven system (i.e. the metric tide).

Outline of the Remainder of This Book

The book is designed to be read in order. This is so that I can build upon concepts as they appear, as well as ease into concepts supporting the insights raised by the interview results. This includes a greater appreciation of the study's methodology and what this means for the interpretation of any results. The final chapter, however, can be read alone, but from my point of view this would be a shame. Overlooking the chapters also means that you miss out on appreciating the interactions and personalities of individual characters that I have had the privilege to talk to throughout this study. Stylistically, I use the evaluators' voices to describe their experiences and the approaches debated and adopted within the group.[3] This I hope will demonstrate how individual evaluators spoke as one "eye".

Chapter 2 will describe the main theoretical approaches and literature necessary for the interpretation of the remaining chapters. It explores peer review as a group-led process and examines what this means for the evaluation of ambiguous objects such as Impact. I also use this chapter to introduce the concept of a dominant definition, providing much of the necessary discourse for the development of this book's theories and interpretations. Chapter 3 will outline the evaluation rules that governed the REF2014, which I refer to as evaluation mechanics (Lamont 2009). It is impossible to view the results and findings uncovered in this study without also considering how mechanics steered them. Chapter 3 will also discuss the mechanics' role in facilitating versus infiltrating the process, and whether this was intended or not, presenting descriptive typologies for mechanics surrounding ambiguous objects.

Chapter 4 will then capture the conceptualisations of Impact that were expressed by panellists prior to the evaluation taking place and explore how the group developed strategies for its valuation. These conceptualisations will be explored using current models of societal impact assessment from the literature and the challenges faced by Impact evaluators in practice. These pre-evaluation conceptualisations of Impact will also be cross-referenced with views expressed after the evaluation process was complete, and will explore examples and reasons for any instances of change on the individual level. Throughout this chapter we will also start to understand the importance of "the group" and will glimpse how evaluators began to negotiate their own conceptualisations of Impact with those of others, within peer review panels.

Chapter 5 will explore the interplay between different evaluator types and examine what it means to be a peer for Impact relative to concepts of representation and expertise. The REF2014 Impact assessment process was unique in that it combined traditional academic peers as evaluators, but essentially expanded the definition of a peer to include experts with experience beyond academia. Therefore, I examine the value added to the assessment and to the assessment process of the user-evaluator. Essentially, did the inclusion of users make any difference? I explore instances of when different evaluator types clashed, agreed and negotiated their standpoints in the evaluation process. I also get a unique and painfully funny (cultural-cringe) insight into how users valued the contribution of academics and vice versa and the influence of this on the outcomes. Chapter 6 will lead on to explore the more general group behaviour across the panels to examine how a consensus was formed and discuss how this, if at all, framed the assessment of Impact. Here I am sensitive to issues related to group dynamics as outlined by Levi (2015) and groupthink (Janis 1982) and reflect on these risks. In particular, like Lamont (2009), I am concerned with the organisational and temporal constraints that effectively force groups to "satisfice" or do good enough, as opposed to adopting a more robust expert-led decision-making process. This chapter goes beyond the user/academic divide within groups to explore the wider, group-level dynamics adopted to assess Impact. From the group perspective, I examine the structure of the assessment process and how change in group dynamics can influence the assessment outcome. The final chapter will review what has been learnt in the previous chapters and present some practical recommendations for facilitating the assessment of Impact using peer review.

Notes

1. This term "beyond academia" is taken directly from the REF2014 Impact definition, which is described in more detail in Chap. 3.
2. The Impact criterion has been conformed for REF2021 and will increase in value from 20% in REF2014, to 25% of the overall evaluation in REF2021.
3. Throughout the text, where I use the evaluator's voices, I denote each with a code. The structure of the codes used with the quotations from participants in the results follow a pattern. The first two digits refer to the panel to which the evaluator belonged. For example, P0 denotes the Main Panel and P1 sub-panel 1 (Clinical Medicine). In many cases an evaluator belonged to more than one panel and if so their multi-membership is shown through the first part of the code, that is, P1P2 means that the panellist was a member of both sub-panel 1 and sub-panel 2. The second part of the code represents the criterion that the evaluator assessed, being one of three possibilities. That is, "Out" where the evaluator only assessed the Outputs criterion; "OutImp" where the evaluator evaluated both the Outputs and Impact criteria; and "Imp" where the evaluator only assessed

Impact. The next part of the code is an individual identification number, and the last part in brackets represents whether the quotation is taken from the pre-evaluation (PRE) or post-evaluation (POST) interviews.

References

Aubé, C., V. Rousseau, and S. Tremblay. 2011. Team size and quality of group experience: The more the merrier? *Group Dynamics: Theory, Research, and Practice* 15 (4): 357.

Baron, R.S. 2005. So right it's wrong: Groupthink and the ubiquitous nature of polarised group decision making. *Advances in Experimental Social Psychology* 37: 219–253.

Bernardin, H.J., H. Hennessey, and J. Peyrefitte. 1995. Age, racial, and gender bias as a function criterion specificity: A test of expert testimony. *Human Resource Management Review* 5 (1): 63–77.

Bornmann, L., G. Wallon, and A. Ledin. 2008. Does the committee peer review select the best applicants for funding? An investigation of the selection process for two european molecular biology organization programmes. *PLoSOne* 3 (10): e3480.

Bourdieu, P. 1975. The specificity of the scientific field and the social conditions of the progress of reason. *Information (International Social Science Council)* 14 (6): 19–47.

Chubin, D.E. 1994. Grants peer review in theory and practice. *Evaluation Review* 18 (1): 20–30.

Chubin, D.E., and E.J. Hackett. 1990. *Peerless science: Peer review and US science policy*. Albany: State University of New York Press.

Comer, D.R. 1995. A model of social loafing in real work groups. *Human Relations* 48 (6): 647–667.

Cooper, J., K.A. Kelly, and K. Weaver. 2001. Attitudes, norms, and social groups. In *Blackwell Handbook of social psychology: Group processes*, ed. M.A. Hogg and R.S. Tindale, 259–282. Oxford: Blackwell.

Dahler-Larsen, P. 2007. Evaluation and public management. In *The Oxford Handbook of public management*, ed. E. Ferlie, L.E. Lynn Jr., and C. Pollitt. Oxford: Oxford University Press.

———. 2011. *The evaluation society*. Palo Alto, CA: Stanford University Press.

———. 2012. Constitutive effects as a social accomplishment: A qualitative study of the political in testing. *Education Inquiry* 3 (2): 171–186.

———. 2014. Constitutive effects of performance indicators: Getting beyond unintended consequences. *Public Management Review* 16 (7): 969–986.

Derrick, G.E., and G.N. Samuel. 2014. The impact evaluation scale: Group panel processes and outcomes in societal impact evaluation. *Social Science and Medicine*, in press.

Epley, N., and T. Gilovich. 2006. The anchoring-and-adjustment heuristic: Why the adjustments are insufficient. *Psychological Science* 17 (4): 311–318.

Epley, N., B. Keysar, L. Van Boven, and T. Gilovich. 2004. Perspective taking as egocentric anchoring and adjustment. *Journal of Personality and Social Psychology* 87 (3): 327.

Esser, J. 1998. Alive and well after 25 years: A review of groupthink research. *Organizational Behavior and Human Decision Processes* 73 (2/3): 116–141.

Faigman, D.L., J. Monahan, and C. Slobogin. 2014. Group to individual (G2i) inference in scientific expert testimony. *The University of Chicago Law Review* 81 (2): 417–480.

Gallo, S.A., J.H. Sullivan, and S.R. Glisson. 2016. The influence of peer reviewer expertise on the evaluation of research funding applications. *PLoS One* 11 (10): e0165147.

Hall, D., and S. Buzwell. 2013. The problem of free-riding in group projects: Looking beyond social loafing as reason for non-contribution. *Active Learning in Higher Education* 14 (1): 37–49.

Hemlin, S., and S.B. Rasmussen. 2006. The shift in academic quality control. *Science, Technology, & Human Values* 31 (2): 173–198.

Holbrook, J.B., and R. Frodeman. 2011. Peer review and the exante assessment of societal impacts. *Research Evaluation* 20 (3): 239–246.

Huutoniemi, K. 2012. Communicating and compromising on disciplinary expertise in the peer review of research proposals. *Social Studies of Science* 42 (6): 897–921.

Janis, I.L. 1982. *Groupthink: Psychological studies of policy decisions and fiascoes.* Boston, MA: Houghton Mifflin Company.

Kerr, N.L., R.J. MacCoun, and G.P. Kramer. 1996. Bias in judgement: Comparing individuals and groups. *Psychological Review* 103: 687–719.

Lamont, M. 2009. *How professors think: Inside the curious world of academic judgement.* Cambridge, MA: Harvard University Press.

Langfeldt, L. 2001. The decision-making constraints and processes of grant peer review, and their effects on the review outcome. *Social Studies of Science* 31 (6): 820–841.

———. 2006. The policy challenges of peer review: Managing bias, conflict of interests and multidisciplinary assessments. *Research Evaluation* 15 (1): 31–41.

Latane, B., K. Williams, and S. Harkins. 1979. Many hands make light the work: The causes and consequences of social loafing. *Journal of Personality and Social Psychology* 37 (6): 822–832.

Lee, C.J. 2012. A Kuhnian critique of psychometric research on peer review. *Philosophy of Science* 79 (5): 859–870.

Lee, C.J., C.R. Sugimoto, G. Zhang, and B. Cronin. 2013. Bias in peer review. *Journal of the American Society for Information Science and Technology* 64 (1): 2–17.

Levi, D. 2015. *Group dynamics for teams*. London: Sage Publications.

Luukkonen, T. 2012. Conservatism and risk-taking in peer review: Emerging ERC practices. *Research Evaluation* 21: 48–60.

Manville, C., S. Guthrie, M.-L. Henham, B. Garrod, S. Sousa, A. Kirtkey, S. Castle-Clarke, and T. Ling. 2015. *Assessing impact submissions for REF2014: An evaluation*. Cambridge: RAND Europe.

Merton, R.K. 1973. *The sociology of science: Theoretical and empirical investigations*. Chicago: University of Chicago press.

Porter, A.L., and F.A. Rossini. 1985. Peer review of interdisciplinary research proposals. *Science, Technology, & Human Values* 10 (3): 33–38.

Roumbanis, L. 2016. Academic judgments under uncertainty: A study of collective anchoring effects in Swedish Research Council panel groups. *Social Studies of Science* 47: 1–22.

Samuel, G.N., and G.E. Derrick. 2015. Societal impact evaluation: Exploring evaluator perceptions of the characterization of impact under the REF2014. *Research Evaluation* 24 (3): 229–241.

Simms, A., and T. Nichols. 2014. Social loafing: A review of the literature. *Journal of Management Policy and Practice* 15 (1): 58.

Taylor, J. 2011. The assessment of research quality in UK universities: Peer review or metrics? *British Journal of Management* 22 (2): 202–217.

Travis, G.D.L., and H.M. Collins. 1991. New light on old boys: Cognitive and institutional particularism in the peer review system. *Science, Technology, & Human Values* 16 (3): 322–341.

van Arensbergen, P., I. van der Weijden, and P. van den Besselaar. 2014. The selection of talent as a group process. A literature review on the social dynamics of decision making in grant panels. *Research Evaluation* 23 (4): 298–311.

Viner, N., P. Powell, and R. Green. 2004. Institutionalized biases in the award of research grants: A preliminary analysis revisiting the principle of accumulative advantage. *Research Policy* 33 (3): 443–454.

2

Peer Review of Impact: Could It Work?

This is a human endeavour, so I think a lot of judgements came into it as
part of the issue, I think, but human judgements are, including this one,
are, you know, imprecise, coloured by many different things.
P0OutImp1 (Post-evaluation)

This book is concerned with peer review processes conducted in groups,
similar to those governing the type of peer review associated with grant
and promotion applications. The other peer review, the peer review of
manuscripts, has received a lot of attention in the literature and arguably deals with different notions of excellence. Group panel peer review
processes are considered the poorer-research cousin of the scholarly peer
review of manuscripts, with research predominantly focused on the latter. This is mainly because the other peer review does not suffer from the
same methodological challenges faced by peer review panel research.
Indeed, the problem with peer review is that it is still a black box that
requires researchers to get "inside" and much of the main criticisms are
focused on this lack of transparency. The reasons for this are both logis-
tical (it is hard to get sufficient access to study this empirically) and

© The Author(s) 2018
G. Derrick, *The Evaluators' Eye*,
https://doi.org/10.1007/978-3-319-63627-6_2

methodological. A small handful of studies have been granted permission to get "inside" to observe and appraise panel processes (Arensbergen 2014; Lamont 2009; Langfeldt 2004); however, much of what we have learnt further justifies fears about the process, rather than waylaying them. Unfortunately, access is rarely granted by either those within the black box or those who oversee it, further inhibiting significant progress in this field. Politically speaking, the blackness of the box is preferred to maintain an illusion of expertise and objectivity that drives the legitimacy of peer review as the "gold standard" evaluation tool of choice.

Methodological Considerations of Being Inside

In lieu of being inside, I developed the "in vitro approach" to study peer review evaluation processes. Summarised in Fig. 3.1 (Chap. 3) and transposed onto the REF2014 evaluation timetable, this approach juxtaposed and compared evaluator responses during two sets of interviews: one conducted with evaluators before the evaluation began (pre-evaluation, $n = 63$) and then another after the evaluation was complete (post-evaluation, $n = 57$). This approach captured pre-conceived ideas and opinions, and evaluators had, and then map (using recollections captured in the post-evaluation interviews) the evolution of these ideas through in-group interplay without interfering with the process itself. Interviews allowed the participants to, within reason, take charge of the interview, and from this I could draw reasonable hypotheses about the group dynamics that occurred during the evaluation process, and identify issues that were unresolved due to a lack of deliberation, and therefore at risk of groupthink. Specifically, I captured how the interaction of raw, baseline views expressed prior to the evaluation process (as well as prior to the calibration exercises or evaluation experience gained) were resolved in committee, what themes were dominant and the influence of these in-group decisions on the evaluation outcome. Capturing these views prior to any group interaction meant that I could reliably pinpoint any instances of change that occurred as a result of the process, hypothesise the interactions that would occur between evaluators and then confirm these with the post-evaluation analysis.

This approach was developed as a way of compensating for the difficult and near impossible task of directly observing peer review panel processes, including the REF2014. For all intents and purposes, the in vitro approach allowed me to successfully paint a picture of the Jackson Pollack-like mess that is the peer review evaluation panel debate around Impact. However, its drawback as a tool is inevitable. It involved a long and complex analysis, requiring continuous qualitative comparison of interviews between participants, types of evaluators and within panels, alongside other markers of influence and power. In lieu of direct observations, however, it is by far the most robust research design available for this type of research.

As this type of methodology still requires a high level of experimental design and organisation, I restricted the analysis to one of the 4 main panels (Main Panel A) within the UK's Research Excellence Framework, which included for the first time a formal, ex-post evaluation of "Impact" where evaluation outputs were tied to funding allocation decisions. I interviewed 62 evaluators (including 6 Output only assessors; 47 Output and Impact assessors; and 9 Impact only assessors) in the pre-evaluation interviews conducted prior to the Impact assessment, and 57 of the same interviewees again in the post-evaluation interviews (including 6 Output only assessors; 44 Output and Impact assessors; and 7 Impact only assessors).[1] The evaluators interviewed in the pre-evaluation interviews were the same in the post-evaluation interviews, and only 5 evaluators declined to be interviewed again, a 92% return rate. Extra care was taken to ensure that a critical mass of evaluators were included, carefully balancing characteristics such as gender, academic rank and career stage across all panels to ensure that reasonable comparisons of evaluator interaction within and between panels could be captured. The analysis only included evaluators from Main Panel A and its sub-panels to avoid the problem associated with comparing fields, as this group of panels focused only on health, medical and biomedical sciences. Restricting the analysis to one Main Panel avoided the ongoing debate about the definition of Impact, since for this panel the research is a little more developed here. It also allowed me to minimise the influence of any overt disciplinary differences in the panel's customary rules (Michèle Lamont and Huutoniemi 2011).

An additional methodological caveat was that the panels I studied were composed of experts from clinical and applied backgrounds, but more interestingly these panels also included "Users". Users were thought to bring stakeholder-based expertise to the evaluation process. Their inclusion implies that the academics are not "expert" enough to be trusted with the assessment of societal impact. This is a fascinating addition. The structure of the evaluation meant that interviews included evaluators who had evaluated the outputs beforehand, in addition to Impact, as well as those who had only evaluated the Impact and those who had only evaluated the Outputs. This meant that the research design had a naturally occurring control group built in. This in turn meant that in terms of the robustness of the research, triangulation could cross reference between groups of evaluators (Impact only, Output only, and Impact and Output), types of evaluators (Academic and User) and different panels within Main panel A, before and after the evaluation (pre- and post-evaluation interviews), as well as by individual evaluator attributes (age, gender, organisation, scientific background and experience of Impact). This project was without a doubt a research playground that I felt absolutely privileged to access.

Peer Review Laid Bare

Peer review has been likened to a black box. This hides not only the unaccountability of the evaluators who work within it, but also the influence of personal biases, vendettas, and the professional ambitions and competition that may frame deliberations and influence outcomes. Acknowledging the failings of peer review is nothing new, nor is the recognition that research is, at times, a competitive clash of egos. This black box can hide prejudices, and cannot always be relied upon to make the right decision. All we see are the outcomes, and for many trying to crawl their way up the academic career ladder this is all that matters. However, within the black box of peer review, all the cynicism, doubt, political incorrectness, nepotism and general bias can manifest itself in a decision-making process to award funding. All this happens without transparency and public responsibility of the people making these decisions. In research regarding peer review, the change of focus from the attributes of submissions to one that focuses on the way that academic groups arrive at a consensus is revolutionary in this field; however, there is a lack of empirical evidence of how criteria are operationalised in evaluative practice (Arensbergen 2014; Lamont 2009; Langfeldt 2001, 2004; Pier et al. 2017). For me, it is a glorious thing to research as it reveals research as the gritty, competitive interaction that we all suspect it is, and moves past its idealised public reputation as objective, meritocratic guardian of knowledge.[2] The change in research focus away from outcome and to process also changes the principles of its proposed legitimacy as a tool. This includes understanding its additional role as a political as well as an academic construct (Cetina et al. 1991; Knorr-Cetina 1983, 1991), for the valuation of research.

Group-based peer review has a long history for the evaluation and rewarding of competitive grants and fellowships (Hackett and Chubin 2003), and its role as the gold standard of research evaluation (Chubin and Hackett 1990) is based on a number of underpinning principles. Broadly speaking, this *"system(s) of institutionalized vigilance"* (Merton 1973) in the self-regulation of the research community reaches a common judgement through what (Olbrecht and Bornmann 2010) described as mutual social exchange, where the final judgement is based on the common judgement of all evaluators, or "peers". Its reliance on "expert"-driven decision making has ensured the political and public legitimacy of the process as well as a pillar of academic self-governance. As such, an important underpinning principle of peer review is its reliance on a democratically deliberative evaluative model (Greene 1997, 2000) which emphasises the importance of inclusion, representation and dialogue (Dahler-Larsen 2007; Solomon 2006). In this model, groups work out differences in opinions in practice by reaching a consensus through deliberation (Solomon 2006). For Impact, the deliberative approach of peer review becomes participatory (Greene 1997; Mark and Shotland 1985) as it extends to including stakeholder views under the broad umbrella of "expertise". This ensures that the evaluation outcome is the sum of many opinions, and not just one authoritative voice. Ideally, this group approach reduces bias, but in practice it also risks certain biases being confounded through support of more than one deliberating voice. As a black box process, the in-group equalisation (or destabilisation) means that there is safety in peers (or experts) being completely honest in their assessments of proposals. In addition, for the evaluators there is safety in being able to assess your peers without fear of your decisions coming back to haunt you at conferences or academic dinners. It also allows researchers the freedom to voice what they really think (professionally), although the drawback of this is that at times this also gives them free reign to say what they really think personally. Nonetheless, it gives researchers a sense of security to be academically and unforgivingly open in their assessment of value. The final underpinning principle legitimising peer review is that outcomes are assured to be based on the combined expert opinion, and therefore perceived as fair by the academic community. Peer review remains the only decision regarding the allocation of public funds that is made by people with absolutely no accountability to the public, or for their decisions. The guarantee of expertise compensates, at least in part, for peer review's black box nature. Likewise, for funding agencies, there is political safety in the lack of transparency where the decisions made can be defended by the sanctimony of the peer review process, as well as the decisions made by experts. This also reduces the possibility of people questioning the decisions made, and the endless paperwork and cost of investigating or rectifying these decisions.

Only those present in the hallowed peer review chambers occupied by the evaluators actually know what goes on in this black box, although each seasoned academic professor will have their own opinion on how to navigate this system. These include tips on who to collaborate with, who to cite and what characteristics to look for in a potential reviewer.[3] This knowledge is based on their own personal experience in winning and losing grants, as well as being peer reviewers themselves, but it is based less on empirical evidence. It is this acquired knowledge of excellence that every young, slightly naïve and definitely scared researcher obtains from their academic peers, which suggests that the process of peer review is not as black as it would seem. The assumption of peer review is that, at the end of the day, the best proposals are funded. Unfortunately, investigation of past performance of selection processes is characterised by large numbers of false positives (granted applications performing less than rejected applicants) and false negatives (rejected applicants performing higher than granted applicants) (Bornmann et al. 2008; Cole et al. 1981; Giraudeau et al. 2011), and this has resulted in the opinion that success in grants is more the *"luck of the reviewer draw"* (Cole et al. 1981, 885), or *"more like a lottery that could just as well be taken care of by a computer"* (Roumbanis 2016), than a systematic assessment of excellence. However, these revelations do not, as one would expect, result in a political devaluing of science. Rather, acknowledging its failings, as well as its benefits, has the power to position applicants as more prepared to handle the sometimes incomprehensible outcomes of the process. It also allows funding agencies to organise the criteria, approach and assessment process to reflect the political, social and economic goals and ambitions of the time, as has been the case for societal impact. This random, luck-dependent process is as complex as it is essential for the academic self-governance of research, a characteristic that is repeated within academic communities globally irrespective of the cultural, linguistic and other differences.

Indeed, the ferocity with which academics defend its role means that alternatives to peer review, when presented, are rarely considered equal. Roy (1985) was less than sympathetic to peer review, stating that its role as an evaluation tool of choice was the result *"of the inherent elitism of the hard sciences and its arcane linguistic barriers [that] have enabled some scientists to claim that science should play by special rules"*, and that *"there is now a generation of scientists who have experienced no other means of obtaining research funding and hence feel their entire research career to be at risk when any questions are raised about the peer-review system"* (Roy 1985). If nothing else, Roy's (1985) concerns were echoed in the unsolicited warning I received from a concerned colleague cautioning me that *"Critiquing peer-review doesn't always win friends among academic colleagues"*. These are damning assertions, but like Roy (1985), I refuse to justify the existence of peer review simply because there are no alternatives. For me, any comparison made with alternatives is unfair, and the community's blind defence of peer review while accepting its obvious faults and drawbacks seems to justify Roy's (1985) concerns about the prospect of implementing any possible alternative for the assessment of scientific impact. For ambiguous notions of Impact, however, the jury is still out.

Why Evaluate Impact?

Impact can be a very personal achievement for researchers. Its realisation is hardly ever a straightforward affair, with, at times, many unseen hurdles addressed through unorthodox behaviour by the researchers. In one extraordinary example, Prof Barry Marshall in 1984 famously devoured a cup of *Heliobacter pylori* in order to prove his own theory that the cause of stomach ulcers was bacterial, leading directly to more effective treatment options. These personal hurdles are difficult to explain, and even more difficult to describe in a rational manner to a group of peers all on their own personal Impact pilgrimages and with their own interpretations of what is a courageous step towards Impact. Impact is therefore difficult to evaluate using any rational, linear construction, tool or lens. For Smith (2001), evaluating societal impact required an *"instrument [that] should (a) fit with current ways of evaluating research, (b) look to the future also, (c) be efficient for both assessors and the assessed, and (d) work in practice"* (p. 528; see also van der Meulen and Rip 2000).

The political motivations behind evaluating Impact are clear, and from a public investment accountability point of view, its purpose is seductive. Governments are increasingly keen to receive a return on their initial investment. Ideally, this return would be felt as less spending in other areas of government responsibility, such as healthcare, agriculture and business investment. In an era of ever-increasing budgets and public demands on services, research investment is a great hope in relieving this burden. From a research perspective, formally assessing and recognising Impact is a way of closing what I refer to as the *"recognition deficit"*, where researchers who were previously engaged in activities designed to have an Impact were not recognised through traditional academic evaluation channels. Prof Barry Marshall was one of these until his Nobel Prize win, and subsequent status as a public hero. Independent of any significant academic recognition of professional esteem (Nobel Prize) or media frenzy, these activities are not yet widely valued in academia and instead remain secondary in importance, in that Impact was what an academic did when they were not good enough to be a "real" academic, and so achievements beyond academia were not reflected in promotion, grant and/or employment decisions. In many cases, the academics involved were motivated more by a sense of altruism (Haynes et al. 2011) than an inability to excel in a traditional realm of academia, and yet in the vast majority of situations, excellence in Impact was not seen as central to one's career progression. Indeed, engagement in Impact takes valuable time away from the production of academic articles, books and grant applications—all essential goals for a successful academic career. It comes as no surprise that academics are less than enthusiastic about spending time on something that is unlikely to be recognised formally. And yet, ensuring that research remains relevant and applicable to society is at the centre of research's social contract (Gibbons et al. 1994; Nowotny et al. 2001). The Impact agenda has changed this belief, placing it closer in importance to traditional academic notions of excellence. There is still a long way to go in achieving equal status between the two research outputs, and in narrowing this recognition deficit. The REF2014's formal inclusion of Impact was undoubtedly a major step towards formally recognising research's societal contract, and recognising those researchers who have successfully achieved this in their careers.

What Is "Impact" in National Research Evaluation Policies?

In the absence of any evaluative precedent, Impact as a formalised criterion remained an ambiguous object in practice. There has been a rush to label this concept as reflective of the type of societal benefits that research promises (Bornmann 2012), including labels like 'third stream benefits', 'enterprise science' or 'knowledge transfer', all implicitly referring to the specific tangible outcomes of these wider societal benefits, specifically their economic benefits. In contrast, other labels have tried to broaden the nature of societal impact by considering Impact as economic, societal/social impact; cultural; and environmental; or as more general, non-specific 'societal benefit'. There is a danger in adopting one particular label over another because it risks the follow-on effect of also narrowing the assessment focus, as in many situations more than one focus plays a role in realising Impact (Bornmann 2013; Spaapen and Van Drooge 2011). Further, the overlap of economic and non-economic impacts has been previously noted as a 'fuzzy boundary' (Salter and Martin 2001) that is difficult to distinguish during an evaluation which focuses solely on Impact, as opposed to a journey involving continual engagement. Continually referring to Impact in broad, associative terms, however, also narrows the options available for its evaluation by leaving the object ambiguous and open for interpretation by panels.

Nonetheless, for the sake of government policies surrounding Impact as an evaluation object, different organisations and governments are constantly attempting to define research (Grant et al. 2010). Australia has maintained a long-running research evaluation framework, Excellence in Research for Australia (ERA), which until recently has been focused on evaluating traditional research outputs through indicator-informed peer review. However, the need "...*to create and embed a culture of and expectation for impact within Australian universities and wider society*" (Universities 2015) has resulted in a potential object that emphasises the importance of industry "engagement" as a proxy for Impact. The emphasis on industry engagement (still currently in development) is the result of an observation that a focus on producing academic articles "*thwart[s] engagement with industry*" (Finkel 2015), and the corresponding comments from Prime Minister Malcolm Turnbull about ending the "publish or perish culture" (Knott 2015). This is a more directed, intentional focus than those under consideration by countries such as Finland, Sweden and New Zealand, where the definition is more in line with the broad approach adopted by the UK and the US. However, at the other end of the spectrum is the more subtle conceptualisation of the term offered by The Netherlands. In the latest iteration of the Standard Evaluation Protocol Vereniging van Univeriteiten (VSNU), the criterion "relevance to society" is referred to as "*the quality, scale and relevance of contributions targeting specific economic, social or cultural target groups, of advisory reports for policy, of contributions to public debates, and so on*" *(VSNU 2015)*. Here, the definition, like in the UK, is quite broad, but the concept relates more to broader concepts of valorisation of research than in the REF2014 definition, which does not include proxies such as "engagement". Despite these differences, there are a number of commonalities including having a "*benefit to society*" or influence "*beyond academia*", both concepts present in the UK REF2014, the US's National Science Foundation (NSF) Broader Impacts criterion, and in the European Research Council's definition, which refers to *"customer and societal benefits"*. This contrasts with the conceptualisation of Impact as being utilised for financial or economic benefits alone, although text-mining of policy documents suggests an over-utilisation of the terms in documents describing the criteria (Derrick et al. 2014). Nonetheless, other non-national innovation policies have illusions of public engagement associated with Impact. These are in line with research's societal contract (Gibbons et al. 1994; Nowotny et al. 2001) but also with government through the development of evidence-informed policies, and industry towards some financial or economic benefits. And yet, other words for the concept have included "influence", "extrinsic merit", "societal outcomes" and, my favourite, "grand challenges". This policy buzz-term elicits the illusions of a joint venture between the public and research in tackling the world's problems through applying research evidence. Indeed, it is this term that echoes Bodmer's and Wolfendale's intentions towards a relationship between research and the public that is two-way and based on the assumption of a duty of researchers who are in receipt of public funds towards making the world a better place.

Purpose of Audit Frameworks as Research Governance Tools

Assessment exercises, both globally and in the UK, are important corner-stones for the academic community. For better or worse, they set clear and achievable targets for individuals, organisations and governments about the appropriate outcomes and future goals of publicly funded research, and are linked to incentivising socially and politically desirable research behaviours. The general consensus is that assessments should locate and fund areas of research (institutions, fields, teams, individuals) who are performing the best, to reward good performers and encourage lower performers to perform at a higher level (Herbst 2007). Practically, however, audit exercises are cumbersome to implement and the constitutive effects (Dahler-Larsen 2014) can be uncontrollable. They have been labelled as *"football-style performance analysis"* in the UK, mainly because, inevitably, the results are organised into league-table-like rankings; and as *"unnecessary red tape"* in Australia. By imbedding competitive elements into research practice by funding "winners", decisions around funding allocation become a tool to nudge (Thaler Richard and Sunstein Cass 2008) research behaviour in desirable directions. Empirical evidence supporting them as efficient allocation mechanisms is still mixed (Abramo et al. 2015; Auranen and Nieminen 2010; Hicks 2012; Ingwersen and Larsen 2014; Sandström et al. 2014; Sivertsen and Schneider 2012). Constitutive or unintended effects are an inevitable consequence of being watched (Dahler-Larsen 2014; De Rijcke et al. 2016)—a type of neo-academic Heisenberg theory—but they can also be used as a way of directing behaviour in politically desirous directions (Deem et al. 2007; Leisyte and Dee 2012; Willmott 2011) that are not all negative (Andersen and Pallesen 2008). Traditionally, winning has been dependent on publishing in high-impact journals or books, collaborating internationally, winning competitive funding or building strong research teams—hallmark concepts of research excellence, widely accepted by the academic community.

The extent to which national assessment frameworks can augment norms of excellence is linked to the selection of criteria used and connecting their performance to research funding distribution. Some, such as the UK's REF (previously Research Assessment Exercise (RAE)), are directly linked to the allocation of public funding to Higher Education Institution (HEIs) conducting research, while others such as Australia's ERA are all but independent of the allocation of block funding for universities. There is a middle ground adopted by many countries. The *sexenio* in Spain, for example, uses an assessment of research quantity and quality to reward groups extra funding to be distributed amongst employees equally through their salaries (Derrick and Pavone 2013; Fernández-Zubieta et al. 2015). Critics have argued that imposing these frameworks upon researchers is a type of research managerialism, one that runs counter to academic freedom and autonomy (Deem et al. 2007). Instead the system works to replicate and formalise community-agreed notions of academic excellence. The issue for critics should not be dependent on the existence of the frameworks themselves, but on the criteria used to mobilise and enable them as incentives. Hicks (2012) emphasises that in order to better understand the role of assessment exercises as governance tools in general, we must not focus on the intricacies of individual systems, specifically the criteria, but instead on how criteria are operationalised during evaluations as tools and lenses.

The purpose and resulting influence of research assessment frameworks in legitimising new norms of research excellence are therefore more tightly integrated than previously acknowledged. Whereas some studies have viewed them as externally-imposed managerial tools promoting an externally derived, incentive-led academic nudge, they fail to recognise researchers as anything other than operating at the mercy of these frameworks. As such, they depict researchers who are passive participants neither aware nor in control of their own behaviour. If we consider the depth of debate that happens around the implementation of certain criteria, we notice that contrary to claims of limiting academic freedom and other extreme opinions of their effects, the operationalisation of criteria still remains in the hands of the academic community. In the face of changing assessment criteria, expert-led peer review continues to emerge as the evaluation tool of choice, the gold standard tool. Establishing these formal evaluations is therefore a way of legitimatising and formalising a level of academic self-governance under the guise of a reflexive and accountable research assessment framework, rather than fuelling an academic revolution towards politically desirable outcomes. If nothing else, this paints academics as far beyond the passive, malleable role assumed by past studies. Instead, research assessment frameworks act to give researchers the autonomy necessary to do research as they see fit, and reward aspects of excellence that they value. Since 2014, in the UK, this now includes "Impact".

The UK's Research Excellence Framework (REF2014) Critique

In line with the influence of perverse incentives on academic practice, the UK assessment framework in its various guises has suffered its fair share of warranted and unwarranted attacks. Unlike many commentators (academic and otherwise) with an interest in this field, I do not adopt the normative stance of negativity towards the REF2014. To do so, I believe, is both destructive and pointless. Instead, I adopt a more practical approach that accepts the *nuevo*-reality that research accountability is not going anywhere and further ongoing research assessment is part of formally operationalising that accountability. So, instead of being destructive for the sake of it, or having a negative voice just to ensure that I am the one being the loudest, I seek to work with these new realities, and concentrate on how to get these evaluation frameworks to work better. Nonetheless, I must dedicate a small part of this book to cover the range of criticisms that have been weathered specifically by the REF2014 and are relevant to the issues pertinent to this book.

With Impact described as *"Frankenstein's monster"* (Martin 2011), critics doubted the possibility of robustly evaluating the societal impact of research. The main lines of controversy (Smith et al. 2011) focused on the extra burden placed on both individuals and organisations in preparing submissions around this ambiguous object; concerns regarding generalisations about how Impact is realised in different fields (and the potential devaluing of some fields over others as a result); and the potential threat imposing a criterion of excellence beyond academia on academic autonomy. In fact, the enormous cost to organisations in preparing for the REF2014 and the Impact criterion has been used as an argument against regular evaluation frameworks and against the implementation of frameworks in Italy (Geuna and Piolatto 2016). Costs associated with academic autonomy were also highlighted. Here, evaluation frameworks are a by-product of the increasing marketisation, massification and neo-liberalisation of higher education (Watermeyer and Hedgecoe 2016). These lines of research assume that the academic ivory tower is to be protected at all costs and this is in spite of increasing calls for public accountability of research (Watermeyer 2015). Instead, formal assessment requirements are seen as impinging on academic self-governance, and any change in traditional academic behaviour (positive or negative), such as constructing a colourful narrative, is directly associated with a type of 'managerialism' that is invading higher education and research (Chubb and Watermeyer 2016). These arguments may be well articulated, but they tend to profess the virtues of a system of the past, where research was completely self-governed, was conducted for research's sake only, and was therefore devoid of all public accountability. In this view, Impact assessment is seen to be impinging on the ideal world of academia and the researcher's role as a *guardian of objective truth* (Watermeyer 2016). For me, who takes a more balanced approach, these views are destructive, and concentrate on demonising a system that will not disappear, rather than focusing on how to make the system work better.

Focusing on Impact specifically and submissions to the UK government's call for evidence about the REF2014, Smith et al. (2011) use Bourdieu (1975, 1984, 1997) to explore how the introduction of the Impact criterion as a "new" element in research evaluation represented threats to researchers' autonomy and academic freedoms. Bourdieu (1997, 14) argued that knowledge production is more autonomous the more the audience is limited to direct competitors or peers (Bourdieu 1975). Therefore, for the REF panels the act of giving user-evaluators membership on the evaluation panel, side by side with academic peers, threatens this autonomy. Indeed, the involvement of users would jeopardise the very tenet of peer review. One submission in the last RAE2008 (Engineering evaluators) noted that "it would be a regrettable and backward step, if they became marginalised by being involved only in the assessment of Impact" (cf. Smith 2001). They therefore proposed an advisory role for users only. Scientific production is considered separate, and incompatible with politics and other non-scientific modes of cultural production, sentiments similar to Merton (1973), and to some extent Gibbons et al. (1994) and Nowotny et al. (2001). The introduction of criteria that consider influence "beyond" academia therefore represents a constant negotiation between sources of academic autonomy and external power (political or economic), as well as the tenets of transparency and accountability of funding decisions. Inherent in these arguments is the labelling of Impact as a non-productive aspect of research, and the time constraints that prevent academics from further participation in these activities, and the risk of pursuing Impact only for it to be rendered irrelevant (Smith et al. 2011). Although the perception of time constraints is based on the researcher's understanding of "doing impact" as something extra, rather than criteria to reward what they are engaging with unknowingly (de Jong et al. 2015).

Evaluating Impact—Models, Proxies and Assumptions

This book is not concerned with mapping the evaluation process against any pre-determined assessment model for Impact. Instead I emphasise that models for impact evaluation are created in practice, within peer review processes and not separate from this dynamic interplay. There is therefore little reason to go into any in-depth discussion about any model in particular, or how models differ in their loci of evaluation. I do acknowledge that they exist and have played a dominant role in the development of impact assessment in the UK. As such, a brief discussion of their main attributes is warranted here.

Despite the plethora of models available to describe how Impact from research is realised and how it may be evaluated, linear perspectives, whether these include feedback loops or various stakeholder perceptions, still dominate. Side by side with these logic model approach is a standard and still dominant theme that research feeds a reservoir of knowledge in the hopes of future downstream practical applications (Pielke and Byerly 1998). Further, these linear assumptions assume that creating Impact is "someone else's" job, that a researcher's responsibility is restricted to creating "good science", and that making Impact is the job of non- or even lesser scientists existing beyond academia. The linear reservoir model promotes the conditions for societal progress, but does not promote a role or need for scientists to explicitly aim or push towards particular societal outcomes. If at all, researchers are brought into the impact process at the end of the research project (Frodeman and Parker 2009) as an add-on, separate from rather than part of scientific endeavours. Examples abound where the achievement of Impact has inspired irrational behaviour, not within the traditional remit of being an academic; the example of *Heliobactor pylori* is evidence of this. Although these stories amount to a public level of hero worship, peers are unwilling to incentivise these irrational, non-academic behaviours by rewarding them formally through research evaluation. One issue with assessing non-academic Impact using academic tools is the ingrained assumption from peers that *"doing impact"* [sic] is beyond their remit. This is further confounded in processes dictated by these peer opinions. A conflict therefore exists between the way that research is traditionally done and the belief systems about what it means to be an academic and what is appropriate behaviour relating to that role. In the absence of newer, more innovative evaluation tools for assessing excellence *"beyond academia"*, tensions and judgements of individual peers within evaluation groups are more persuasive than external, political needs for dynamic research heroes. As a result, we see a never-ending negative cycle between external demands for a socially reflective research system and an evaluation network that is unwilling to incentivise what they perceive as non-academic behaviour.

In models of impact realisation, from traditional research to societal outcomes, an orientation towards linearity dominates, and this reverberates in how evaluators approach its assessment. Each model has emphasised a different marker and/or proxy for determining (1) if Impact has occurred and (2) how it is to be valued; and still promotes a neo-linear conceptualisation of Impact in its evaluation. Despite existing in theory only, these frameworks have both directly and indirectly influenced the development of the REF2014 evaluation process under investigation.

The PayBack framework (Buxton and Hanney 1996) has been the most influential of these models, feeding directly into the development, pilot and mechanics of the UK's REF2014 Impact assessment guidelines. Its applicability to the REF2014 is that it is particularly relevant for ex-post evaluations, which has already been seen in a number of successful applications in the health and medical sciences in the UK (Wooding et al. 2005, 2011), as well as internationally (Donovan et al. 2014; Oortwijn et al. 2008). PayBack uses a narrative case study approach with a series of framework outcomes and feedback loops to capture and focus, organise and analyse individual impact cases. Similar models such as the Research Impact Framework (RIF) (Kuruvilla et al. 2007, 252) allow for the organisation and capture of evidence in the construction of impact case studies, but do little to inform group panels on how to value different cases of impact. Social Impact Assessment Methods for research and funding instruments through the study of Productive Interactions (SIAMPI), on the other hand, professes to offer a "suite" of avenues in which the process of impact realisation is tracked using "productive interactions". Productive interactions come in different forms (Direct, Indirect and Financial interactions) (Spaapen and Van Drooge 2011), and are basically "tracks" of exchanges between researchers and stakeholders that, if used, define them as "productive" (Molas-Gallart and Tang 2011; Spaapen and Van Drooge 2011). Since Impact is a consequence of these "successful/productive interactions", it can be difficult for evaluators to draw a clear distinction between the productive interaction as a proxy or flag and the Impact itself.

The alternative prospect of developing a sole indicator may sound unnecessarily reductionist considering a broad conceptualisation of Impact, as well as potentially dangerous, given the recommendations against the sole use of indicators for evaluation (Hicks et al. 2015), but it is also attractive in the face of the widely acknowledged complexity of its nature as an evaluation object. In metric-driven models, the emphasis is on the comparison of final outcomes, and the creation of quantitative evidence underpinning these outcomes as evidence of Impact. Though passionate in their defence, they do not address important questions such as when Impact occurs and the time taken for its realisation. Instead, these models view Impact as an event, or accumulation of events (productive interactions or not) that can be measured quantitatively. All indicator models are based on logic models and, by their nature, enforce the concept of linearity in subsequent evaluations. Additionally, only including research-driven interventions and using cost-effectiveness or cost-utility data to estimate incremental benefits, these models further promote a linear conceptualisation of impact realisation. Their successful use in estimating the net gains from research investment in a number of health areas such as cardiovascular research (Wooding et al. 2011) and musculoskeletal disorders (Wooding et al. 2005) increases their lure. However, as with all metric-driven models, to reach these final estimations a number of simplifying assumptions must be made regarding time lags, and the proportionality of attributed research outputs, further confusing and confounding their evaluation.

A parallel bias exists against Impacts that is not as readily amenable to quantitative representation. Indeed, regardless of how these indicators are developed, in many evaluations their interpretation and value is dependent upon subjective judgements by evaluators and panels. Models such as the monetisation models (Johnston et al. 2006) automatically promote a notion of value in economic or economic-related outcomes (expressed as cost savings, net gains through quality adjusted life years (QALYs), commercial profits, etc). This is also despite the "fuzzy boundary" acknowledged between economic and non-economic benefits from research. This assumption within evaluation practice inadvertently diverts attention away from the importance of more salient, difficult to capture features, some of which were included by HEFCE as potential impacts in their instructions for panels (HEFCE 2010).

This is not to say that indicators are not important in the evaluation process, especially one that is mediated by peers. Rather, reliance on indicators isolated from expert judgement biases the evaluation simply because some Impact is not adequately represented through quantitative metrics. Adopted in practice, this risks the panel adopting an overly pragmatic approach. However, when used in combination with other tools of judgement, indicators provide powerful pieces of evidence, even if they are not representative of Impact. Studies have identified up to 60 different indicators as necessary to tackle the task of Impact evaluation comprehensively (Martin 2011), none of which can be used alone. Instead, developing indicators to support evaluation decisions has more influence in evaluative practice than imposing one model to the exclusion of all others. The key difference is that metric-driven models can be designed to complement subjective decisions, rather than to supplement them, allowing for the judgement to be made by others and not the indicators.

Group Processes in Peer Review Panels

How people work together towards a common goal, or "group behaviour", lies behind much of what we currently understand about peer review processes. The idea of using theories from behavioural psychology to understand peer review panel processes has been mooted before, and a good summary of the main points and interactions is provided by van Arensbergen et al. (2014). Altering the focus on valuation away from the attributes of the applicants/applications to one that focuses on the way academic groups make decisions is revolutionary for this field. However, by means of extension, it is from theories of group behaviour that I draw many of the understandings that are investigated in much of this book; I adapt these theories and extend them to include the interaction between evaluator types, and the consideration of power within panels during peer review. This perspective also acknowledges the inconvenient political truth that these decisions are less about objective notions of research excellence and more about who is in the room, and how well they interact with each other. Peer review panels are great examples of group processes as they are, by their nature, highly functional and task orientated. This is combined with an understanding that academic peers are very tight-knit, highly interconnected and interpersonal; in other words, everyone knows everyone else.

Previously, Lamont (2009) used Bourdieu's theories to situate her own work on panel interactions and the cultural capital researchers bring to their operation; however, for the concept of societal impact, researchers are less habituated than they are for more traditional concepts of scientific excellence. For notions of Impact beyond academia, their social and political capital is significantly reduced. It is this lack of habituation for Impact that makes it so interesting. It gives us an opportunity to see what happens when scientific experts are called upon to assess something that is not only outside of their professional experience but also outside of their comfort zone. It is primarily for this reason that I, unlike Lamont (2009), do not use Bourdieu within this book. Evaluators bring the cultural capital of previous peer review experience of scientific excellence, but their cultural capital is more ambiguous for that of Impact. This goes for any argument for *interactional expertise* within panels that has been used previously to justify the use of peer review to evaluate interdisciplinary research. If nothing else, interactional expertise enforces the importance of group-level interaction to navigate ambiguous criteria such as Impact. It is too simplistic to conclude from this study, therefore, that evaluators lacked the type of symbolic capital necessary to engage in the evaluation of Impact. Instead, what is seen is that the process of the debate paints a more complex, dynamic and interesting picture.

When assessing Impact, evaluators are required to judge its wider value, using a different perspective, one that exists beyond academia. Therefore, without a clear precedent for effective evaluation, differences in what is believed to be valuable Impact are likely to be more pronounced within a discipline where there are already conflicting viewpoints about what constitutes excellence (Derrick et al. 2011; Haynes et al. 2011). Past research has shown that peer review panels regard any new evaluation criteria as separate from concepts of "excellent research" (Huutoniemi

2010), as shown by studies of panel assessments of the concept of "frontier research" (Luukkonen 2012) and risk adopting a conservative approach, as was seen for Interdisciplinarity (Laudel and Origgi 2006). Luukkonen (2012) also suggested that in panel assessment situations, submissions proposing unorthodox claims of "frontier research" that were contrary to the personal experience of the panel reviewers needed to meet a higher burden of proof during assessment. Indeed, Lamont (2009) argues that the cognitive value of submissions cannot be assessed in a way that is separate from the assessor's *"sense of self and relative positioning"*, suggesting that the interpretation of excellence in societal impact may be heavily based on an evaluator's personal experiences and values, as well as the combination of these values in peer review groups. Reviewer bias, where evaluators do not interpret or apply evaluative criteria in identical ways, may be more pronounced in situations where personal conceptions of the criteria are deemed as more reliable yardsticks for evaluation than untested, unfamiliar guidelines. In situations where experiences, definitions and values of Impact vary between individual panellists, it is difficult to predict how these differences would be resolved during group evaluation discussions.

Capturing the interplay of values, opinions, interests and expertise within a panel is therefore key in understanding how panels navigate ambiguous evaluation objects like Impact. In addition, it is the very concept of peer-led expertise in peer review that implies a type of academic judgement that is not immune to various forms of cognitive and institutional bias (Bourdieu 1975; Chubin and Hackett 1990; Derrick and Samuel 2014, 2016; Hemlin and Rasmussen 2006; Huutoniemi 2012; Langfeldt 2006; Travis and Collins 1991), and when we are dealing with a criterion that is exogenous to the community-led concept of traditional research excellence, these biases are prone to becoming more pronounced.

Group Think and Impact Evaluation

Theories associated with group processes provide a better understanding of the social dynamics inherent in peer review. The group dynamics approach assumes that individual members of a group, no matter the strength of their individual intentions and opinions about a task to be completed (evaluating societal impact), are sensitive to the opinions and pressures from other group members.

Groups, like individuals, have shortcomings, and contrary to what the peer review literature professes, there is no guarantee that groups of experts will make better decisions together than one expert alone. Indeed, group interaction is influenced by the power or status of individuals within the group, and the perception of this power by other panellists. This interaction and exchange of value-laden power perceptions can work to motivate group members and increase the amount, and quality, of information that is discussed and assessed. However, group interaction can also result in poorer decision making because shared responsibility creates a situation where everyone withdraws and no one takes the lead, better known as social loafing (Comer 1995; Hall and Buzwell 2013; Latane et al. 1979; Levi 2015; Simms and Nichols 2014), amplifying the influence of bias. Group decision-making processes should not be confused with the concept of groupthink. Unlike the normal interplay between values that inevitably occurs within groups, groupthink in some situations can become dangerous as individual members submit to group conformity and uniformity, rather than being classified as an out-group, thereby discouraging independent critical thinking. Janis' (1982) example of the Bay of Pigs "fiasco" is an instance of group processing becoming the victim of groupthink.

Academia is not immune to the influence of groupthink and relying on the "wisdom of the crowds" in decision making situations (Mollick and Nanda 2015). Groupthink is when group members are preoccupied with the goal of reaching a consensus rather than reaching the "correct" decision (Aldag and Fuller 1993; Janis 1982; Solomon 2006). Reaching the correct decision requires the continued interchange of values and opinions through peer deliberation. Groups that are vulnerable to groupthink are therefore not motivated to detect any possible weaknesses in their decisions, or to critically appraise alternative decisions, and this in turn can be potentially damaging for peer review outcomes, both academically and politically. Studies of groupthink (Janis 1982) have identified a number of risk factors associated with the development of groupthink. Unfortunately for peer review, many of these risks echo the reasons academia promotes peer review as the evaluation standard of choice. Janis (1982) believed that groups were prone to suffer from groupthink if they were cohesive, had highly directive leadership and were insulated from external experts. These characteristics are all evident in modern peer review structures and forms, and to a lesser extent in academic departmental hierarchies and operations. In addition, when a degree of accountability is absent, the risk of groupthink is higher and, again, academic peer review is characterised by the lack of accountability on academics for the decisions made in determining the allocation of public funds. Since peer review panels can be regarded as an organised, practical attempt to arrive at reasonable agreements despite: differences in outlook among individual members; those who are making decisions based solely on their own expertise; and those who are highly interconnected, the decision-making paradigm is particularly susceptible to risks associated with group-based heuristics.

Irrespective of the risk of making the wrong decision in groups is the fact that while operating to a common goal, the group develops its own identity and set of norms. For peer review, this means that the individual norms and values brought by individuals to the group situation are normalised to a group norm, by which all proposals are judged. Understanding this groupthink therefore provides a lens to interpret the relationships that are formed within the peer review panel, and helps explain the strategies chosen by the panel to value the object. This theory therefore considers peer review as an ongoing, complex social, emotional, political and philosophical interaction.

More recently, Roumbanis (2016) used the theory of "anchoring effects" to explain the decision-making process within peer review panels. By observing evaluation panels for the Natural and Engineering Sciences for the Swedish Research Council, he concluded that grant success from peer review was increasingly a matter of chance and anchoring rankings of proposals were sensitive to an anchoring effect. Moreover, *there is frequently agreement about which proposals are near the top, and which are near the bottom*" (p. 17), but that organisation of the rankings in the middle emerged through a large number of group-based anchoring, adjustments and reappraisals made during the session. Referred to as *"collective anchoring effects"*, or anchoring effects made at the group level—the idea is that the concept of double heuristics introduces the idea that individuals, each with their own capacities to judge, each with biases and blind spots, are aggregated by an organised procedure, and this second-order procedure generates its own heuristics, with its own biases and limitations (Roumbanis 2016). He noted that panel groups can be regarded as an organised, practical attempt to arrive at reasonable agreements despite differences in outlook, an assertion that I absolutely agree with when it comes to peer review.

More specifically, Travis and Collins (1991, 327) refer to the concept of "cognitive particularism" when referring to how panellists reach a group decision through peer review. This concept, which refers to the cognitive boundaries that naturally exist between different disciplines and methodological approaches, can be used to explain both agreements and disagreements between panellists in session. However, this does not mean that any evidence of this cognitive particularism automatically implies a source of bias. In the authors' words: *"It is not that panel members are not of goodwill, but that they simply do not fight so hard for subjects that are not close to their hearts"* (Travis and Collins 1991). Lamont (2009) also showed how academics from different disciplines work together to reach a group-based consensus in academic decision making. What we do know is that when there is a better discipline match between applicant and reviewer, review scores are significantly higher than when there is no match (Porter and Rossini 1985). In other words, when an expert is assessing a proposal in his area of expertise, he is more likely to reward it positively.

The reasoning surrounding group-based peer review is primarily associated with the size and breadth of the proposals under consideration. It is almost impossible to be a sufficient expert in all fields to comment as an expert on all proposals, and for this reason some have argued that group-based peer review is not "true" peer review. Nonetheless, panel processes prevail because, quite simply, a panel of 10 reviewers will have more intellectual and physical (if we are talking of a long-drawn out process) resources to draw from than one or even two individual evaluators. Inherent in meeting this goal is the concept of "consensus building", which is achieved through integrating information and negotiating values through debate and discussion.

Lamont's (2009) panel discussions were steered by informal rules, generally known by all panellists. These are unwritten rules that become "group norms" about what are appropriate and inappropriate terms of behaviour. Through these unwritten rules, groups are able to cordially work towards building a group consensus with which to guide the evaluation. Implicit in this assumption is that within the group, panellists can disregard their own preferences in order to single out the best proposals through dialogue and discussion. Second is the assumption that if this cannot be done, then as a group and through this dialogue the explicit biases or preferences of one evaluator can be compensated for by the existence of opposing and equally extreme biases of another evaluator within the group. Indeed, panel discussion is used as a tool to ensure fair evaluation processes, and to reduce differences between reviewers (Fogelholm et al. 2012; Olbrecht and Bornmann 2010). This consideration is recognised by many funding agencies that use academic groups as an evaluative tool of choice, specifically to reduce the influence of corrupting external biases (Lamont 2009). The problem exists when all panellists exhibit the same underlying, unconscious or implicit bias that shadows the objective, expert-led assessment of all proposals. In this regard, the selection of evaluators for the peer group, as well as considering how they work together, is an important pre-evaluation consideration.

There are obvious tensions inherent in the creation of a group consensus, particularly the effects that reviewer disagreements may have on decisions (Mayo et al. 2006; Porter 2005). However, Harnard (1985) in his criticisms of the Cole et al. (1981) study suggested that even though consensus was the aim of peer review, a certain degree of disagreement was not only healthy, but an informative and essential aspect of scientific activity, and therefore of peer review (Harnad 1985). It was, he argued, more valuable for subjective discussion to have disagreement, rather than to believe that its existence was evidence of some type of scientific shortcoming. Further, Lamont found that group debate was vital for creating "trust" within panels, stating that "debating plays a crucial role in creating trust: fair decisions emerge from dialogue among various types of experts, a dialogue that leaves room for discretion, uncertainty and the weighing of a range of factors and competing forms of excellence" (Lamont 2009, 7), although such discussions are not always necessary to improve the reliability of any resulting evaluations (Fogelholm et al. 2012). In this book, providing sufficient temporal and intellectual space to ensure robust in-group deliberation is key for avoiding groupthink.

The Emergent Dominant Definition of Impact

Whereas the consensus building and the resulting committee culture were related to how the committee understands the strengths and weaknesses of the contribution of all group members, the dominant definition is the unconscious collection of decisions made by the group about the evaluation object. As one evaluator described how his group progressed through the evaluation, *"...I call it mood music—that movement away from disruptive critical appraisal to constructive critique"* P0OutImp6(POST). Previous research has focused on the committee culture that develops around an evaluation process and its power over the direction of that evaluation (Huutoniemi 2012; Langfeldt 2001, 2004); however, the dominant definition is focused solely on how the committee focuses on the valuation of a specific object (as was the case for Impact). In other words, the committee culture refers to how the group comes together during the evaluation, but the dominant definition reflects the evaluator's eye and guides the group's selection of valuation strategies around the evaluation object. During peer review, as a number of different evaluation objects are under consideration, it is important to focus on how the group orientates itself around each object individually, especially if they are formally required and distinct from other objects (such as the case for Impact), to understand how submission attributes are valued. An evaluation object is not restricted to a criterion, although formal inclusion in an overall evaluation is a requirement. More broadly, the concept of an evaluation object goes beyond the evaluation construct to include how the group approaches valuation in practice. In this way the concept of *"Interdisciplinarity"*[4] does not become a specific evaluation object unless it is (a) formally required as a consideration and (b) requires a separate evaluation process to determine its value. In the REF2014, Impact was an evaluation object as it required an evaluation process that was separate from other criteria (Outputs and Environment).

A dominant definition around an object combines the act of forming a consensus and the influence of the committee culture, as the evaluation process progresses. The idea was developed from Foucault's concept of dominant discourse (Arribas-Ayllon and Walkerdine 2008), and the relationship with power, Collins and Evans' (2002) idea of interactional expertise stemming from tacit knowledge sharing, as well as more general theories related to social constructivism. Developing the dominant definition recognises that within these peer review panels, power relationships exist and influence the direction of the debate (implicitly and explicitly), and also how ideas and concepts around the evaluation object gain (and lose) allies within deliberations. It is a theory that reflects a tug-of-war towards forming the evaluator's eye. It acknowledges the direction of evaluation decided by groups that are sensitive to outwardly declared as well as internally perceived influences of power.

Identifying the dominant definition in practice, whether through observations or the in vitro approach employed here, is difficult, as on a group level it is employed unconsciously, and reflects implicit decisions a panel makes towards the value of the object, *"…how the panel implicitly behaved" P0P2OutImp1(POST)*. For that reason, it becomes difficult to pin down. It becomes the evaluation's *"mood music"*, and at the point when panel deliberation moves away *"…from disruptive critical appraisal to constructive critique"*. We can identify evidence in its existence as panellists refer to how, *"…over time, there was a coming together P3OutImp2(POST)*, and they referred to their *"…gut feeling of how this thing is going" P5Imp1(POST)*, when they talked about how the group valued Impact as an object. The implicit nature of the dominant definition, however, means that it is difficult for even the panellists to refer to it with hindsight: *"So once you've got an agreed set of definitions, although I can't remember them precisely now, six months later" P2Imp1(POST)*. Although the repeated use of *"we"* and group pronouns emphasise how the group both developed and took ownership of the evaluator's eye around Impact: *"And kind of worked out that we knew what we were measuring against, we were marking against" P0P2OutImp1(POST)*, and *"… we gained something of a kind of common mind-set if you want" P3OutImp3(POST)*. The practice of applying the dominant definition is seen in how panellists returned to re-evaluate submissions assessed earlier, armed with the lens that the group had developed together in practice: *"…we revisited a number of things that had done either very, very well or very, very badly, and reappraised them in the light of having completed the whole series of work" P2Imp5(POST)*. This also reflects how the dominant definition, hand in hand with the development of a committee culture towards the generation of a group consensus, evolves as the evaluation progresses. A strong committee culture is therefore reflected in how well the dominant definition is applied in practice, as well as the extent to which the panellists, as a group, take ownership of the evaluation process and its outcomes. In this way, the dominant definition, and how it relates to specific evaluation objects, becomes the evaluator's eye, that *"constructively (sic) critiques"* submissions according to the implicit mutual construction of individual evaluator perspectives about them.

Notes

1. A Likert survey was used at the end of each round of interviews to test the validity of the qualitative analysis performed. This Likert survey used statements of the dominant themes emerging from the interviews to test the extent they reflected the opinions of the group. Only dominant themes that emerged from the analysis, and confirmed by the Likert surveys were used.

2. This term is taken directly from Chubb, J., Watermeyer, R. (2016) Artifice or integrity in the marketization of research impact? Investigating the moral economy of (pathways to) impact statements within research funding proposals in the UK and Australia. *Studies in Higher Education* 1–3. Doi:10.1080/03075079.2016.1144182.

3. Many applications these days offer applicants the courtesy of nominating reviewers. This reduces the burden on funding agencies and journals to search for a reviewer, and seemingly gives people a sense of control of the applications' destiny.

4. Research investigating how concepts of Interdisciplinarity are evaluated by peer review panels, are commonly professed to be a model that also forms the basis of how we consider how Impact is evaluated. Katri Huutoniemi, *Evaluating Interdisciplinary Research* (10: Oxford: Oxford University Press, 2010).

References

Abramo, G., C.A. D'Angelo, and F. Rosati. 2015. Selection committees for academic recruitment: Does gender matter? *Research Evaluation* 24 (4): 392–404.

Aldag, R.J., and S.R. Fuller. 1993. Beyond fiasco: A reappraisal of the groupthink phenomenon and a new model of group decision processes. *Psychological Bulletin* 113 (3): 533.

Andersen, L.B., and T. Pallesen. 2008. "Not just for the money?" How financial incentives affect the number of publications at Danish research institutions. *International Public Management Journal* 11 (1): 28–47.

Arribas-Ayllon, M., and V. Walkerdine. 2008. Foucauldian discourse analysis. In *The Sage Handbook of qualitative research in psychology*, ed. Carla Willig and Wendy Stainton-Rogers, 91–108. London: Sage.

Auranen, O., and M. Nieminen. 2010. University research funding and publication performance—An international comparison. *Research Policy* 39 (6): 822–834.

Bornmann, L. 2012. Measuring the societal impact of research. *EMBO Reports* 13 (8): 673–676.

———. 2013. What is the societal impact of research and how can it be assessed? A literature survey. *Journal of the American Society of Information Science and Technology* 64 (2): 217–233.

Bornmann, L., G. Wallon, and A. Ledin. 2008. Does the committee peer review select the best applicants for funding? An investigation of the selection process for two european molecular biology organization programmes. *PLoSOne* 3 (10): e3480.

Bourdieu, P. 1975. The specificity of the scientific field and the social conditions of the progress of reason. *Information (International Social Science Council)* 14 (6): 19–47.

———. 1984. *Distinction: A social critique of the judgement of taste*. Cambridge, MA: Harvard University Press.

Bourdieu, Pierre. 1997. Capital cultural, escuela y espacio social. *Siglo* xxi.

Buxton, M., and S. Hanney. 1996. How can payback from health services research be assessed? *Journal of Health Services Research* 1 (1): 35–43.

Cetina, K.K., J. Clark, C. Modgil, S. Modgil, I.B. Cohen, K. Duffin, S. Strickland, R. Feldhay, Y. Elkana, and R.K. Merton. 1991. Merton's sociology of science: The first and the last sociology of science? *JSTOR* 20 (4): 522–526.

Chubb, J., and R. Watermeyer. 2016. Artifice or integrity in the marketization of research impact? Investigating the moral economy of (pathways to) impact statements within research funding proposals in the UK and Australia. *Studies in Higher Education* 1–13. https://doi.org/10.1080/03075079.2016.1144182.

Chubin, D.E., and E.J. Hackett. 1990. *Peerless science: Peer review and US science policy*. Albany: State University of New York Press.

Cole, S., J.R. Cole, and G.A. Simon. 1981. Chance and consensus in peer review. *Science* 214 (4523): 881–886.

Collins, H.M., and R. Evans. 2002. The third wave of science studies: Studies of expertise and experience. *Social Studies of Science* 32 (2): 235–296.

Comer, D.R. 1995. A model of social loafing in real work groups. *Human Relations* 48 (6): 647–667.

Dahler-Larsen, P. 2007. Evaluation and public management. In *The Oxford Handbook of public management*, ed. E. Ferlie, L.E. Lynn Jr., and C. Pollitt. Oxford: Oxford University Press.

———. 2014. Constitutive effects of performance indicators: Getting beyond unintended consequences. *Public Management Review* 16 (7): 969–986.

de Jong, S.P., J. Smit, and L. van Drooge. 2015. Scientists' response to societal impact policies: A policy paradox. *Science and Public Policy* 43 (1): 102–114.

De Rijcke, S., P.F. Wouters, A.D. Rushforth, T.P. Franssen, and B. Hammarfelt. 2016. Evaluation practices and effects of indicator use—A literature review. *Research Evaluation* 25 (2): 161–169.

Deem, R., S. Hillyard, and M. Reed. 2007. *Knowledge, higher education, and the new managerialism: The changing management of UK universities*. Oxford: Oxford University Press.

Derrick, G., I. Meijer, and E. van Wijk. 2014. Unwrapping "impact" for evaluation: A co-word analysis of the UK REF2014 policy documents using VOSviewer. *Proceedings of the Science and Technology Indicators Conference*.

Derrick, G.E., A.S. Haynes, S. Chapman, and W.D. Hall. 2011. The association between four citation metrics and peer rankings of research influence of Australia researchers in six fields of public health. *PLoSOne* 6: e18521.

Derrick, G.E., and V. Pavone. 2013. Democratising research evaluation: Achieving greater public engagement with bibliometrics-informed peer review. *Science and Public Policy* 40 (5): 563–575.

Derrick, G.E., and G.N. Samuel. 2014. The impact evaluation scale: Group panel processes and outcomes in societal impact evaluation. *Social Science and Medicine*, in press.

———. 2016. The evaluation scale: Exploring decisions about societal impact in peer review panels. *Minerva* 54 (1): 75–97.

Donovan, C., L. Butler, A.J. Butt, T.H. Jones, and S.R. Hanney. 2014. Evaluation of the impact of National Breast Cancer Foundation-funded research. *The Medical Journal of Australia* 200 (4): 214–218.

Fernández-Zubieta, A., A. Geuna, and C. Lawson. 2015. Mobility and productivity of research scientists1. *Global Mobility of Research Scientists: The Economics of Who Goes Where and Why* 105.

Finkel, A. 2015. Research Engagement for Australia (REA): Measuring research engagement between universities and end users. Presentation to Universities Australia.

Fogelholm, M., S. Leppinen, A. Auvinen, J. Raitanen, A. Nuutinen, and K. Väänänen. 2012. Panel discussion does not improve reliability of peer review for medical research grant proposals. *Journal of Clinical Epidemiology* 65 (1): 47–52.

Frodeman, R., and J. Parker. 2009. Intellectual merit and broader impact: The National Science Foundation's broader impacts criterion and the question of peer review. *Social Epistemology* 23 (3–4): 337–345.

Geuna, A., and M. Piolatto. 2016. Research assessment in the UK and Italy: Costly and difficult, but probably worth it (at least for a while). *Research Policy* 45 (1): 260–271.

Gibbons, M., C. Limoges, H. Nowotny, S. Schwartzman, and P. Scott. 1994. *The new production of knowledge: The dynamics of science and research in contemporary societies*. London: SAGE.

Giraudeau, B., C. Leyrat, A. Le Gouge, J. Leger, and A. Caille. 2011. Peer review of grant applications: A simple method to identify proposals with discordant reviews. *PLoSOne* 6 (11): e27557.

Grant, J., P.-B. Brutscher, S. Kirk, L. Butler, and S. Wooding. 2010. *Capturing research impacts: A review of International practice*. Documented briefing. RAND Corporation.

Greene, J.C. 1997. Evaluation as advocacy. *Evaluation Practice* 18: 25–36.

———. 2000. Challenges in practicing deliberative democratic evaluation. *New Directions for Evaluation* 2000 (85): 13–26.

Hackett, E.J., and D. E. Chubin. 2003. *Peer review for the 21st century: Applications to education research*. Ed. National Research Council. Washington, DC.

Hall, D., and S. Buzwell. 2013. The problem of free-riding in group projects: Looking beyond social loafing as reason for non-contribution. *Active Learning in Higher Education* 14 (1): 37–49.

Harnad, S. 1985. Rational disagreement in peer review. *Science, Technology, & Human Values* 10 (3): 55–62.

Haynes, A.S., G.E. Derrick, S. Chapman, S. Redman, W.D. Hall, J. Gillespie, and H. Sturk. 2011. From "our world" to the "real world": Exploring the views and behaviour of policy-influential Australian public health researchers. *Social Science & Medicine* 72: 1047–1055.

HEFCE. 2010. REF2014: Panel criteria and working methods. http://www.ref.ac.uk/media/ref/content/pub/panelcriteriaandworkingmethods/01_12.pdf. Accessed 1 Mar 2016.

Hemlin, S., and S.B. Rasmussen. 2006. The shift in academic quality control. *Science, Technology, & Human Values* 31 (2): 173–198.

Herbst, M. 2007. *Financing public universities*. New York: Springer.

Hicks, D. 2012. Performance-based university research funding systems. *Research policy* 41 (2): 251–261.

Hicks, D., P.F. Wouters, L. Waltman, S. De Rijcke, and I. Rafols. 2015. The Leiden Manifesto for research metrics. *Nature* 520 (7548): 429.

Huutoniemi, K. 2010. *Evaluating interdisciplinary research*. Oxford: Oxford University Press.

———. 2012. Communicating and compromising on disciplinary expertise in the peer review of research proposals. *Social Studies of Science* 42 (6): 897–921.

Ingwersen, P., and B. Larsen. 2014. Influence of a performance indicator on Danish research production and citation impact 2000–12. *Scientometrics* 101 (2): 1325–1344.

Janis, I.L. 1982. *Groupthink: Psychological studies of policy decisions and fiascoes*. Boston, MA: Houghton Mifflin Company.

Johnston, S.C., J.D. Rootenberg, S. Katrak, W.S. Smith, and J.S. Elkins. 2006. Effect of a US National Institutes of Health programme of clinical trials on public health and costs. *Lancet* 367 (9519): 1319–1327.

Knorr-Cetina, K.D. 1983. *The ethnographic study of scientific work: Towards a constructivist interpretation of science*. London: Sage.

———. 1991. Epistemic cultures: Forms of reason in science. *History of Political Economy* 23 (1): 105–122.

Knott, M. 2015. *Academic publications to become less important when funding university research*. Sydney: Sydney Morning Herald.

Kuruvilla, S., N. Mays, and G. Walt. 2007. Describing the impact of health services and policy research. *Journal of Health Services Research & Policy* 12 (suppl 1): 23–31.

Lamont, M. 2009. *How professors think: Inside the curious world of academic judgement*. Cambridge, MA: Harvard University Press.

Lamont, M., and K. Huutoniemi. 2011. Opening the black box of evaluation: How quality is recognized by peer review panels. *Bulletin SAGW* 2: 47–49.

Langfeldt, L. 2001. The decision-making constraints and processes of grant peer review, and their effects on the review outcome. *Social Studies of Science* 31 (6): 820–841.

———. 2004. Expert panels evaluating research: Decision-making and sources of bias. *Research Evaluation* 13 (1): 51–62.

———. 2006. The policy challenges of peer review: Managing bias, conflict of interests and multidisciplinary assessments. *Research Evaluation* 15 (1): 31–41.

Latane, B., K. Williams, and S. Harkins. 1979. Many hands make light the work: The causes and consequences of social loafing. *Journal of Personality and Social Psychology* 37 (6): 822–832.

Laudel, G., and G. Origgi. 2006. *Introduction to a special issue on the assessment of interdisciplinary research*. Oxford: Oxford University Press.

Leisyte, L., and J.R. Dee. 2012. Understanding academic work in a changing institutional environment. In *Higher education: Handbook of theory and research*, ed. J.D. Smart, 123–206. New York: Springer.

Levi, D. 2015. *Group dynamics for teams*. London: Sage Publications.

Luukkonen, T. 2012. Conservatism and risk-taking in peer review: Emerging ERC practices. *Research Evaluation* 21: 48–60.

Mark, M.M., and R.L. Shotland. 1985. Stakeholder-based evaluation and value judgments. *Evaluation Review* 9 (5): 605–626.

Martin, B.R. 2011. The Research Excellence Framework and the 'impact agenda': Are we creating a Frankenstein monster? *Research Evaluation* 20 (3): 247–254.

Mayo, N.E., J. Brophy, M.S. Goldberg, M.B. Klein, S. Miller, R.W. Platt, and J. Ritchie. 2006. Peering at peer review revealed high degree of chance associated with funding of grant applications. *Journal of Clinical Epidemiology* 59 (8): 842–848.

Merton, R.K. 1973. *The sociology of science: Theoretical and empirical investigations*. Chicago: University of Chicago press.

Molas-Gallart, J., and P. Tang. 2011. Tracing 'productive interactions' to identify social impacts: An example from the social sciences. *Research Evaluation* 20 (3): 219–226.

Mollick, E., and R. Nanda. 2015. Wisdom or madness? Comparing crowds with expert evaluation in funding the arts. *Management Science* 62 (6): 1533–1553.

Nowotny, H., P. Scott, and M. Gibbons. 2001. *Re-thinking science: Knowledge and the public in an age of uncertainty*. Argentina: SciELO.

Olbrecht, M., and L. Bornmann. 2010. Panel peer review of grant applications: What do we know from research in social psychology on judgement and decision making in groups? *Research Evaluation* 19 (4): 293–304.

Oortwijn, W.J., S.R. Hanney, A. Ligtvoet, S. Hoorens, S. Wooding, J. Grant, M.J. Buxton, and L.M. Bouter. 2008. Assessing the impact of health technology assessment in the Netherlands. *International Journal of Technology Assessment in Health Care* 24 (03): 259–269.

Pielke, R.A., and R. Byerly. 1998. Beyond basic and applied. *Physics Today* 51 (2): 42–46.

Pier, E.L., J. Raclaw, A. Kaatz, M. Brauer, M. Carnes, M.J. Nathan, and C.E. Ford. 2017. 'Your comments are meaner than your score': Score calibration talk influence intra- and inter-panel variability during scientific grant peer review. *Research Evaluation* 26 (1): 1–14.

Porter, A.L., and F.A. Rossini. 1985. Peer review of interdisciplinary research proposals. *Science, Technology, & Human Values* 10 (3): 33–38.

Porter, R. 2005. What do grant reviewers really want, anyway? *Journal of Research Administration* 36 (2): 5–13,13.

Roumbanis, L. 2016. Academic judgments under uncertainty: A study of collective anchoring effects in Swedish Research Council panel groups. *Social Studies of Science* 47: 1–22.

Roy, R. 1985. Funding science: The real defects of peer review and an alternative to it. *Science, Technology, & Human Values* 10 (3): 73–81.

Salter, A.J., and B.R. Martin. 2001. The economic benefits of publicly funded basic research: A critical review. *Research policy* 30 (3): 509–532.

Sandstrom, U., U. Heyman, and P. Van den Besselaar. 2014. The complex relationahip between competitive funding and performance. In *Context counts: Pathways to master big and little data – STI*, ed. E. Noyons, 523–533. Leiden: CWTS. https://doi.org/10.13140/2.1.5036.6728.

Simms, A., and T. Nichols. 2014. Social loafing: A review of the literature. *Journal of Management Policy and Practice* 15 (1): 58.

Sivertsen, G., and J. Schneider. 2012. Evaluering av den bibliometriske forskningsindikator.

Smith, R. 2001. Measuring the social impact of research—Difficult but necessary. *British Medical Journal* 323: 528. https://doi.org/10.1136/bmj.323.7312.528

Smith, S., V. Ward, and A. House. 2011. 'Impact' in the proposals for the UK's Research Excellence Framework: Shifting the boundaries of academic autonomy. *Research Policy* 40 (10): 1369–1379.

Solomon, M. 2006. Groupthink versus the wisdom of crowds: The social epistemology of deliberation and dissent. *The Southern Journal of Philosophy* 44 (S1): 28–42.

Spaapen, J., and L. Van Drooge. 2011. Introducing 'productive interactions' in social impact assessment. *Research Evaluation* 20 (3): 211–218.

Thaler Richard, H., and R. Sunstein Cass. 2008. *Nudge: Improving decisions about health, wealth, and happiness*. New Haven, CT: Yale University Press.

Travis, G.D.L., and H.M. Collins. 1991. New light on old boys: Cognitive and institutional particularism in the peer review system. *Science, Technology, & Human Values* 16 (3): 322–341.

van Arensbergen, P. 2014. *Talent proof. Selection processes in research funding and careers*. Den Haag: Rathenau Instituut.

van Arensbergen, P., I. van der Weijden, and P. van den Besselaar. 2014. The selection of talent as a group process. A literature review on the social dynamics of decision making in grant panels. *Research Evaluation* 23 (4): 298–311.

Van der Meulen, Barend, and Arie Rip. 2000. Evaluation of societal quality of public sector research in the Netherlands. *Research Evaluation* 9 (1): 11–25.

Watermeyer, R. 2015. Lost in the 'third space': The impact of public engagement in higher education on academic identity, research practice and career progression. *European Journal of Higher Education* 5 (3): 331–347.

———. 2016. Impact in the REF: Issues and obstacles. *Studies in Higher Education* 41 (2): 199–214.

Watermeyer, R., and A. Hedgecoe. 2016. Selling 'impact': Peer reviewer projections of what is needed and what counts in REF impact case studies. A retrospective analysis. *Journal of Education Policy* 31 (5): 651–665.

Willmott, H. 2011. Journal list fetishism and the perversion of scholarship: Reactivity and the ABS list. *Organization* 18 (4): 429–442.

Wooding, S., S. Hanney, M. Buxton, and J. Grant. 2005. Payback arising from research funding: Evaluation of the Arthritis Research Campaign. *Rheumatology* 44 (9): 1145–1156.

Wooding, S., S. Hanney, A. Pollitt, M. Buxton, and J. Grant. 2011. Project retrosight: Understanding the returns from cardiovascular and stroke research: the policy report. *Rand Health Quarterly* 1 (1): 16.

3

Evaluation Mechanics

> I think it's an irresistible idea, unfortunately.
>
> *POP2OutImp1, Post-evaluation*

Let me start this chapter by reiterating that this book does not aim to deconstruct or evaluate the REF's place as an assessment tool in regulating the UK academic community, or by extension the role of audit exercises as academic governance tools globally, despite being *"an irresistible idea, unfortunately"*. The UK is by no means a novice in national research audit exercises, having conducted these in various guises since 1986 (Bence and Oppenhein 2005). The UK therefore brings a long history of evolving criteria and evaluation guidelines that has reinforced peer review as central to the operationalisation of these evaluative frameworks. This book's preparation went hand in hand with a series of academic articles, and it became clear that it was almost impossible to write a book about Impact evaluation processes that was completely separate from the political associations of the REF2014. The REF2014 is extremely emotive for its critics, and at many times the technicalities of the evaluation were used in defence of any perceived criticism or slight on its existence. As

© The Author(s) 2018
G. Derrick, *The Evaluators' Eye*,
https://doi.org/10.1007/978-3-319-63627-6_3

such, an endless list of reviewers would, perhaps unconsciously and unfairly, project their frustrations of the REF2014 process onto their consideration of the article's merits, rather than observe the studies of the evaluation process as independent from these internal frustrations. Therefore, within this chapter and amid a discussion of REF2014 evaluation rules and guidelines, I emphasise that the REF2014 is not my dependent variable. Rather the REF2014, as the world's first evaluation framework with a formal, ex-post criterion of Impact, conveniently provided the opportunity to explore the practice of its assessment rather than being the object of study.

In this chapter, I explore the rules and procedures underpinning the REF2014's evaluation of Impact. I label these as "mechanics" to reflect the ways in which they operated to guide the evaluation process and, by extension, the behaviour of panellists. The existence of mechanics reinforces the role of peer review as a political and social construct that balances public accountability with the appearance of academic autonomy. As with all democratic deliberation-based evaluations, however, certain boundaries are required to ensure that all voices are heard (Greene 2000) and that the group remains focused on the evaluation object. Mechanics provide these boundaries as a form of "assisted sense making" (Mark et al. 2000), but overdependence on these in preference to deliberation as a consensus-building tool risks negating any benefits associated with peer review as an evaluative tool by supplementing deliberation as a problem-solving tool, and risks groupthink. In this way, mechanics are essential players in dictating the evaluation process that has been overlooked in similar studies of peer review as a goal-orientated approach where such side effects are ignored (Vedung 1997; Dahler-Larsen 2012). Here, I further classify how these mechanics operate during the assessment as either *facilitative* or *infiltrative*, together with a consideration of their intended or unintended effects. I extend Dahler-Larsen's work on constitutive effects as I see how these mechanics work within an evaluation process, similar to how any indicator influences behaviour towards an evaluation. A constitutive effect is one that considers how measurement indicators around an evaluation object help to define the social realities of which they are part (Dahler-Larsen 2011, 2014), and one that points to a constructed nature of evaluations and outcomes. As such, mechanics operate as an in-group indicator by providing guidelines and signposts to the evaluators about how to value the object, thereby guiding the process. Whereas Dahler-Larsen's work specifically views a constitutive effect as something that occurs external to the evaluation and refers to the behaviour of applicants (submissions), here I flip this perspective to one that views how these mechanics have an effect (unintended or not (Dahler-Larsen 2014)), within the evaluation process. In other words, I consider how constitutive effects manifest themselves in vivo.

After introducing the concept of evaluation mechanics as actors in the peer review process, I explore evaluators' pre-conceived beliefs around Impact relative to the perceived role of the evaluation mechanics. By combining the pre-evaluation panellists' views together with the objectives of each mechanic, I begin to explore the types of conflicts that would exist in practice between the mechanics' intentions and the pre-conceived ideals evaluators had about Impact. I explore how evaluators anticipated issues in implementing the mechanics in practice, and how they developed strategies to avoid issues.

Facilitative and Infiltrative Mechanics

Rules, guidelines and structures are to be expected in large-scale research evaluation frameworks. Lamont (2009) sees these structures as machinery of the evaluation that may act to define and constrain evaluation outcomes, limiting deliberation in panels. In contrast, I see these machineries as potentially facilitating tools and not necessarily ill-intended. Such facilitation is essential if an evaluator's experience of the object is limited. The structures put in place for the REF2014 were designed to adhere to a notion of transparency and reflexivity in public policy decision making by making decision-making parameters clear for submitting HEIs.

It is not unreasonable to expect a level of guidance, especially when tasking evaluators with navigating an ambiguous object such as Impact. This is independent of academic arguments that suggest that establishing an "Impact database" like Web of Science or Scopus which would index all possible societal benefits stemming from each academic article (Bornmann 2012; Bornmann and Marx 2014) is the only way to facilitate its assessment. Without reflecting too deeply on the sheer impossibility of indexing all types of Impacts systematically and attributing each to individual research articles, this argument has been a seductive, predominant and ongoing theme in research impact assessment. The act of valuing Impact doesn't happen through a database, or by reducing it as a concept. Rather, valuation is the result of conflicting expert views and reaching a compromise-based consensus. Peer review as an evaluation tool facilitates this consensus building; however, it transposes a subjective human element into a seemingly objective process. Thus, mechanics provide necessary boundaries in the process to ensure its efficiency and, despite its black box nature, a degree of transparency. To make the invisible visible, or at least responsible from the peer review black box.

For an ambiguous evaluation object, such as Impact, there is a risk associated with evaluation through peer review either through (a) unstructured deliberation with no outcome (inefficient, time consuming and therefore expensive), which questions the ability and authority of "experts" involved in the discussions; or (b) an unstructured deliberation with an outcome where it is unclear on what grounds an assessment was made. For the second option, the evaluation can also be time consuming and expensive; there is an increased risk for groupthink if evaluation shortcuts in decision making are taken in the face of time limits and in-group pressure. Although peer review is, at its most basic level, a pragmatic process, the effects of these shortcuts can be circumvented by providing boundaries in the evaluation via mechanics. In addition, in line with transparency and accountability, mechanics were made available prior to the evaluation to guide HEIs to develop their submissions. However, this chapter does not explore how the mechanics facilitated the submission process, but instead investigates how they act in the peer review evaluation process, and the influence of mechanics played a large role in both stages of this evaluation. The divide is whether they act to infiltrate or facilitate the evaluation process, and this depends on the evaluators' ability to utilise the mechanics to construct their own reality, and not be constrained by them. Being constrained implies that the evaluation group is unable to mould the relevance of the mechanics for their needs, restricting the freedom underpinning democratic deliberation as a tool towards consensus building. In these cases, the evaluation outcomes will resemble the mechanics. I refer to these as *"artefacts"*, and their presence in the evaluation outcomes indicates an infiltrative mechanic. This is because the mechanic provides the lens with which all submissions are to be valued, acting to dictate the process. Examples of artefacts are seen in the studies of peer review that have found how evaluation outcomes correlate with proxy bibliometric indicators of the same object (Rinia et al. 1998; Aksnes and Taxt 2004; Bornmann and Daniel 2005; Bornmann et al. 2008; van den Besselaar and Leydesdorff 2009; Franceschet and Costantini 2011). In this example, the provision of bibliometric indicators infiltrated the evaluation process, leaving behind artefacts in the evaluation outcomes. In these cases, it is safe to assume that the evaluation process was not grounded in the expert-driven deliberation that is the hallmark of peer review, and instead was driven by mechanics as proxies for expert assessments. Providing panels with infiltrative mechanics risks replacing, rather than reflecting, the benefits associated with expert-driven deliberative judgements such as peer review.

Higher Education Funding Council for England (HEFCE) acknowledged the importance of allowing the REF2014 panels to govern themselves by allowing panels to choose if and how publication metrics would be used to facilitate the evaluation of the Outputs criterion (HEFCE 2010), but the process was less autonomous for Impact. For navigating a new and untested evaluation criterion, using a panel of Impact evaluation novices, the mechanics offered an aid to guide the evaluation, rather than to unintentionally steer it. However, evaluation mechanics can have both intended and unintended effects on the evaluation process. In the above example of using bibliometric indicators in assessments of scientific excellence, the provision of the indicators was intended to be facilitative but had the unintended consequence of infiltrating and thereby directing the evaluation. Mechanics with intended effects imply some type of purpose or agency behind their implementation, by the evaluation designers or by the evaluators themselves. Utilising the mechanics as intended ensures that the evaluation outcomes reflect their purpose, thereby leaving artefacts. Interpreting their influence (facilitative or infiltrative) on a group level rather than just on the individual level means that the analysis is sensitive to the role they played in strengthening or defeating arguments during group deliberations. This distinction is important because if more than one evaluator is influenced by mechanics, then a claim of their infiltrative nature is more valid.

Typologies of Evaluation Mechanics

Mechanics can be either infiltrative or facilitative, as well as having intended or unintended consequences. As such, I extend Dahler-Larsen's (2007, 2012) concept of constitutive effects, to describe four typologies of how evaluation mechanics influence an evaluation process. I use the words "unintended" and "intended" loosely, so as not to imply any type of political motive in their use but instead look at unintended effects as something that is counter to their seemingly good intentions (Norman 2002). These four typologies are shown in Table 3.1, and combine facilitative (F) and infiltrative (I_1) influences with intended (I_2) and unintended (U) consequences for the evaluation process. I label these as Type 1 through to Type IV and distinguish each by juxtaposing pre- and post-evaluation recollections from panellists about the process of evaluation and their orientation of the object relative to these mechanics, as well as examining the extent to which the mechanics are detectable in the evaluation outcomes (i.e. they leave behind artefacts).

Type 1 mechanics are those that act to infiltrate the evaluation process (Infiltrative, I_1), but restrict the ability of evaluation groups to produce evaluation outcomes independent from their influence. In Type 1 situations, there is usually some type of agency behind the mechanic that desires that evaluation outcomes reflect a pre-determined intention or design (Intended, I_2). In many cases, this direction is determined by some force external to the evaluation process. In such cases this evaluation might

Table 3.1 Typologies of evaluation mechanics and their effects

	Infiltrative (I_1)	Facilitative (F)
Intended (I_2)	Type I	Type II
	($I_1 - I_2$)	($F - I_2$)
Unintended (U)	Type III	Type IV
	($I_1 - U$)	($F - U$)

masquerade as an idealised peer review process, but prohibits the panel's ability to adopt independent evaluation strategies, resulting in transferring artefacts to the outcomes. Identification of Type 1 is achieved by cross-referencing the mechanic with the evaluation outcomes, noting any similarities between the two.

In contrast, Type II mechanics might have intended (I_2) consequences but do not restrict the ability of the evaluation group to interpret these notions for themselves. This means that the intentions are left intentionally open for interpretation (i.e. to evaluate notions of academic excellence, interdisciplinarity, or Impact). This is not to say that the evaluation allows the group to throw caution to the wind and work independent of any guidance or nudge (Thaler Richard and Sunstein Cass 2008), but rather the group is permitted to interpret and apply any provided mechanic as they choose. In these situations the mechanics merely serve to stimulate and facilitate (F_1) debate by anchoring (Epley et al. 2004) discussion points, rather than constrain or direct the evaluation process. In terms of a pragmatic peer review, where the process requires some type of infrastructure, this typology is the most desirable as it allows the outcomes to be expert-driven and deprives them of artefacts. As Type II mechanics are unlikely to produce artefacts in the evaluation outcomes, it can be difficult to clearly separate analytically from Type IV mechanics by an analysis of the outcomes alone.

Type III and Type IV mechanics are the first of the mechanics that have unintended effects. These unintended effects are difficult to identify prior to the evaluation stage because their nature is not yet known. Unintended consequences are only identified through hindsight and are difficult to prevent. However, to inform future evaluations, a line can be drawn between unintended effects that exist because of mechanics that facilitate the process (Type IV) and those that infiltrate the process (Type III). Type III are identified by their artefacts but it is difficult to experimentally assess the extent to which their infiltrative nature was intentional. Their existence questions whether the panel was sufficiently expert or confident to handle the evaluation object independent of the mechanic. This risks the relevance of using peer review as an evaluation tool and can be a good indication that an alternative may be necessary.

Type IV rarely exists. This is because facilitative mechanics by nature cannot have unintended outcomes without changing the nature of the evaluation object itself. When this occurs, it is difficult to directly associate this typology with the evaluation process of the desired object without prompting a refocus of the evaluation aims. The incidence of a static Type IV is therefore rare in practice.

REF2014 Evaluation Mechanics

As the world's first formal, ex-post Impact criterion, guidance is necessary to compensate for the ambiguity of the evaluation object. A table of the mechanics offered to submitting HEIs and evaluators outlining at what stage the mechanics were utilised (before, during or after the evaluation) is provided in Table 3.2. Mechanics available before the evaluation, at the submission stage, were used by submitting HEIs to support the development of their Impact submissions. Some mechanics were available at multiple stages of the evaluation process. For example, Main Panel A as a mechanic was only available during the Evaluation stage, but the Impact

Table 3.2 List of REF2014 Impact mechanics at stages of the evaluation process

Submissions (pre-evaluation)	Evaluation	Interpretation (post-evaluation)
Units of Assessment	Units of Assessment	Units of Assessment
Impact definition	Impact definition	Impact definition
Star ratings (U-4*)	Star ratings (U-4*)	Star ratings (U-4*)
Sub-criteria (Significance and Reach)	Sub-criteria (Significance and Reach)	Sub-criteria (Significance and Reach)
Submission guidelines		Submission guidelines
Impact case study template		
Impact template		
	Main Panel A	
Panel membership		
	Peers and experts	
	Panel working methods	Panel working methods
		Report on panel working methods
	Calibration exercises	

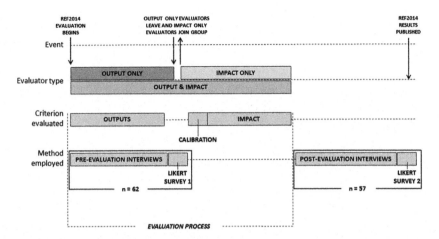

Fig. 3.1 The evaluation process as a structural mechanic transposed with the in vitro methodology adopted in this study (A criterion for Environment was included as 15% of overall REF2014 evaluation). The consideration of Environment is not explored here as it was not central to the study's objective and was not mentioned by participants as central to their approach to assessing Impact

definition was available across all three stages. As a structural mechanic not included in Table 3.2, the order in which each criterion was evaluated is important and underpins the discussion in the forthcoming chapters. Each criterion was evaluated by panels in the following order: first Outputs (65%) were assessed over a period of 4–6 months, then Impact (20%) and finally Environment (15%). Figure 3.1 shows how this structural mechanic is transposed with this study's in vitro methodology.

Whereas this book focuses on the evaluation of Impact, reference to the evaluation of the Outputs is constantly made in the interviews as it was assessed just before the Impact assessment began. The pre-evaluation interviews were conducted at the intersection when the Outputs finished and when Impact began. Here, and before the calibration exercises, there was an interchange of evaluators, resulting in a changed group membership and dynamic. The evaluators who were responsible for evaluating the Outputs-only were removed from the group, and the user-evaluators responsible for only assessing the Impact criterion joined. These Impact-only evaluators were new to the group dynamics that had already been

Table 3.3 Description of Star ratings awarded to Outputs (65%), Impact (20%) and Environment (15%)

	Outputs (65%) ratings	Impact (20%) ratings	Environment (15%) ratings
4 stars	Quality that is world-leading in terms of originality, significance and rigour	Outstanding impacts in terms of their reach and significance.	An environment that is conducive to producing research of world-leading quality, in terms of its vitality and sustainability.
3 stars	Quality that is internationally excellent in terms of originality, significance and rigour but which falls short of the highest standards of excellence.	Very considerable impacts in terms of their reach and significance.	An environment that is conducive to producing research of internally excellent quality, in terms of its vitality and sustainability.
2 stars	Quality that is recognised internationally in terms of originality, significance and rigour.	Considerable impacts in terms of their reach and significance.	An environment that is conducive to producing research of internationally recognised quality, in terms of its vitality and sustainability.
1 star	Quality that is recognised nationally in terms of originality, significance and rigour.	Recognised but modest impacts in terms of their reach and significance.	An environment that is conducive to producing research of nationally recognised quality, in terms of its vitality and sustainability.
Unclassified	Quality that falls below the standard of nationally recognised work. Or work which does not meet the published definition of research for the purposes of this assessment.	The impact is of little or no reach and significance; or the impact was not eligible; or the impact was not underpinned by excellent research produced by the submitted unit.	An environment that is not conducive to producing research of nationally recognised quality.

Source: http://www.ref.ac.uk/panels/assessmentcriteriaandleveldefinitions/. Accessed 22 March, 2017 formed, as the Outputs-only and Outputs-Impact evaluators had already worked together, and formed relationships during the Outputs assessment process.

Below, I describe each evaluation mechanic relevant to this study and explore how panellists perceived the utility of the mechanic prior to the assessment taking place. An exploration of the use of mechanics during the evaluation process as well as their nature (Type I, II, II or IV) is included later in the chapter.

In-Group Structures and Star Ratings

Unlike the Outputs criterion, which was performed primarily by peer review in isolation (HEFCE 2010), Impact was evaluated by group-based peer review. Although each sub-panel conducted separate evaluations in separate groups, the overarching role of the Main Panel (discussed below) in governing the evaluation in each of the sub-panels, as well as the fact that many evaluators sat on more than one sub-panel, means that I can treat the Main Panel and 6 sub-panels as one complete panel methodologically. Therefore, unless otherwise stated, the interactions within panels are treated as if the panels were acting between themselves, as one evaluators' eye.

There were commonalities between sub-panels, including the use of the users in smaller subgroups and panel discussions. From the interviews I discern that all panels, except one (sub-panel 6), assessed Impact independently in smaller sub-groups of 3 panellists, including at least one user-evaluator and two academic sub-panel members, per case study (Table 3.4). Sub-panel 6 decided to assess Impact using a roundtable model where all case studies were discussed by the entire panel. This was the panel's choice in response to the relatively low number of case studies to consider. All other panels used a large group-based assessment as a way of resolving disagreements from the sub-groups, to calibrate scoring (post-sub-group calibration) across sub-groups and to finalise scoring. Panel deliberations were used to address the discrepancies in valuation that occurred within the sub-groups, or to calibrate evaluators informally before they separated into smaller sub-groups. In various forms, panel

Table 3.4 How sub-panels approached the evaluation

	Main Panel A					
	Sub-panel 1 Clinical Medicine	Sub-panel 2 Public health, health services and primary care	Sub-panel 3 Allied health professions, dentistry, nursing and pharmacy	Sub-panel 4 Psychology, psychiatry and neuroscience	Sub-panel 5 Biological sciences	Sub-panel 6 Agriculture, veterinary and food sciences
Core calibration exercise	X	X	X	X	X	X
Roundtable discussion	X					X
Sub-groups with at least 1 User-evaluator	X	X	X	X	X	
Post sub-group calibration in whole panel	X	X	X	X	X	
Use of champions to present case to panel	X					

Table 3.5 Proportion of submissions awarded 1–4 stars for each criterion

		4*	3*	2*	1*	U(0)
Clinical Medicine	Outputs	23.1	53.5	21.3	1.1	1
	Impact	76.4	19.6	3.3	0.3	0.4
	Environment	59.4	36.1	4.5	0	0
Public health, health	Outputs	22.6	48.6	25	3.1	0.7
services and primary care	Impact	68.3	26.5	5.2	0	0
	Environment	70.7	25.8	2.2	1.3	0
Allied health professions,	Outputs	21.4	55.7	20.1	1.9	0.9
dentistry, nursing and	Impact	47.2	40.8	10.4	0.6	1
pharmacy	Environment	50.1	35.5	13.4	1	0
Psychology, psychiatry and	Outputs	25.9	45.8	24.6	3	0.7
neuroscience	Impact	60.9	29.1	8.1	1.6	0.3
	Environment	58.3	28.7	10.6	2.3	0.1
Biological sciences	Outputs	29.3	48.9	19.1	1.3	1.4
	Impact	47.8	41.1	9.5	0.6	1
	Environment	57.9	36.1	4.5	1.5	0
Agriculture, veterinary and	Outputs	18.2	50.7	27.7	2.6	0.8
food science	Impact	64.3	20.9	10.3	2.8	1.7
	Environment	68.9	22.4	6	2.1	0.6

deliberation played a large role in checking the consistency of scoring, calibrating scoring across sub-groups, to discuss contested cases, and a larger role in ensuring that Impact was assessed fairly. Through this discussion, panellists were made aware of their own scoring behaviour relative to others, as well as the broader concerns faced by other members of the panel.

This style of evaluation corresponded with the information from the working methods of Main Panel A and sub-panels (HEFCE 2010), a RAND Europe report on the evaluation process (Manville et al. 2015). These open sessions were essential to open dialogue and develop a larger committee culture and a dominant definition, and to construct strategies to assess Impact.

The Impact Definition

The UK is not alone in its desire to assess the impact of its publically funded research. In the US, from 1981 to 1997, the NSF included the ex-ante criteria of *"Utility or relevance of the research"* and *"Effect of the research on the infrastructure of science and engineering"* alongside the assessment of traditional, intrinsic values of research (Frodeman and Parker 2009). From 1997 onwards, this was compressed into one criterion of the *"broader impacts"* but unlike the REF2014 it has remained an ex-ante consideration of research's engagement with education, public outreach and broadening the diversity of those involved in the research (capacity building). Other countries have also experimented with notions of ex-ante societal impact, such as Australia, The Netherlands and New Zealand. HEFCE's REF2014 evaluation, as an ex-post consideration, collapsed all these notions into a criterion called "Impact". A definition was provided to associate Impact with notions of research excellence that exist *"beyond academia"*. As a mechanic, the definition was provided at the pre-submission stage to HEIs, as well as to evaluators during the evaluation. It stated that Impact was

> *...an effect on, change or benefit to the economy, society, culture, public policy or services, health, the environment or quality of life, beyond academia. (Research Excellence Framework 2011, 26)*

The formulation of this definition was the result of a review of international approaches (at the time) to research impact assessment (Grant et al. 2010), and a pilot exercise also run by HEFCE in 2009 (2010; Technopolis 2010). The definition was praised for its inclusivity in that it recognised that Impact is the result of many, different and complex pathways. As a mechanic, it was important to develop guidelines that would provide sufficient clarity but was still suitably broad and generic to encompass all possible Impacts and pathways. In addition, the definition emphasised two key components: that Impact encompassed a *"change or benefit"* and that this change had occurred *"beyond academia"*. Nonetheless, its ambiguity as an object was intended and it allowed panels a certain level of flexibility with its interpretation in practice. The intention was not to constrain submissions or the evaluation process, and HEFCE had stated that panels were to consider any Impact that met its broad definition mechanic (HEFCE 2010). However, a key determinant of the extent to which this mechanic would be infiltrative is to consider the extent to which an emphasis on a *"change or benefit"* was present in how the panel valued Impact.

At times, the Impact definition went against the personal opinions and pre-evaluation views of what was an important Impact:

Yeah, because I think the way that we're being asked to assess Impact is much more material. I think my definition of Impact is very broad. The definition that we have been asked to assess ... is much more narrow, much more focused. P1OutImp2(PRE)

Where a conflict between an evaluator's personal opinions regarding Impact and the *"REF view"* existed, evaluators acknowledged that their approach during the evaluation stage would be to value a notion of REF Impact, rather than prioritise Impacts that they felt were important. All evaluators (users as well as academics) referred to their personal views of the object as "broad", broader than the REF-provided mechanic:

I have a very broad view of what impact is, which isn't the same as the REF view, which is very much about saying it must be outside the academic sector and so academic to academic is not Impact, for me though I think there is an Impact in that. P1Imp1(PRE)

In these cases, evaluators offered alternative notions of Impact beyond the REF definition such as more nuanced views of *"whether it has changed the field in one way or another"* that was *"not recognised by REF"* *P4OutImp3(PRE)*; and that *"sufficient emphasis"* was not placed on *"... books that can have a very wide Impact beyond the purely scholarly and move into spreading the word in terms of the educated public or the interested public" P5OutImp3(PRE)*. There was therefore a valuation gap between the personal views of Impact and what was being asked of the submissions by the Impact definition mechanic. Tension existed towards valuing aspects of public engagement as Impact and the REF-provided definition's emphasis on "a change or benefit". Evaluators' notions of Impact existed beyond even the REF's broad and inclusive definition. The way that evaluators could enforce their view over and above the influence of this mechanic would be indicative of its typology.

Despite the difference in views about Impact between the mechanic and the evaluators pre-evaluation, a minority explicitly stated that they were committed to sticking to the REF2014 definition as a guide. This indicated potential risk of the definition infiltrating the evaluation process. For these evaluators, Impact *"It's not for me to define, is it? I mean, I just follow what it says in the book. It's really not for me to have any particular view on it"* *P4OutImp1(PRE)*, and therefore in the absence of any conflict between the mechanic and an evaluator's expert opinion of the evaluation object, *"All I do is read what it says in the document so that's what I've been trying to follow or I really try to follow, when we actually get the stuff"* *P4OutImp1(PRE)*. This echoes a pragmatic approach to Impact that was presented in Lamont's (2009) study of more traditional notions of research excellence. In practice, the Impact definition was all-inclusive: *"we are definitely trying to stay within the circle of what is in the REF document and I do think all of the bullet points at least within our sphere have some mileage"* *P2OutImp7(PRE)*. With Impact, however, it reflected the evaluators' inexperience with Impact as an evaluation object.

The Impact Case Study and Template

The qualitative case study was chosen as the submission method for the REF2014. This is by far the most arduous and expensive of impact assessment mechanics (Donovan 2011). Other methods such as metrics and capturing information about knowledge exchange interactions were considered during the pilot exercise, but the case study approach was still adopted to capture and assess broad claims of ex-post impact. To ensure that the evaluation process did not become too arduous, the length and structure of each impact case study (ICS) was restricted to a maximum of four pages, with departments submitting one impact case study per 10 FTE staff (2011). Within each submission, pieces of underpinning research were nominated (publications, books, performance pieces, etc.) and then, using a provided template, the impact was explained. The case study template followed a simple structure with sections on: (1) Summary of the Impact; (2) Underpinning Research; (3) References to the research; (4) Details of the Impact and (5) Sources to corroborate the Impact.

To be eligible as Impact, the underpinning research must have been considered as, a minimum threshold, no less than 2 stars in quality

(*"quality that is recognised internationally in terms of originality, significance and rigour"*) (HEFCE 2010, 2011), to avoid the group being preoccupied with research excellence proxies for the assessment of Impact, as well as to guard against the ill-effects of Impacts stemming from bad research. Pieces of underpinning research had to have been published no earlier than 1993, with the Impacts to have followed between 2008 and midnight of the 31st July, 2013 to control for time-lag advantages. The Impact template, which was an additional requirement to be submitted alongside the (ICSs, used a narrative to describe how each university department approached and supported Impact. Since the REF2014, it has been recommended that this component be absorbed into the Environment criterion for future assessments, but it is not the main focus of concern for this book. The assessment of the Impact criterion was completed by reviewing both the four-page case studies submitted by each HEI, as well as the Impact template.

Both the ICSs and the Impact templates depended heavily on the use of narrative to justify the worth and sell the value of Impact. The narrative played a major role in constructing notions of the Impact as valuable and outstanding (4 stars). Evaluators acknowledged how they were aware of how many HEIs had employed professional writers to construct each ICS, a consequence of the REF2014 Impact criterion that has been widely acknowledged. This professional construction wherein the value of the Impact might be *"a bit of hyperbole" P4OutImp4*, or ICSs might be *"lying a little bit"* and that panellists might be *"blinded by people who are good storytellers" P3OutImp8(PRE)*.

> ...*in all these case studies, they are all good but also glamorous case studies and all of them will be lying a little bit, I think ... they will be kind of making the claim just slightly bigger than they could justify. P2OutImp2(PRE)*

In these cases, the evaluation process as subjective and reliant on human judgement would be sensitive to the potential persuasion of the narrative contained within the ICSs as *"I think there is more potential for pulling wool over the eyes with a clever writer in the ICSs" P2OutImp8(PRE)*. This would downplay the legitimacy of the process by making it into *"a bit of a beauty contest"*, re-directing the evaluators' eye away from the value of Impact. As one evaluator put it:

> But they're [the group]not going to understand all the different potential out-comes or the different places that outcome—that the Impact outcomes are being claimed with as much sophistication as they understand, if you like, the core defined research. When case studies are framed, we've made a massive impact in this field of practice somewhere. It's highly unlikely that people on the Impact panels are going to have a really deep knowledge of that field of practice in order to be able to make a proper expert judgment of whether those claims are in fact credible or not.... Because we're going to be looking at loads and loads and loads of ICSs, and they're going to be saying, well, we made a big difference over there and we made a massive difference over here. There's no way that we're going to be able to be experts in all of those different domains, some of which will not be very specialist or niche. We're just going to have to take a lot of what's in the case studies pretty much on trust and as read. P3Imp2(PRE)

This concern did not relate to an internal weakness of the panellists as experts, but instead a lack of expertise (*"proper expert judgement"*) around valuing the object. There was further doubt that a panel, even one as extensive as the REF2014 panel, would have the necessary objective expertise to remain immune to the seductive construction of the ICS narrative. The option available to panels, therefore, was to *"take a lot of what's in the case studies pretty much on trust and as read"*, whereas others were committed to checking the validity of each claim of Impact to isolate the *"hyperbole"*:

> I think in some cases you'll have to sort of check exactly whether everything that they've written is quite—Is it a bit of hyperbole. Is it exaggerated as they write it? That might require some work to identify hyperbole. That might require a little background reading, I think to do that. P4OutImp4(PRE)

The challenge faced by the panellists was to isolate an assessment of value free from the influence of any narrative spin, and by doing so ensure that the peer review of Impact remained firmly based on expert-driven judgements in vivo: *"I think the challenge is going to be for us on the panel it kind of seems to be the spin—seeing what was really there and whether the evidence supports the claim" P3OutImp5(PRE)*. For less sceptical evaluators, there was a belief that the true value of Impact, when written honestly, would be clear and not require any stylised narrative to promote its value:

> *If you just write the honest document from the start right ... by the time you are finished if you've done the job right, it will be looking like the Impact is absolutely clear, obvious and marvellous and all that stuff. That's a trick of writing these kinds of things. P6OutImp2(PRE)*

The anticipated strategies of the evaluators, because of their awareness of the influence the narrative of this mechanic would involve, as one evaluator put it, maintain a measure of "intelligent scepticism": (*"I'd be taking a pinch of salt with it, I'd say, in a sort of an intelligent scepticism" P3Imp2(PRE)*) and would attempt to reach a consensus that was independent of any unfair, stylistic advantages built into the ICS narrative.

Main Panels and Sub-panels

In total, the REF2014 included 4 Main Panels (A-D) which included up to 6 smaller sub-panels or Units of Assessment. Each sub-panel was associated with a research discipline and included up to 51 research experts or peers as panellists. I was only interested in Main Panel A and its associated sub-panels, which evaluated over 50,000 academic outputs and over 1600 Impact case studies. These panels shared a disciplinary focus loosely based around Health, Medical and Biomedical research.

Panels for the assessment of Impact were made up of academic evaluators, who were also involved in the Outputs criteria assessment, and user-evaluators. Across Main Panel A and its sub-panels (Fig. 3.2), 51 user-evaluators were involved in the Impact assessment. User-evaluators were included as a way of garnering the "user perspective" on Impact, an external perspective. Their influence on the evaluation process is explored in Chap. 5. Their association with governments, industry and other third sectors was believed to ensure that a stakeholder perspective was provided, but they were not involved in the Outputs assessment, only joining the panel once this was complete.

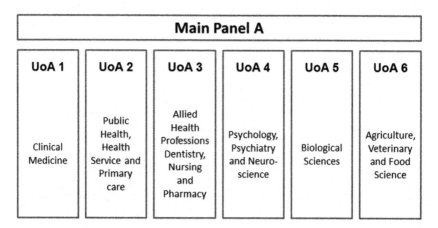

Fig. 3.2 The Main Panel A and associated sub-panels

The Role of the Main Panel

In this study, the 6 sub-panels were governed by one, overarching Main Panel (Fig. 3.2). One of the key roles of the Main Panel was to provide a forum for discussing issues that arose within sub-panels during the assessment. This could be small technical details, such as to confirm evaluation rules (mechanics) on the eligibility of outputs or co-authorship claims; or more complex, such as to resolve evaluation issues in the definition of the star levels. Members of the Main Panel were focused on the consistency of the evaluation process across the sub-panels, especially in relation to the Impact criterion (Manville et al. 2015). It therefore acted as a governing oversight body focused on process rather than a direct mediator, or as an equal evaluator in discussions within sub-panels.

These were mediated by an ongoing feedback process between the Main Panel and sub-panels that monitored and acted upon any major variances between the assessments emerging from the sub-panels, a type of ongoing re-calibration. These issues were usually resolved at regular Main Panel meetings, which included sub-panel Chairs and sub-panel Chair members. The focus of the Main Panel was therefore to maintain consistent standards of assessment, and to ensure fairness and equity across all sub-panels that had been calibrated to international standards of excellence: to be an evaluation "big brother".

Significance and Reach

The concepts of Significance and Reach were offered as sub-criteria to guide assessments related to the valuing of Impacts. Impact was to be seen as more valuable if it scored highly in these two sub-criteria categories. The term "Significance" referred to the intensity of the influence or effect, whereas "Reach" was the spread or breadth of influence or effect on the relevant consistencies (HEFCE 2010). Perhaps despite natural, human-led proclivities, it was stressed that Reach was not to be restricted to purely geographical terms, but rather based on the spread or breadth to which the potential constituencies have been affected. As a mechanic, these sub-criteria were directly related to the star ratings awarded to the Impact (discussed later). As can be seen in Table 3.3, the description of Impacts worthy of 4 stars was framed around their performance of these two sub-criteria, with 4-star Impacts meaning that Impacts were *"outstanding in terms of their reach and significance"*, and in contrast 1-star Impacts reflected merely *"modest Impacts in terms of their reach and significance"*. Panels were instructed to make one, overarching assessment of the value of the two sub-criteria, rather than assessing each separately. Therefore, even though 4-star Impacts would need to perform well in both Significance and Reach, it was less clear if awarding 3- and 2-star Impacts would prioritise a better performance in either criterion, to the detriment of the other. The instruction to make an overarching assessment therefore bypassed the need to valorise the importance of each sub-criterion over the other. Panels were still allowed to create their own pragmatic "rules of thumb" (HEFCE 2010) with which to navigate the assessment of Impact relative to these sub-criteria and therefore be facilitative and not infiltrative. During analysis, I was sensitive to the way in which these sub-criteria were embedded within the dominant definition of Impact, as well as the way they framed the group's chosen evaluation strategies around Impact. Likewise, I was sensitive during the analysis of how panellists utilised the terms "Significance" and "Reach" when referring to their own evaluation approach to Impact.

Prior to the evaluation, the evaluators wrestled with how to weigh the importance of each sub-criterion for health research Impact. In particular, there was a conflict between how to value those Impacts that had produced a minor discovery (low in Significance) but in a disease area that would influence a large population of people (high in Reach), versus those major leaps forward in discovery (high in Significance) but on a small population (low in Reach). The comparative examples used by the evaluator below compared discoveries in Alzheimer's disease and therefore affecting millions of lives with discoveries that would influence fewer people because the disease area was rarer:

> ...what we talk about is the reach, meaning how broad is this Impact, is it something which has had impact just in Aberdeen or just in Scotland or across UK or across Europe or across the whole world, that level which you could say there is a scale or level to the reach of the Impact. And then there is a numerical one that's infected ten people or has it affected hundred people or a thousand people or million people, those are things which don't necessarily comment on the one quality of the work, but it might be one way of expressing the extent of the impact, but only one way and that would be disciplined specific thing. So clearly if you could—if you had something which had an effect on Alzheimer's disease, which affects so many people or diabetes, you could imagine if that was potentially has got the chance of having a very high Impact. Some piece of work, which is an absolute breakthrough in a much more niche like disease, which affects fewer people, let's say Myasthenia Gravis, it doesn't matter you can choose any such example. I wouldn't comment on the difference and equality of the underpinning research, but you could say that the scale of the Impact is different; simply it's just a pragmatic thing. P5OutImp5(PRE)

This type of inner conflict was common among many panellists, and reflected their awareness that attributing a value of Impact could discriminate against western and non-western diseases, as well as Impacts that occurred in developed versus developing nations. The desire for some method of quantifiable value to these sub-criteria was evident in how people conceptualised the Reach sub-criteria: *"The fact that the reach is this big, to my mind, would put it at least at first glance alongside an improved hypertension regime that may affect 40 percent of the population, but provides a moderate benefit"* P4OutImp2(PRE). Here, words associated with *"moderate"* benefits that would affect *"40 per cent of the population"* echoed the evaluators' unease about valuing Impact relative to these barometers.

Further still was the difficulty in resolving how to apply these sub-criteria mechanics relative to the mechanic offered to value Impact and assign star ratings. Prior to the evaluation process, this led to a strategy that would use a *"binary scoring system"* to determine if Impact had occurred, and then assess the sub-criteria as indicative of the star ratings:

> *At this stage of the process in some ways I think we should have almost a binary scoring system: did this have impact in your view or did it not? And if it did, it did, so what's the problem? Because actually the significance and the reach aspects are the ones that are going to give it a four, three or two star. P6OutImp2(PRE)*

Again, however, evaluators wrestled with whether a higher level of Significance over Reach or vice versa could be *"forced onto a four-star scale"*:

> *So I can see having both of them get a higher score than having one or either of them … having a lower level of both. There have been some cases that have high levels of both or one or the other could, you can easily see how that could suddenly turn into a forced four-star scale. P2OutImp6(PRE)*

Evaluators anticipated an approach to assessing Impact that would not require a reduction to reflect these smaller, sub-criteria. They were determined instead not to let these procedural mechanics interfere with the evaluation process. This was despite these two mechanics being interlinked. However, as many evaluators professed a desire to follow the REF Impact evaluation mechanics, invoking the language of "Significance" and "Reach" would occur at a later consideration of the Impact (post-evaluation). When employed in practice, these mechanics would influence the way in which evaluators would translate their own individual opinion of the Impact's value to the star ratings as an outcome.

Calibration Exercises

In recognition of the newness of Impact and to guarantee consistency, a series of calibration exercises were conducted with each panel (www.ref. ac.uk 2014; Derrick and Samuel 2017). A more in-depth examination of the calibration exercises and their influence on the evaluation process is the subject of a separate article which utilises the pre- and post-evaluation interviews (Derrick and Samuel 2017).

The calibration exercises as a mechanic were essential tools used to initiate robust discussion and provide an opportunity for panel members to clarify expectations and form a common lens to guide the impact evaluation (Derrick and Samuel 2017). The parity of information provided by HEFCE regarding the structure of these calibration exercises prior to the evaluation taking place has meant that most information regarding these exercises has had to be solely derived from the pre- and post-evaluation interviews. From the information we do have, we know that the calibration exercises were conducted separately for the Outputs and then again for the Impact criteria. For Impact, the calibration exercise example ICSs had cross-disciplinary relevance including health and social policy. The participants in the main calibration exercise were members of the Main Panel, rather than within the sub-panels. Calibration exercises occurred at the beginning of the process and then again before the scoring was finalised. The ongoing interchange between the Main Panel and sub-panels ensured that the exercises in calibration were filtered through to the sub-panels to ensure that consistency and fairness of evaluation was maintained in the sub-panels.

The necessity of the calibration exercises was acknowledged by evaluators as an opportunity to *"try and sort things out"*: *"But none of us really are very sure how we're going to go about this and we will have a calibration exercise at the beginning and try and sort things out"* P3OutImp1(PRE). Calibration would also allow a safe space for the evaluators to *"discuss these potential areas of conflict before we do it for real"* P2OutImp7(PRE). In the absence of some type of mechanic or indicator to base evaluations, the panel had little experience with the possibilities of Impact that they would possibly encounter during the real evaluation:

> And I'm sure that will help a lot, but at the present moment I'm not sure that the panel is in a good position to be able to assess the impact of research across the diversity of the panel. P3OutImp3(PRE)

There was hope that the calibration exercises would facilitate the evaluation process specifically to help the panel reach a mutually agreeable consensus: *"I assume we'll have calibration exercises and from that will come a process that we are all content with"* P3OutImp9(PRE). Training evaluators is a common tool to facilitate consensus building and increase intra-reviewer reliability[1] (Derrick and Samuel 2017), but the extent to which they can infiltrate the process, thereby framing the process in a desirable direction and producing specific outcomes, has been overlooked.

Evaluation Mechanics in Practice

In addition to working out a dominant definition surrounding the Impact object, the group needed to develop valuation strategies around using each of the mechanics made available to facilitate this process. Facilitative mechanics allow this to be done in practice more than infiltrative mechanics. Since the ultimate outcome of this evaluation process was an estimation of Impact's value commensurate with the 1–4 star rating scale provided, the panel also needed to go through a process of interpretation around these mechanics.

Deliberation as a vital basis of peer review played a large role here concentrating not on the question of "What is the object?" but on valuation strategies of "how to evaluate" the object. The primary concern of these panels was how to navigate the object using a mechanic-driven conceptualisation that was, at times, counter to their own expert view. To be Type II (an ideal form), the mechanic should not limit the group's ability to modify and shape it for their own purposes. Panellists expressed their own, personal conceptualisations of the nature of Impact using the language of the evaluation mechanics, and inferred limitations in these mechanics offered. Instead they constructed strategies to compensate, even before the evaluation had begun. Here, I began to comprehend just how influential these mechanics would be in framing the valuation process. However, this was only for valuing constructions of REF Impact, and not a more organic Impact that was anticipated by evaluators prior to the evaluation. As with all group processes that are overly dictated by short deadlines and therefore ruled by pragmatic approaches, there is a risk of groupthink if the panel relinquishes control of the evaluation process to these mechanics during the evaluation, thereby detouring deliberation as a primary problem-solving tool. Evaluation mechanics that support a groupthink approach do not permit panels to mould their intentions, and redefine them in practice, therefore infiltrating the process. For Impact, an infiltrative mechanics with intended effects (Type I) should be avoided. Here, using the post-evaluation interviews I examine how panels fashioned these mechanics to reflect their own, group-generated valuation of Impact. I first discuss these mechanics generally before discussing each specifically as they were identified in the interviews. Examining these mechanics in practice and building on panellists' pre-conceptions of their use allowed me to explore how mechanics can operate as one of the four typologies outlined in Table 3.1.

From the post-evaluation interviews, it was clear that all mechanics (criteria according to P2Imp1 below) were vital during the evaluation process. Although P2Imp1 refers to the evaluation as *"impossible to do without the criteria [sic]"*, there was also a degree to which the panel judgement was allowed to supersede the mechanics, and influence the valuation:

> Well it would have been impossible to do it without the criteria, but the criteria are starting points for making the judgement, and then there's a degree of inference that you bring to the process in order to reach your judgement. P2Imp1(POST)

A *"degree of inference"* was permitted, but this is not to classify them as facilitative (Type II or IV) too soon. Mechanics were not only tools to stimulate discussion but also had agency in the way evaluators used them to validate certain viewpoints, and gain allies during deliberation. By having agency, and considering their influence of galvanising competing viewpoints, mechanics became unintentionally infiltrative (Type III) even though they were initially used to stimulate debate only. In this way, the use of the mechanics could swing between being Type II and Type III in the way they both (1) structured the evaluation on REF Impact (facilitative with intended consequences, Type II), and also (2) sway other group members and ally evaluators towards certain Impact narratives (infiltrative with unintended consequences, Type III).

It was unclear if, in the absence of these mechanics, the panel would have reached the same conclusion, a clear question to determine the extent to which mechanics were infiltrative. Indeed, at times, the mechanics were referred to as the *"Bible"*, even though their power was restricted to reasoned arguments within the group, helping to align allies with complementary ideas:

> *...the REF teams were able to refer back to the REF guidance which after all was a Bible for our assessment, whatever your view of Impact or otherwise. The REF guidance was the thing that you should be referring back to. P3Imp2(POST)*

The above quote, with its rejection of personal opinion around the object in favour of the mechanic, was followed up with an assertion from the same evaluator about the need for the panel to focus on assessing REF Impact only. This lens arguably hands the mechanics more power to influence the evaluation process and, by extension, its outcomes: *"The job I needed to do is to apply the REF guidance... This is what the guidance says and that's what we're here for..." P3Imp2(POST)*. This approach echoed a minority of evaluators who, in the pre-evaluation interviews, expressed a strategy of assessing Impact on REF terms even if this was counter to their personal orientation to the object. Considering that this was a minority view from individuals prior to the evaluation, it was clear that the mechanics had more influence, or this view was supported by more powerful individuals than I had initially considered. Two options are available to explain this discrepancy: first, that the mechanics were Type I and their infiltrative nature was intentional in their design; and second, that the decision to frame the evaluation by powerful individuals within the group worked by polarising the group thereby influencing the group's evaluation strategy.

It is possible that different sub-panels utilised the mechanics in different ways, on different levels, resulting from different evaluation challenges, but adherence to the mechanics was a similar theme across all sub-panels and the overarching Main Panel, another source of in-group power. For Panel 3, a multidisciplinary panel, there was a greater likelihood of reliance on the structure dictated by the mechanics, but a similar trend observed of the group to heavily rely on the mechanics that suggests that any degree of flexibility in the mechanics allowed was not employed in practice:

> *We stuck very much to the letter of what was in the instructions. That was what we did. I mean, we just went back again and again to those sorts of briefing documents that we were using, always relied on that. P4OutImp1(POST)*

The use of mechanics as a way of swaying arguments within delibera-tions, and recruiting allies within the process, was also noted in recollec-tions of how, if deliberations about Impact valuation deviated from conceptualisations of REF Impact, the mechanics were used to refocus deliberations. This was predominantly seen around the Impact definition mechanic, as well as the HEFCE panel guidelines more broadly (HEFCE 2010). At times, the evaluation mechanics were used as bargaining chips in session, and to frame arguments against emerging ideas that some evaluators did not agree on:

> *…people often drifted away from what was actually said in the document about how they should be assessed. Some of them could be relatively easily addressed by just saying well, actually, the rules are very clear on this. P0OutImp2(POST)*

The mechanics demonstrated a remarkable influence on the valuation process of Impact and as such extended their influence beyond the object, to a more complex strategic tool utilised by all evaluators against compet-ing arguments. This degree of inflexibility implies an infiltrative influ-ence; one evaluator inferred that this was not a perspective they agreed with, but that they felt compelled to use: *"I think you have to distinguish between the issues as to whether we, (a), understood the rules that allowed us to judge things, and, (b), whether we agreed with them" P1OutImp4(POST).* This suggests a more complex role of mechanics that minimises the abil-ity to track any direct, explicit influence (intended or not) they may have as they become interwoven in the panel's interplay. Considering them as having agency within the panel to direct and to be used to re-direct delib-erations suggests that their influence over the panel was greater than the individual expert conceptualisations brought to the panel by each evaluator. Classifying them therefore requires a look at each mechanic individually, as well as considering if their artefacts are discernible in the evaluation's outcomes. To this end, below I explore two of these mechanics in more detail: the use of the 1–4 star scoring scale, as well as the sub-criteria, Significance and Reach. I examine how panels utilised these mechanics as well as, where relevant, the extent to which artefacts were left behind in the evaluation outcomes.

Scoring Behaviour of Group Around Impact

Assigning scores to Impact was less about providing a numerical reflection of its value than about "sending a signal": *"I think it's a bit like marking students' assignments. The actual grades are not objectively a measure of the quality. They are a signal. Those scores are a signal"* P3OutImp2(POST). *In practice, evaluators had no ability to adjust the range of scores available to them to value Impact. This was considered by evaluators as inadequate as, in their expert opinion, some Impact was worth in excess of 10, 15 or 50 stars. This meant that panellists resorted to utilising this mechanic to award stars as a signal of quality only, and not as a measure of value.* The following quote from an evaluator on the Clinical Medicine sub-panel outlines this difficulty:

> *And the other thing that came very, very strongly was we weren't marking that on a grade from one to four or zero to four. We were marking—there was—I don't know how to put this, but it was this idea that there could be 5 star and 10 star and 15 star impact. There was some incredible stuff we saw in Clinical Medicine. We saw some amazing things which had really altered everything, a massive, massive change. But if we had used some kind of statistical analysis to say, well, because it was amazing that's a four then everything else has to be kind of rated down in order that we only have 20 percent four star or something. We were told very clearly no, it's not about that. It's about the four is a four is a four and this is a six, this is outstanding, but this thing here which has got lesser impact, it's still a four. P1Imp1(POST)*

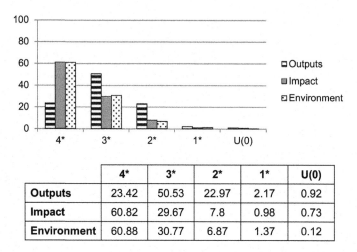

	4*	3*	2*	1*	U(0)
Outputs	23.42	50.53	22.97	2.17	0.92
Impact	60.82	29.67	7.8	0.98	0.73
Environment	60.88	30.77	6.87	1.37	0.12

Fig. 3.3   Main Panel A and sub-panel scoring behaviour over each criterion

This tendency can also be used to explain the overwhelmingly large proportion of Impact from this sub-panel to be awarded 4 stars (Fig. 3.3). Across the sub-panels, 60.82% of Impact received 4-star ratings, compared to 23.42% for the Outputs criterion. The mechanic did not permit the panel to custom it during practice, despite some panellists expressing a desire for it to be more "fine grained": *"my subpanels would have liked a finer grading with a greater number of points to be able to give to the ICSs to pick the super impact, as opposed to the very, very good impact or an excellent impact" P5OutImp5(POST)*. Instead the star scale mechanics required panellists to orientate their evaluative practice around it, by awarding no more than 4 stars. In this way, the mechanic acted as Type I, being infiltrative and having clearly intended consequences.

On the other hand, an unintended consequence of the mechanic was that it encouraged an evaluative process that was more generous than that employed for the evaluation of the Outputs criterion; this provides an alternative explanation for the high proportion of Impact receiving 4-star ratings. Looking at this tendency in more detail, over the entire 1-to-4-star spectrum, we see how 90.5% of Impact submissions were award 3 or more stars, with the pattern of Outputs outcomes being more discriminate across the spectrum. Table 3.4 gives a finer-grained perspective of scoring behaviour across the sub-panels. All sub-panels scored the Impact at 3 stars and above, whereas they scored Outputs at 3 stars and below. This tendency for generosity was directly referred to in the interviews with evaluators who adopted a default approach to Impact scoring where submissions would lose stars, rather than earn them: *"default position to this, there's everything is a four star let's see how you fail" P2OutImp5(POST)*. This approach was endorsed by powerful evaluators from within the panel who encouraged this approach to scoring: *"I recall some fairly strong guidance from the senior people from the main panel saying that the schedules should always err on the side of positive rather than negative" P1OutImp1(POST)*. Further, when deliberating panellists conflicted in their awarding of star ratings, the group would assume a tendency to "round up". This re-enforced a culture of generosity in practice: *"but on the whole, we were encouraged to always kind of round up rather than round down" P2OutImp8(POST)*. This unintended generosity ended up having a political angle as the group acknowledged an approach to celebrating research, as a way of entrenching its value to the UK: *"Their feeling was that ICSs that they saw and read were all marvellous and we should reflect that marvelosity, which we did" POP2OutImp1(POST)*.

This is not to say that all Impact was given 3 stars and above; on some occasions (8.8% of submission) a score of 2 stars or below was awarded. In these cases, using the scoring scale as a "signal" and not as a measure of quality was also important because some ICSs were not as impressive to the group: *"The twos were exceptional and it was just simply the Impact wasn't that impressive and the story wasn't that impressive. So it got a two" P2OutImp5(POST)*. The downgrading of stars, especially in comparison to the panel-wide trend favouring high star ratings, provides a strong signal to the submitting institution based on the construction of the narrative.

Significance and Reach

As explored earlier, having two separate terms was problematic not only because they could clash, but because this implied that at some time a choice between these two terms would need to be made, to distinguish the ratings awarded. As interlinked terms within one mechanic, it remained the group's decision as to how these terms would be utilised during the evaluation process. In this way, the mechanics were intended to be facilitative, allowing evaluator panellists to alter the emphasis of Significance and/or Reach during their valuation of Impact. In the post-evaluation interviews, panellists expressed how these sub-criteria did indeed help to *"clarify the issues that we had"* P2OutImp5(POST), but a consequence was that evaluators would be forced to make a value judgement around Impact. In other words, they would need to make a judgement about the "societal" value of Impact. For health research this was difficult, and evaluators *"...didn't feel like it was our job to make these judgements about when how [valuable] peanuts were compared to babies and 200 million people in Pakistan and Nepal"* P3OutImp1(POST). One evaluator reflected on the dangers of such a *"lexigraphic approach"* (infiltrative) towards balancing this mechanic during the evaluation. The danger of its use was two-fold:

> *I felt, one, it probably wouldn't discriminate between Impact and that we were in danger of scoring everything too high. And secondly, I didn't think it would reflect reasonable views about what was a really important and massive Impact from others that were maybe less important or indeed almost trivial.* P2OutImp2(POST)

We have already explored the tendency to score Impact generously, and this can be interpreted as an artefact, as such a group response is evident in the evaluation outcomes, and evidence of Type I. Using Significance and Reach as sub-criteria is inextricably linked to the star ratings, so we could assume that they would be Type I as well. One evaluator did admit an inflexible approach to applying these mechanics. From the pre-evaluation interviews, panellists used the terms Significance and Reach prior to the evaluation process, indicating that this mechanic could have infiltrated the evaluation earlier than expected. The evaluator continued to reason that they thought the mechanics were unintentionally infiltrative (Type III) to guard against evaluators making social value judgements. However, the evaluator also admitted that these types of judgements were unavoidable in evaluations, including peer review. The unintended effect of these infiltrative mechanics (Type III) would therefore be to protect evaluators from making *"perverse"* social judgements:

> *I understood why our main panel had issued that strong guidance to be lexigraphic because they didn't feel that we should be making the social value judgments. My position was, well, if you are lexigraphic, you're making social value judgments anyway, but you're making really perverse ones. P2OutImp1(POST)*

Making value judgements within evaluations is not evidence of malpractice or the unsuitability of peer review as a tool for impact evaluation; however, for notions of social value, they did provide an interpretive shield for such inevitably uncomfortable judgements: *"It's a pseudo-precise language like significance and reach, okay, to hide the fact that it's a purely subjective exercise P6OutImp2(POST)*. This is important for the legitimacy of peer review for impact assessment as it is *"not about making social value judgements" P2OutImp1(POST)*, and the consequence of making these judgements outside of the peer review black box is that *"...I think on the whole, we kind of pondered that and then shied away from making that sort of assessment P2OutImp8(POST)*. This has been previously discussed as a reason why researchers are reluctant to engage with an assessment of research's social value through formalised criteria (Holbrook 2010; Holbrook and Hrotic 2013). Although these mechanics were intended to be facilitative in providing a basis for discussion, their use as a lens to conceptualise Impact and dictate its outcomes (star ratings, "change or benefit") acted more as Type I than an idealised Type II.

Conclusion: What Have We Learnt About Evaluation Mechanics?

In this chapter I have shown how the evaluators constructed their own realities around the value of Impact pre-evaluation relative to the mechanics available to them. I have argued that these mechanics can work to either infiltrate or facilitate the evaluation process and have corresponding intended or unintended consequences. The extent to which they infiltrate the process with intended effects (Type I) risks the benefits associated with allowing expert-driven deliberation to underpin the evaluation process. This is not to say that this infiltration is intentional. It is beyond the scope of the data here to conclude this, but in providing mechanics that infiltrate and essentially dictate the process, one jeopardises the legitimacy of the outcomes if they are not based on a deliberative interplay of expert views that comes from robust deliberation as a primary problem-solving tool in peer review groups. It also risks the validity and relevance of using a deliberative evaluation model such as peer review as a tool to evaluate ambiguous concepts such as Impact, as well as its various related buzz-terms. Although a certain level of guidance by mechanics is to be expected in all research evaluation processes, their influence should not supersede deliberation as the basis of more ideal forms of expert-driven evaluation.

Ideally, mechanics should intend to be facilitative with known consequences that (Type II) remain independent of external factors. Mechanics should not require that evaluators orientate themselves around them lest they be infiltrative. Instead, evaluators must familiarise themselves with the mechanics on offer, and then mould the mechanics, and their use, towards forming a group consensus and dominant definition. Infiltrative mechanics are easily identified by the artefacts they leave behind in the evaluation outcomes (intended or not), but the extent to which and the way they were infiltrative, as opposed to Type IV mechanics, is identified by understanding the evaluation process, and not solely the outcomes. Studies that overlook the evaluative process by solely analysing the characteristics of the evaluation outcomes risk their conclusions being reflective of the evaluation mechanics, rather than of the object. This has happened in a number of studies involving an ex-post, retrospective analysis of the REF2014 evaluation outcomes (London and Science 2015; Manville et al. 2015).

The post-evaluation interviews showed how for some mechanics, evaluators felt constrained, whereas others had a more facilitative effect. Their consequences, whether intended or not, were not always negative. In the example of Significance and Reach as sub-criteria, evaluators anticipated the problems in valuing each indicator separately, but in practice, when used together, the sub-criteria guarded against evaluators making value judgements over and above more robust assessments. This is a beneficial unintended effect, even though the mechanic still operated as Type III. On the other hand, the star rating scale acted as a Type I mechanic, as it constrained the ability of evaluators to reward the quality of the Impact, and instead limited their outcomes to a *"signal"* of value. However, an unintended consequence, echoing a Type III mechanic, was that it allowed evaluators to adopt a generous approach to scoring that was counter to their practice surrounding more traditional academic criteria. This unintended consequence played a political role in allowing the evaluators to use the evaluation as an advocacy tool in *"celebrating the value of British science"*.

The post-evaluation interviews only focused on analysing the effects of some mechanics (Significance and Reach; Scoring scales and the Panel guidelines in general) but not others. The way the others were used, in particular the Main Panel, Impact definition and the Evaluation structure, was so embedded in evaluator interplay and valuation process that its influence is explored within these themes in the forthcoming chapters. However, ahead of this, I was particularly concerned about the effect the evaluation structure (Fig. 3.1) would have on the evaluation process. Specifically, the decision to ask the evaluation group to address the Impact criterion, in the shadow of the Outputs criterion, deserves some attention. In the forthcoming chapters, I am sensitive to reports of how evaluating an ambiguous concept, directly following a more traditional, habitual criterion of Outputs, influences panel behaviour. Furthermore, I was sensitive as to how the interchange of evaluators (Impact-only evaluators in, and Outputs-only evaluators out) affected how a new committee culture was developed. The strength of their group identity or culture and the space for them to develop their dominant definition are vital to assessing the relevance of a deliberative evaluation tool for Impact. For newcomers to the panel, the difficulty lay in how to challenge and infiltrate these already formed, and in some cases extremely strong, group norms in order to ensure that their voices were heard during panel deliberations. I am therefore sensitive to how interrupting an existing panel dynamic was difficult for these new panellists. The ability of these outsiders to position themselves within the group such that they could actively influence the evaluative practice is a key consideration as I move to a consideration of group-level dynamics around Impact.

In conclusion, however, from the results of this chapter it is vital that peer review groups are able to harness the facilitative aspects of these mechanics and resist their pernicious influence on overly prescriptive evaluative approaches. Being able to balance the benefits and drawbacks of evaluation mechanics in evaluative practice is therefore vital in navigating an ambiguous concept such as Impact.

Notes

1. I use the term "intra-reviewer reliability" intentionally as I wanted to reflect the evaluators' eye in consensus building in this panel. Other research uses inter-reviewer reliability, but does not see the evaluation outcomes resulting from group interplay in the same way as this book.

References

Aksnes, D.W., and R.E. Taxt. 2004. Peer reviews and bibliometric indicators: A comparative study at a Norwegian University. *Research Evaluation* 13 (1): 33–41.
Bence, V., and C. Oppenhein. 2005. The evolution of the UK's research assessment exercise: Publications, performance and perceptions. *Journal of Educational Administration and History* 37 (2): 137–155.
Bornmann, L. 2012. Measuring the societal impact of research. *EMBO Reports* 13 (8): 673–676.
Bornmann, L., and H.-D. Daniel. 2005. Committee peer review at an international research foundation: Predictive validity and fairness of selection decisions on post-graduate fellowship applications. *Research Evaluation* 14 (1): 15–20.
Bornmann, L., and W. Marx. 2014. How should the societal impact of research be generated and measured? A proposal for a simple and practicable approach to allow interdisciplinary comparisons. *Scientometrics* 98 (1): 211–219.
Bornmann, L., G. Wallon, and A. Ledin. 2008. Does the committee peer review select the best applicants for funding? An investigation of the selection process for two european molecular biology organization programmes. *PLoSOne* 3 (10): e3480.

Dahler-Larsen, P. 2011. *The evaluation society*. Palo Alto, CA: Stanford University Press.

————. 2012. Constitutive effects as a social accomplishment: A qualitative study of the political in testing. *Education Inquiry* 3 (2): 171–186.

————. 2014. Constitutive effects of performance indicators: Getting beyond unintended consequences. *Public Management Review* 16 (7): 969–986.

Derrick, G.E., and G.N. Samuel. 2017. The future of societal impact assessment using peer review: Pre-evaluation training, consensus building and inter-reviewer reliability. *Palgrave Communications*. https://doi.org/10.1057/palcomms.2017.40

Donovan, C. 2011. State of the art in assessing research impact: Introduction to a special issue. *Research Evaluation* 20 (3): 175–179.

Epley, N., B. Keysar, L. Van Boven, and T. Gilovich. 2004. Perspective taking as egocentric anchoring and adjustment. *Journal of Personality and Social Psychology* 87 (3): 327.

Franceschet, M., and A. Costantini. 2011. The first Italian research assessment exercise: A bibliometric perspective. *Journal of Informetrics* 5 (2): 275–291.

Frodeman, R., and J. Parker. 2009. Intellectual merit and broader impact: The National Science Foundation's broader impacts criterion and the question of peer review. *Social Epistemology* 23 (3–4): 337–345.

Grant, J., P.-B. Brutscher, S. Kirk, L. Butler, and S. Wooding. 2010. *Capturing research impacts: A review of International practice*. Documented briefing. RAND Corporation.

Greene, J.C. 2000. Challenges in practicing deliberative democratic evaluation. *New Directions for Evaluation* 2000 (85): 13–26.

HEFCE. 2010. REF2014: Panel criteria and working methods. http://www.ref.ac.uk/media/ref/content/pub/panelcriteriaandworkingmethods/01_12.pdf. Accessed 1 Mar 2016.

HEFCE. 2011. Assessment framework and guidance on submissions. REF 2014.

Holbrook, J.B. 2010. The use of societal impacts considerations in grant proposal peer review: A comparison of five models. *Technology & Innovation* 12 (3): 213–224.

Holbrook, J.B., and S. Hrotic. 2013. Blue skies, impacts, and peer review. *A Journal on Research Policy & Evaluation*. https://doi.org/10.13130/2282-5398/2914.

King's College London and Digital Science. 2015. *The nature, scale and beneficiaries of research impact: An initial analysis of Research Excellence*

Framework (REF) 2014 impact case studies. King's College London and Digital Science.

Lamont, M. 2009. *How professors think: Inside the curious world of academic judgement.* Cambridge, MA: Harvard University Press.

Manville, C., S. Guthrie, M.-L. Henham, B. Garrod, S. Sousa, A. Kirtkey, S. Castle-Clarke, and T. Ling. 2015. *Assessing impact submissions for REF2014: An evaluation.* Cambridge: RAND Europe.

Mark, M.M., G.T. Henry, and G. Julnes. 2000. *Evaluation: An integrated framework for understanding, guiding and improving policies and programs.* San Francisco, CA: Jossey-Bass.

Norman, R. 2002. Managing through measurement or meaning? Lessons from experience with New Zealand's public sector performance management systems. *International Review of Administrative Sciences* 68 (4): 619–628.

Rinia, E.J., T.N. van Leeuwen, H.G. van Vuren, and A.F.J. van Raan. 1998. Comparative analysis of a set of bibliometric indicators and central peer review criteria: Evaluation of condensed matter physics in the Netherlands. *Research Policy* 27 (1): 95–107.

Technopolis. 2010. REF research impact pilot exercise lessons-learned project: Feedback on pilot submissions.

Thaler Richard, H., and R. Sunstein Cass. 2008. *Nudge: Improving decisions about health, wealth, and happiness.* New Haven, CT: Yale University Press.

van den Besselaar, P., and L. Leydesdorff. 2009. Past performance, peer review and project selection: A case study in the social and behavioral sciences. *Research Evaluation* 18 (4): 273–288.

Vedung, E. 1997. *Public policy and program evaluation.* New Brunswick and London: Transaction Publishers.

www.ref.ac.uk. 2014. Consistency across UOAs: REF2014. http://www.ref.ac.uk/2014/results/analysis/consistencyacrossuoas/. Accessed 20 Sep 2016.

4

Introducing Impact to the Evaluators

> One of the most intriguing aspects of impact has been how little
> comprehension of impact — what impact is—there has been and how
> difficult a concept it has been to crystalize.... I mean, the definitions are
> fluid, but the concept is terrifically important.
> *Evaluator (Sub-panel 4), Pre-evaluation*

In 1976, a German researcher first linked the use of sunbeds to the risk of skin cancer.[1] In 2006, a 26-year-old Australian girl, Clare Oliver, was diagnosed with advanced melanoma. Instead of resigning herself to her fate, Clare used her final months to launch a campaign that highlighted the dangers of the solarium industry in Australia, which led to the creation of new policies regulating their use (Sinclair and Foley 2009). In a few short months, Clare had managed to convince policymakers to heed the 1976 piece of German research, and put its recommendations into action. By the time Clare had passed away, she had successfully pushed all melanoma-risk-orientated research[2] to an Impact, an achievement that had taken researchers over 30 years to achieve without her.

© The Author(s) 2018
G. Derrick, *The Evaluators' Eye*,
https://doi.org/10.1007/978-3-319-63627-6_4

Impact is a sticky process, and is rarely linear. Beyond the obvious question of why it took so long for the dangerous solarium industry to be regulated is the question of why it took so long for research first published in 1976 to inform policy. The answer lies in the fact that the link between research and Impact is not clear cut. It is therefore difficult to design appropriate research assessment approaches that are sensitive to the ambiguity of Impact as an object for evaluation. For Impact evaluation, issues with causality, attribution and time-lag underpin how necessary steps for achieving an Impact (especially for health) such as randomised controlled trials, systematic reviews, policy drafts, government committee meetings, and by-chance productive interactions between researcher and government are recognised and appropriately rewarded during assessment. Also, Impact does not necessarily end when a policy is implemented, but can continue to gain value in the changes and benefits such as how many lives, how much health funding, how many jobs created and so on. This also changes the value of Impact over time. The ongoing question for the practice of Impact evaluation remains how to value these ongoing ambiguous interactions and outcomes. In many ways, peer review appears a suitable tool for sorting through this mess. Impact assessments require a subjective, human-based judgement of value, and peer review provides a forum to air and resolve conflicting value judgements brought by individuals through group dynamics. The added advantage of peer review is that it is based on expert judgements, and this carries political weight.

What was asked of the REF2014 evaluators was a mammoth task. Effectively, each evaluator was required to defend, negotiate and compromise their own views of Impact's value during panel deliberations towards building a group-based consensus and then to consider all competing ideas brought by other panellists. On top of that, evaluators had to create strategies around its evaluation that would navigate the object's shortcomings. This was not an easy, task but focusing on analysing the process is vital to understand new avenues of assessment since arguments about its nature and how to effectively evaluate it are intertwined (Donovan 2011).

The place of Impact as a formal academic criterion is continually questioned. Rarely has an object been included in formal evaluations with so little understanding of its nature. Although countries have formalised ex-ante considerations of societal impact, they are not yet a formalised percentage of overall peer review panel assessments. This casual approach to assessing ex-ante impact essentially permits a "free pass" for research to consider its outcomes practical and relevant to society.

Although the REF2014 provided the Impact definition as an evaluation mechanic, here I explore how evaluators negotiated their strategies for assessing Impact around their pre-evaluation conceptualisations of the object. In this chapter, I argue that by understanding this evaluation process as dynamic (rather than the sum of conflicting views either pre- or post-evaluation) and the result of group interplay, more relevant Impact evaluation strategies can be constructed that acknowledge the valuation of Impact as practice-based. Models constructed by groups in practice are hence more useful in understanding outcomes than interpretation by transposing a theoretical model onto the process. From the interviews, I show that the characteristics of common Impact assessment models are echoed in how evaluators perceive Impact prior to the evaluation, but are less discernible in how evaluators conceptualise it after the event. That is, the practice trumps the model.

Previous Evaluator Experience of Assessing Impact—The Tick-Box Criteria

I have previously explored how evaluators felt about the prospect of evaluating ex-post Impact for the first time under the REF2014 (Samuel and Derrick 2015; Derrick and Samuel 2016, 2017). It is perhaps not surprising that evaluators felt *"nervous"* about the prospect of Impact. The prospect of evaluating an object without experience or precedent meant that evaluators would naturally use more habituated forms of research evaluation and place greater emphasis on interactional expertise (Collins and Evans 2010; Collins 2007). For ex-post Impact, the danger would be in employing a pragmatic approach to peer review that favoured the adoption of a linear approach underlying all prior models of Impact assessment (Greenhalgh et al. 2016). Any experience evaluating ex-ante

Impact would also assume that evaluators adopted a linear approach, since ex-ante Impact statements give the illusion that Impact can be the result of careful planning and foresight.

I wanted to first test if this was the case by examining the pre-evaluation interviews for when the evaluators had spoken about their previous experiences assessing Impact. At these times, evaluators spoke of *feasibility* as a tool they had adopted for assessing Impact. Assessing ex-post Impact required different approaches than ex-ante, but evaluators' usage of feasibility was interesting as its application in ex-post assessments could bias the panel's conceptualisation of Impact. However, adopting feasibility in ex-ante assessments provided evaluators with a reliable yardstick to make necessary value judgements for Impact:

> *As I've just said, if you are trying to assess something that is proposed rather than has taken place then the whole thing is on the basis of what has not yet happened. So you have to assess how realistic you think—just in the same way as you assess whether they can do the experiment from the way they describe them. P1OutImp6(PRE)*

Realism within their larger concept of feasibility was also important, and in this sense, evaluators described having to "...*be somewhat sceptical of the plans that are in there and try and assess how valid they are*" *P1OutImp6(PRE)*, reflecting a type of organised scepticism towards any ex-post Impact. In the past, evaluators have been reliant on a number of markers to boost their confidence to realistically assess feasibility, including a halo-driven judgement of the reputation of the group or organisation. Track record and or specific experience speaking to the credibility of the proposal would also increase the evaluator's confidence in the assessment made. This approach had worked when assessing ex-ante Impact, and an evaluation of ex-post Impact anticipated the use of a similar lens:

> *If they say that, yes, we will explore commercialization opportunities then is there a track record there? Have any of these guys ever spoken to a company, pharma, diagnostic, or whatever? If they say, oh yeah, we're good to go and we're going to talk to school kids and stuff. Then you say have you done this in the past? Where's the evidence? For me it's a question of how credible it is, really. How realistic the plan is. P4OutImp3(PRE)*

Evaluators' past experiences with assessing ex-ante Impact often involved a casual approach to its valuation side by side with other, more traditional indicators of research excellence. In these situations, Impact took a backseat in importance: *"At the same time, when you read them, I'd still put far more weight on the science" P4OutImp5(PRE)*. As such, its importance was reduced to tick-box criteria: *"It's really more just tick-box criteria for somebody else to evaluate, not necessarily the experts in the field, the researchers" P0OutImp4(PRE)*. And sometimes this was even completely ignored because the evaluators, as a group, agreed that this was not necessarily a vital aspect of the overall proposal:

To be honest, most of the people reviewing those grants completely ignore those sections because they are the same sort of scientists who want to publish in Cell *and all these other fantastic journals and have their impact factors as high as possible. P5OutImp1(PRE)*

With evaluators' previous experiences of Impact based on statements that emphasised a feasible plan and/or pathway, I was concerned with how this would translate to evaluators' approaches in this study. Exposure to Impact presented linearly encouraged an assumption that it can be controlled or pushed. An emphasis on Impact that is, if successful, uncomplicated, planned and evenly executed, step-by-step, was repeatedly used in the pre-evaluation interviews (Samuel and Derrick 2015). However, the evaluators in their past experiences had been sensitive to ex-ante Impact plans that had oversold their anticipated Impact. This showed how evaluators were unlikely to adopt an oversimplified, non-sceptical view of Impact during the REF2014 as well: *"unless you, you're sensible and make sensible statements about the Impact of your research or the potential Impact of your research, it is not going to get funded" P3OutImp3(PRE)* and *"If you turn around and say, well, we're going to stop all cancer because we found this pathway, its bollocks" P3OutImp3(PRE)*. In the pre-evaluation interviews I was told of how these sceptical approaches previously adopted by evaluators had identified *"absolute howlers"* within the submission's construct, claims that promised *"curing cancer in 10 years"* and *"changing the world"*. Even in ex-ante assessments, evaluators had been sensitive to false promises that were adopted because of an oversimplified approach to Impact. In these cases, evaluators had also been sceptical towards how these false promises were disguised within *"fancy writing"* or *"fine words"*. Evaluators therefore had had experiences of combining the tools of feasibility, organised scepticism and a realist approach in practice to deconstruct narrative's and submission's attempts at game-playing. The quote below shows an example of how these tools were combined in an assessment of ex-ante Impact:

> *I'm much more likely to be impressed by someone who can demonstrate that and says we might have a little bit of an Impact than people who claim they're going to change the world, but they have no knowledge of the world they are seeking to change. P2Imp1(PRE)*

Impact assessment experience that had emphasised scepticism towards narratives would prove useful during the REF2014 assessment process, but my concern surrounded how feasibility as a tool would unconsciously promote a linear appreciation of Impact. If the overall object of an evaluation is to reward and incentivise, then to assume that the achievement of Impact, as opposed to scientific impact, is controllable perhaps biases some Impacts over others. Favoured Impacts would be those where linearity was discernible, and the strength with which individual evaluators held onto these views indicated that this would be a widely agreeable approach at the group level as well. As one evaluator explained to me in their post-evaluation interviews, that danger for evaluators was that *"We were all Impact virgins, weren't we?"* POP2OutImp1(POST).

Outside Their Comfort Zone, but Working as a Group

Despite this mammoth task ahead of them, many evaluators told me that they had faith that the process would *"work it out in the end"*. In the post-evaluation interviews, I asked evaluators to reflect on their understandings of Impact as an object compared to their perceptions pre-evaluation. What emerged was how the experience of evaluating Impact was a learning process for the individuals: *"…I mean I think anybody who would go*

through that process would just learn by the experience of doing it in practice"
P5Imp1(POST). As we will start to explore, inexperience in assessing the
object is not necessarily a limitation, and this shared inexperience played
a large role in strengthening the group: *"...I don't think anyone felt that
familiar with Impact that they were able so we're really lucky. Honestly, I
think we were all a little bit wow, and you know, this was new to us all, so I
didn't feel that so much" P2OutImp4.*

Indeed, I started to understand how evaluators referred to the group,
when explaining how they learnt how to navigate Impact. In particular, I
noticed the use of group where the fear and unease of the individual prior
to the evaluation *("Because we hadn't done it before, there was no, sort of,
reference, no standard against which to judge it" P0P2OutImp1(PRE))* was
replaced with the confidence in the evaluation outcomes at the completion of the process. A basis of peer review as the gold standard in research
evaluation is that the responsibility for the outcomes is transferred from
the individual to the group level, and there is safety for the evaluators in
this deferred responsibility. The following sections explore how transferring the evaluation burden to the group level influenced evaluators' confidence in evaluation.

Flagging the Concept of Impact ... Together

In this section, I examine how evaluators reasoned their own conceptualisations of Impact with those provided by the dynamic of the group. Prior
to the evaluation, any move towards adopting a pragmatic approach to
evaluating Impact was understandable as a result of inexperience of individuals either around the object professionally or as a peer reviewer. For
evaluators, Impact as an evaluation object was also ambiguous and broad:
*"...it's a very broad concept of influencing society in one way or another"
P0OutImp6(PRE).* Difficulty around valuing this object that was intangible *("There is always challenge with research because it's an intangible benefit" P1Imp2(PRE))* and nebulous *("Impact is sort of nebulous in a lot of
respects" P0OutImp1(PRE))* was also anticipated. Pragmatically speaking,
defining the concept broadly prior to the evaluation was a way evaluators
could cast the net as far as possible, to capture every possible variant of

the object. This allowed evaluators to remain as inclusive as possible: *"…but I guess things that can help is as broad as it is wide, isn't it?" P2Imp2(PRE)*. Individual evaluators from all panels desired a wide interpretation of Impact. This included evaluators in sub-panels 1–2 where Impact was likely to be less nebulous, and more tangible (*"Impact is so broad … my language is not good enough to be able to encapsulate it in a nugget of usefulness" P1Imp1(PRE))*, and sub-panels 4–6 where Impact was more diverse (*"I don't subscribe to the view that there's only one type of impact. There are lots of different types of impact" P4OutImp3(PRE))*.

For some evaluators, their conceptualisation of a broad object was not matched by the REF Impact definition (mechanic) that they perceived as limiting (*"So I have a very broad view of what Impact is, which isn't the same as the REF view" P1Imp1(PRE))*, and they feared that restricting the object risked overlooking vital impacts that didn't fit the mechanic (*"I think there is relatively little high-quality research that is not impactful. Whether we are going to be measuring that in the REF is another matter altogether" P0OutImp2(PRE))*. There was conflict in how evaluators viewed Impact individually prior to the evaluation process and the boundaries placed around Impact by the REF process. One reviewer in particular felt that contrary to his own personal opinions about Impact the REF definition is what he would use to guide his evaluation behaviour: *"…It's not for me to define, is it? I mean, I just follow what it says in the book. It's really not for me to have any particular view on it" P4OutImp1(PRE)*.

One such example of the conflict between individual, pre-evaluation views about Impact and the REF mechanics was how evaluators had noted the exclusion of public engagement as REF Impact: *"I know what the REF definition is, but that isn't quite the same thing" P1OutImp4(PRE)*.[3] Evaluators felt strongly that public engagement was relevant to be included as Impact, but that the inability to quantify any change or benefit (commensurate also with the boundaries of the mechanic) that resulted from these activities made it difficult to operationalise in practice:

> *I spend a day doing interviews with radio and TV. But is that impactful? It gets the issue into public arena, but does this actually change perceptions to the*

change and demonstrating whether it's changed perceptions or even changed knowledge is actually incredibly difficult. So that's where the 'but' comes in, how do you demonstrate that linkage and that's been difficult sometimes. Sometimes it's been very straight forward. But a lot of the times it's that linkage that is difficult. P2OutImp9(PRE)

Nonetheless, despite its lack of metrics, public engagement and its ability to *"instil excitement in a broader public" P5OutImp3(PRE)* was still considered an important, albeit nebulous Impact by individual evaluators.

In identifying the conflict between individual conceptualisations and the REF mechanics, I started to hear how individuals expected to rely on the group to resolve the differences that existed between individuals, and between individuals and the definition of REF Impact provided by the mechanic. The REF definition was seen as more prescriptive:

Yeah, because I think the way that we're being asked to assess Impact is much more material. I think my definition of Impact is very broad. The definition that we may be asked to assess, use to assess the—in the REF is much more narrow, much more focused. P1OutImp2(PRE)

Also, evaluators were aware that during the evaluation process, individually held views of Impact would need to be resolved with the views of other individuals: *"...I mean, that's where this REF process is going to be quite challenging because different people have a different view about what is Impact" P0OutImp2(PRE)*. This would be difficult, not only because of the variety of views brought to the panel (Samuel and Derrick 2015), but also in how individuals would value each competing conceptualisation of the object:

I just think it's hard because I think I'm still not convinced everybody shares exactly the same definition of what constitutes Impact or where they place the weight or if it's Impact or isn't and unlike, generally there's sort of agreement on what constitutes good quality research. P3Imp1(PRE)

The evaluation would be treated as a learning process where experience would be gained in situ in lieu of experience being brought to the process.

Resolving conflicting individual views would then result in a new group-based dominant definition:

> *But one thing I keep in mind, which is underscored by REF, is that we should be very open to a very broad definition of Impact. And our own definitions of Impact need to be modified by what we read. P5OutImp5(PRE)*

The panel's approach to Impact as a group would be essential to the development (mutual construction (Pier et al. 2017)) of the dominant definition, as well as how strategies were agreed upon to navigate Impact as a broad concept, and its valuation. Evaluators expected that these issues would be resolved through panel deliberation. A lively deliberation was expected, especially in panels that were more multidisciplinary and would want to adopt, pragmatically speaking, *"the widest possible notion of Impact"*:

> *Yeah, it is very multidisciplinary, which is good. I think it's good because it gives you the best chance of reaching the widest possible notion of Impact and not just having a very narrow field with everybody thinking the same. P2OutImp2(PRE)*

Despite being nebulous, evaluators expected that a number of "flags" would indicate to them the value of the Impact. These included references to a number of notions also present in the evaluation process of more traditional notions of research excellence, including Impact being something that stood out from the crowd (*"…so impact—to have Impact, it must be egregious, it must stand out from the crowd otherwise everything has Impact" P1Imp2(PRE))* or made a difference *("…the question for me is what difference does your research make" P3Out2(PRE)*, that had a "so what" moment (*"There is a so-what factor. And that's what Impact's about really, but probably not a very clear definition" P3Out2(PRE)*, or was novel, although it should also be mentioned that a similar number of evaluators didn't think that novelty was an essential aspect of Impact:

> *…it's a little bit of an oxymoron that novelty and impact are related, because they seem to be opposites. Because if something is novel and we don't know what it's going to do, then it couldn't have much Impact at this point. P0OutImp1(PRE)*

These would no doubt be used as thresholds during the evaluation.

Judgements of Impact

So once the concept has been tied down through deliberation, an evaluation is needed. Unlike theoretically thinking about Impact, which one evaluator described as "*a kind of fog that descends when thinking about impact*" *P2Imp1(PRE)*, valuing it means that certain lines, judgements and decisions regarding its value need to be made. In the pre-evaluation interviews, I asked evaluators about their strategies around valuing Impact to identify any tendencies that might manifest themselves in the evaluation process. I use the word "tendency" rather than bias mainly because in the pre-evaluation interviews I didn't want to make the assumption that a tendency would automatically translate itself to a bias. I see a bias as a tendency put into practice, while a tendency is innocent enough on its own. Therefore, any tendencies I identified in the pre-evaluation interviews were to be considered as <u>possible biases</u> only. If we think again of the tug-of-war analogy, if enough evaluators subscribe to a particular tendency, then it is more likely that this is incorporated within the dominant definition of the group, translating into a bias in practice (unconscious or not). The evaluators' eye then reflects this bias. Nonetheless, tendencies presented possible indicators of how an evaluator might behave in practice, and I explore these here.

I was specifically interested in the strategies that evaluators implicitly referred to prior to the evaluation to make hypotheses about how differing individual strategies would be played off against each other within the group. If a strategy was shared by many evaluators or strongly held by the right types of people, then it would more likely be adopted by the evaluation group, becoming "eye". From the pre-evaluation interviews, preferences towards linearity and connectivity were strongly supported. Their faith that "*it would all work out in the end*" was embedded in their hope that linearity would be a key driver of the evaluation despite acknowledging individually (Samuel and Derrick 2015) and understanding from the calibration exercises (Derrick and Samuel 2017) that Impact is not linear. Nonetheless, a desire for linear narratives was strong among evaluators:

"It's quite straightforward, in fact. I'd hope we get a number to look at like that" P3OutImp8(PRE). Within this hope for linearity was the desire for an "iron link" between the underpinning research and the Impact: *"So an iron link between a piece of research and you dying or suffering, I think would be most important" P2Imp2(PRE).* An iron link or clear causality would be considered as strong evidence. Evaluators would have preferred these to be sequential, map-able (*"to provide that sort of UK view of how funding leads to an output and that output then leads to an Impact" P1Imp1(PRE)),* and quantifiable:

> *So that is how you can have—research was done, showed the benefits of exercise got into the clinical guidelines and over time you can track the proportion of the relevant professionals who are implementing the better evidence. P3OutImp8(PRE)*

A preference for linearity anticipated a desired pragmatically-driven, efficient evaluation acting as a "halo" over the evaluation: a "halo" over "linearity", so to speak. Its nature reinforced, at times, other tendencies towards the direct association of excellence research with excellence impact, and there was a belief in this purity of the linear, logic model of impact: *"If research is about excellence and research impact's about the Impact of those excellent ideas, I think we're going to have to remain quite pure on some of the top rated things" P4Imp2(PRE).* This linearity meant that participants assumed logic-model approaches to Impact, and the link in medical and health research between basic and applied research, and translation to adoption (Greenhalgh et al. 2016):

> *So that's the kind of, you know, I have this sort of view all the way across the piece from basic all the way through to applies it, translational and adoption research. P1Imp1(PRE)*

In the absence of experiencing the evaluation, who can blame the evaluators for thinking this way? Most impact models, despite protests that state otherwise, depict Impact linearly (Greenhalgh et al. 2016). If we think Impact as being a matter of time, then it is natural to assume linearity unconsciously, even if we consciously state not to envision it as such:

"…but it's easier when you're thinking about a step-wise process and you're moving along a pathway" P1OutImp3(PRE). Evaluators referred to a linear model which was also strong in how they had approached the assessment of ex-ante Impact in their prior experiences: *"So having Impact requires that you generate the evidence and then that you, in turn you get into guidelines and the people start using that information to change their practice" P4Imp1(PRE).*

At other times, this bias of linearity caused evaluators to express a preference for more downstream Impacts, although this is more reflective of the REF Impact definition mechanic that emphasised a *"change or effect":*

> *So I guess the answer to your question is it's toward the end of that process, isn't it? We're looking for Impact and—not impact from every piece of research has been undertaken, but from, at least, some of the research been undertaken has had a discernible Impact. P2OutImp4(PRE)*

The challenge for the panels was not only to resolve all competing notions of Impact as an object between themselves, but also to develop strategies for its navigation and eventual valuation. A clear preference for an approach that valued linearity was observed and the extent to which it would be translated to group practice would be examined in the post-evaluation interviews. Although such an approach is not ideal, and contrary to the recommendations and knowledge surrounding Impact, its existence in the pre-evaluation interviews represents a tendency only and not yet a bias. Peer review's strength is its grounding in expert-led deliberation and decision making and it would be the group's decision as to whether this tendency would be adopted as a bias in practice. As one evaluator stated, post-evaluation: *"there are often unintended consequences from these otherwise nice ideals" P3OutImp2(POST).*

Examples of Change Post-Evaluation

An old Indian proverb states that "hindsight wisdom is of no use", but for the assessment practice of Impact, hindsight offers us a chance to reflect on what has been learnt, and how we change practice in the future. Through my analysis, I heard how each evaluation group reasoned with competing views of Impact, and about how these were supported by some and dismissed by other evaluators in the group. Although there were strong pre-evaluation tendencies, a clear dominant definition of Impact as an evaluation object and a strategy around its valuation were yet to appear. To identifying the dominant definition, and pinpointing the strategies used by the group, I examined examples of change in individual evaluators by comparing how they conceptualised Impact pre- and post-evaluation. When I say change, I need to be clear about what I defined as a "change". No participant is likely to outwardly admit that they were wrong, and I didn't expect this, nor did I directly seek this type of evidence of change. Instead, as with any group process, change is more gradual, a reasoned process that involves the layering of ideas, rather than flipping them. To use an analogy, the type of change that I was sensitive to was more how the colour red becomes pink, rather than how red changes to green.

Explicit references to change were made by evaluators whose previously held conceptualisations of Impact had been broadened: *"Not so much changed my mind as my awareness was broadened by the process"* P3OutImp3(POST). This described across panels and was not restricted to academic-evaluators:

> *I guess it's giving—yeah, I've taken the slightly wider view, again, it's widened my horizons in terms of things like education and societal impact environment, those sorts if things where you hadn't maybe realized that these things were having as much influence. P5Imp1(POST)*

Adopting a broader perspective of Impact can be interpreted in one of two ways. First, the action of evaluating this unknown and untested criterion can be seen as a learning process (described above), as one participant noted: *"I mean, after doing the exercise, I think we probably were much better at doing it"* P5OutImp3(POST). Subtle references to change were described by evaluators as learning from the evaluation experience: *"Well I guess I've learned that Impact comes from a lot of places and it's not just the classic ones that you think of"* P3OutImp9(POST).

The second interpretation of this change to adopting a broader consideration of Impact was a reaction to how individuals in the group surrendered their perspectives to the group's dominant definition. As a member of a peer review panel, individuals are not immune to the social exchanges and influences from other peer group members (Blau 1964). This results not in an explicit change, but in an altering of perspectives (red-to-pink) that is the reasoned result of being exposed to both dissenting and confirming ideas in practice. This is an example of an in-group compromise, as one evaluator notes post-evaluation; changing his idea around the object was described as *"filing up"*, and he said that he had *"learned a great deal from my fellow panel members"*:

> *I think it will because I went into this completely clueless, and came out with some ideas of what could be Impact and learned a great deal from my fellow panel members. So definitely, yes, I mean, it was filling up actually, entirely. P3OutImp1(POST)*

The question at this point in the analysis remains whether the broadening of ideas about Impact by individual evaluators was common across all panels, or whether it was restricted to this one panel in particular. A summary of the change noted in each Panel 3 example is shown in Table 4.1.

If it was a commonly seen effect, then this would justify the approach by this book of treating all sub-panels as one, overseen by the Main Panel. Panel 3 was an interesting test case for this as it was described as the most multidisciplinary panel of all those included. In fact, one Panel 3 evaluator described it as the *"kitchen sink"* of all panels. Many evaluators from

Table 4.1 Examples of pre- to post- evaluation change in conceptualisation of Impact from Panel 3

Example evaluator	Pre-evaluation conceptualisation	Post-evaluation conceptualisation
P3OutImp5	Linear Measurable Impacts	Broad perspective Measurable through ICS narrative
P3OutImp7	Linear Commercial/Economic Impacts Applied research	Broad Appreciation of policy Impacts
P3OutImp8	Broad but preference for application and utility in Impact	Broad and non-linear

this panel reported that they had altered their previously held ideas of Impact as a result of the evaluation. Overall, all interviewed evaluators from this panel referred to how their ideas about Impact had been broadened. Adopting a broader view might be, as one evaluator described, a little nerve-wracking, but it better equipped individuals for compromise on the group level: *"I think I've got a better idea. I am still a little nervous about its diversity, which is kind of inevitable" P3OutImp2(POST)*. For this evaluator, entering the panel with an open mind and a willingness to compromise resulted in them being more amenable to taking on the definitions of others:

> *An open mind, really, and an ability to work with the criteria, even if they're not ideal. To see what the criteria really means to other people, and then come to some kind of compromise. P3OutImp2(POST)*

Below, I explore three interesting examples of how change occurred for individuals within Panel 3, and how these changes reflect the group moving towards a group-based definition of Impact for its evaluation.

My first example, P3OutImp5, is a female professor with a self-declared track record in clinical and policy impact. In the pre-evaluation interviews, this evaluator emphasised Impact as having had a demonstrable change in public health practice, and tended towards linear strategies for its conceptualisation. She didn't restrict her opinion of Impact in any way because she had doubts as to how research impact could be measured: *"…one of my concerns about the measuring impact for REF has been that these things are very subtle"*. As such, she showed a pre-evaluation preference for Impact that could be tracked and measured. Post-evaluation, the evaluator held onto the belief that Impact was measurable but this illusion was built into the ICS narrative and not a naturally reducible object:

> *It's changed, yeah. I think you can demonstrate it. Yeah, I think there are many different forms it can take. So I think I've kind of got a broader idea of what Impact might look like but I've also got a better understanding of how you might put together an audit trail or an evidence trail to demonstrate that the research you've done has had Impact. P3OutImp5(POST)*

The evaluator told how she now had a *"broader idea of what Impact might look like"*, and that this broadening had induced her to consider Impact that she had either dismissed or not even considered prior to the experience: *"So it's made me go away and think about things where I work that could be shown to have had an Impact, that maybe I wouldn't have thought about in quite the same way before"* P3OutImp5(POST).

Another Panel 3 evaluator (P3OutImp7), prior to the evaluation, showed strong tendencies *"always to apply research into tangible outcomes"* P3OutImp7(PRE) and a preference for Impacts that could demonstrate this (i.e. economic or commercial impacts). This was related to his prior position and an ongoing relationship with a prominent pharmaceutical company, and his experience with commercial impacts (e.g. patents, spin-off companies, etc.) professionally explained his preference for these types of Impact. The evaluator openly declared his orientation towards valuing applied research because he *"…never liked doing research for research's sake"* P3OutImp7 and *"…I think it was the GSK angle, high profile in industry and also professional bodies"* P3OutImp7(PRE). His evaluation tendencies for the Impact assessment were evident in the pre-evaluation interviews, where he quite strongly insisted that *"To me, research impact is the way research is applied and I keep this general, I think it's the application of research to me, is what research Impact means"* P3OutImp7(PRE). Considering the passion, authority and at times ferocity with which these views about Impact were insisted upon by P3OutImp7, it seemed likely that the evaluator would change his behaviour in practice. However, this was made more unlikely since the evaluator was prepared to hold onto this view over and above the boundaries enforced by the REF definition as an evaluation mechanic. Indeed, as explained below in the interview excerpt, the evaluator intended to use the definition as a tool to promote his own views of Impact, rather than the other way around. This would be used not only to galvanise his interpretation in practice, but also to deflect dissent from competing conceptualisations from other individuals in the group:

There's limitless definitions for it in the REF handbook, but you're not going to read it and read it. But for me, I see it as more of an application. How is that research from the bench, observation that you see that is interesting, okay, it looks interesting, to translate itself to something that people can use, administer, take, or actually, initiate further research in a different sphere completely differently. P3OutImp7(PRE)

Other, unconscious signals of power (P3OutImp7 was male, a professor and with over 25 years' experience) would also mean that it would be difficult for dissenting opinions to compete against this definition in influencing the group's dominant definition. As such, this evaluator would be more likely to attract allies within the group to adopt this perspective of Impact than to join others. However, something unexpected happened: he admitted that he was wrong. After the evaluation process, this evaluator gained an appreciation of other Impacts *"and what have you"*, including those less finite ones realised using less direct routes, such as health policies: *"So I think I was more financially driven in my understanding of Impact. But when it came to policy change and what have you I appreciated that a lot more as well after the REF exercise" P3OutImp7(POST)*. When noting this change, the evaluator reflected how *"The wider definition of policy, I think, was good for me to get that appreciation" P3OutImp7(POST)*. As with his fellow Panel 3 member described above, his definition had broadened around Impact, to one that considered more salient aspects that were outside his pre-evaluation conceptualisations of the object.

My last case from Panel 3 was an evaluator who in the pre-evaluation interviews had emphasised linearity as important: *"…that there is something in the real world where you can track its existence back to a piece of research that was done" P3OutImp8*. However, this reviewer did state that his initial knee-jerk reaction towards linearity as a characteristic of Impact was *"perhaps a little naïve"*. He was therefore open to the possibility of considering the role of other factors in realising Impact beyond his pre-evaluation comprehension. However, *"application, utility, outputs is another"* were considered important attributes of impact and in line with his understanding of the REF mechanics. After the evaluation, like fellow panel members P3OutImp5 and P3OutImp7, his conceptualisation broadened to include more nuanced aspects of research impact not amenable to linearity: *"Again, it comes back to the vast range of potential impacts in—we all know it's not linear … and there is a lot more thinking that has to be done … more research to be done on understanding on how to get it"* P3OutImp8(POST). Within this panel at least, the direct and indirect tendencies that evaluators demonstrated towards an idea of Impact that included a linear, directly causal relationship were altered by the evaluation process. As a result, all three of my examples here changed their previously held beliefs about Impact, to a perspective that was more inclusive of Impacts that are non-measurable, and not necessarily restricted to linear trajectories. At this point I cannot say why this happened (see Chap. 6 for a more detailed exploration of why this change occurred), but the existence of changes in these Panel 3 evaluators suggests that the group dynamic played a large role in developing such a consensus. P3OutImp8 reflects on this directly:

…there were some individuals who had the quite fixed views that Impact needed to be something that was making a difference for the lives of people. And it was obviously difficult to convince people that perhaps there were other ways of looking at Impact. P3OutImp8(POST)

Other examples from the remaining panels saw more distinctive changes pre- to post-evaluation. On Panel 4, one female evaluator, a professor, who described herself as engaging with policy, commercial and public impact "very often", had definite ideas in the pre-evaluation interviews of how Impact could be planned and achieved through applied research. From her perspective, applied research pursued *"…after a practical problem … undertaken with a goal of fixing something, or changing something"*. In this way, for applied research, *"…the goal is actually the research"*, and therefore diminished in its value. The evaluator used the example of Teflon on a frying pan and on a spaceship to illustrate this point:

Teflon on a frying pan, versus Teflon on spaceships. The first one was actually basic research with Impact because the research wasn't designed to make non-stick pans. Whereas Teflon on the side of spaceships, well, it was actually, it was setting out to do that. P4OutImp5(PRE)

Using this example, the frying pan Impact would be more valuable than for the spaceship; the spaceship Impact was the intended outcome of the research in the first place. There was less merit associated with pursuing research for a specific goal than discoveries that happened serendipitously. There was therefore little value in research Impact if it was pre-organised: *"So I think about an asteroid impact on earth and research doesn't have an impact in that kind of way. It doesn't necessarily get activated and smack into something"* P4OutImp5(PRE).

After the process, the evaluator still felt, *"personally"*, that applied research was not Impact: *"…My view is that shouldn't count because personally I think commissioned research is not research that has Impact"* P4OutImp5(POST). However, she acknowledged that although her personal view had not changed, her practice had. Instead of holding onto her pre-evaluation ideas, she had surrendered her views to the group, adopting the group's dominant definition and navigation strategies: *"Well, I think now we have to accept that applied research is considered as research of Impact"* P4OutImp5(POST). She was open about this change, commenting that:

> *I accept it, I was wrong [laughter]. And there's an awful lot more applied research going on, you know, which you could argue is a good thing, unless it decreases the amount of other research, which would be a bad thing.* P4OutImp5(POST)

I take one final example from Panel 4 to be compared with the approached adopted by P4OutImp5 and to ascertain the extent to which in-group dynamics were influential in altering evaluators' individually held, pre-evaluation conceptualisations of Impact. In this example, P4OutImp3 (male, professor), prior to the evaluation process, didn't *"…subscribe to the view that there's only one type of impact. There are lots of different types of impact"* P4OutImp3(PRE), but held onto the view of Impact being "beyond academia", which was in line with the REF2014 mechanics. Post-evaluation, he didn't think *"…that my opinion of what constitutes societal impact has changed"*, but that was immaterial because the REF2014 mechanic had strengthened his own conceptualisation of the object in practice and the group's approach had been influenced by it:

So it was kind of clear then when we started talking about Impact that what we have to do by the word impact, the societal impact and it was—I had that perception even then that it had to be something beyond academia. So it had to have actually tangible, real life implications for people. So the criteria that REF came up with sort of add into what I already felt was Impact, and that was actually. P4OutImp(POST)

I am reluctant to draw conclusions at this point regarding the factors responsible for the changes observed by comparing evaluator views before and after the evaluation. I explore the in-group dynamics more thoroughly in Chap. 6; however, the change in views suggests that not only did the group dynamic play a large role in influencing the conceptualisation of Impact but so too did the mechanics. The level of influence of the mechanics has been explored in the previous chapter, and reflections from the evaluators of how the REF Impact definition in particular dictated their practice suggest an infiltrative effect.

What We Are Learning About Peer Review of Societal Impact

The dataset for describing evaluators' views about Impact prior to the world's first formal assessment of ex-post Impact is particularly valuable as it shows views that are untarnished by experience, power or other external influences. The variety of views about Impact held prior to the assessment process (Samuel and Derrick 2015; Derrick and Samuel 2016) shows how there is a need to regularise competing values of Impact that naturally exist in the academic community through practice. This is needed before a meaningful incentive towards achieving impact within a wider notion of research excellence can be achieved. Current models of Impact assessment lack an appreciation of how the social interplay between evaluators influences the construction of their own practice around the evaluation object, during the evaluation process. Adding an alternative focus of Impact evaluation from models to one of evaluative practice and therefore considerations about how a model is mutually constructed (Pier et al. 2017) means that it is no longer sufficient for research to hypothesise the role that *productive interactions, feedback loops* and *indicators* play in realising Impact, and then insist that these models are evident in the evaluation outcomes. Instead, during evaluative practice, these models are twisted, bent and completely torn apart as part of the social interplay within a peer review panel. Previous research shows that when panels applied new and untested criteria in practice they tend towards a conservative approach (Huutoniemi 2010; Luukkonen 2012). In this way, Impact is potentially no different, and the evaluators' adherence to the evaluation mechanics, or their acquiescence to strongly held competing views of other seemingly powerful evaluators, suggests an equally conservative and/or pragmatic approach. In the absence of experience or precedent around the evaluation object, the reliance of group members on each other increases. What emerges is a distinct, one-of-a-kind, pragmatic interpretation of the object that is not only dependent on the values and ideas of Impact brought to the evaluation process, but also how panellists pull others towards them and how they relinquish their own viewpoints in response to better ones. The most influential models and valuation strategies are therefore those that are constructed by the panel, in vivo.

In the section below, I investigate the group-constructed strategies in vivo around Impact. At times, these strategies surrender to the influence of the mechanics (an infiltrative approach), whereas other strategies are the result of panel deliberation, and a mutually constructed valuation lens (the evaluators' eye). I do not pinpoint the dominant definition below (please see Chap. 6), but identify strategies used by the group to navigate and value Impact.

From the Group—What Is/Was Impact?

Assessing Impact in practice meant forming a group consensus and applying the dominant definition. The general feeling of the panels was "... *that Impact was Impact" P3OutImp2(POST)*. Although it is not possible to pin down an explicit description of the implicit dominant definition, it is possible to identify, across participants, key decisions made by the group surrounding how to value aspects of Impact (strategies). These strategies are, as one evaluator outlined, based on a series of judgements, a collective valuation, and not based on the strength of one judgement alone: *"...this was based on judgement, you know, there is no way of reducing this process to some reproducible algorithm..." (P2OutImp8(POST).* Some of these strategies relate directly to the way in which the panel valued certain claims of Impact over others, and so reasonable deductions by the reader can be made about a more explicit dominant definition: *"So Impact is Impact but there were some Impacts that are certainly greater than others" P0OutImp3(POST).* They also represent how the group worked around commonly associated drawbacks of Impact assessment (causality, time-lag and attribution), the boundaries of the evaluation mechanics provided, and an understanding of how to utilise the available expertise within the panel from different evaluator types.

Four distinct strategies to navigate Impact developed by the group were identified by combining results from both the pre- and post-evaluation interviews. These strategies included (1) Considering benefits associated with public engagement; (2) Identifying the linear link; (3) Developing a notion of "centricity" to bypass the drawbacks of causality, time-lag and attribution; and (4) Balancing evidence with trust. By examining each strategy, I identify the evaluators' eye through which all valuations of Impact were made. This evaluators' eye is the result of a reasoned balance between the boundaries permitted by the evaluation mechanics, resolution of competing conceptualisations in situ, and a collective *"gut feeling"* of panellists: *"if it was outstanding, it was outstanding"* *P2OutImp6(POST)*

Public Engagement Impact, with a Little "i"

Although public engagement is an important activity that connects researchers with their public, thereby partially fulfilling their societal contract, it was overlooked as a worthy Impact by REF2014. The Impact definition mechanic restricted claims of Impact to those that had had *"a change or benefit"*, and the examples offered to the panels did not list public engagement. Despite never explicitly excluding public engagement activities as Impact, the mechanics did not facilitate its inclusion unless it could be linked to *"...a change or benefit"*, either economically or otherwise. This was echoed by panellists post-evaluation: *"…it's not enough just to show that you're doing something that the public can come and listen to. You've got to show that something is the consequence of that"* P4OutImp2(POST). Public engagement was therefore only considered as a contributing factor of Impact (i.e. Impact with a little "i"): *"…in a slightly different box to what I would consider to be Impact; like with the small "i" in the general word, because we were there to assess Impact in REF terms"* P3Imp2(POST). In practice, despite this implicit disqualification, how to value public engagement as Impact was constantly debated, reflecting the socialised awareness of panellists of its importance as evidence of a "productive interaction" (Spaapen and Van Drooge 2011). *"There was a huge divergence of views on popular science and Impact in reaching a non-academic community"* P3Imp2(POST).

Although public engagment's place as an Impact was debated, more debate argued over its value relative to competing Impact claims considered by the panel; *"there were clearly some people who thought that we ought to be paying more attention to the number of people suffering from the condition in the world"* P2OutImp8(POST). For these panels, if it was considered, public engagement would need to be viewed as of lesser value than other claims. Compared to other claims of Impact stemming from medical, health and biomedical research, public engagement and its link to increasing public awareness was considered a *"soft Impact"* unless it could be *"translated into something else down the line"*:

> *…being a clinician I'm a little bit more interested in slightly more concrete things like saving people's lives and getting people back into school in the case of children or back into work in the case of adults and so on. Improving awareness I felt was quite a soft Impact to be honest. If that is all you can show, then I think that's quite weak. If you want to impress me with changes of work I'd like to see that translated into something else down the line … how did improving awareness translate into something else.* P4OutImp4(POST)

In fact, there was group-wide discontent that a panel associated with medical and health research would value claims of public engagement over those that "saved lives": *"I think another thing that was not good was*

that people got four stars for a case study that didn't have any effect on patients"
P0OutImp2(POST). The strategy towards public engagement to value
such claims less than other Impacts was supported as the disciplinary
direction by the overarching Main Panel.

In practice, claims of public engagement lost out to other Impacts
because the panel favoured the ability to make comparisons. Public
engagement is difficult to value without a degree of quantitative evidence.
If a claim of public engagement as Impact could provide quantitative
evidence of its Significance and Reach, then reasonable comparisons of
value could be made by the panel. For public engagement, quantifiable
evidence of its Impact, in line with the Impact definition's emphasis on *"a
change or benefit"*, would allow panels to employ a valuation exercise that
would separate strong from weaker claims of Impact:

> *In most cases, where we did see something which has been commercialised,
> we had no problem with that; that was fine. And so the weakest ones were
> the ones where people sort of were basically saying we stimulated a policy
> debate or a conversation. I felt that we felt that was a bit weak.*
> *P2OutImp8(POST)*

As another evaluator put it, claims of public engagement as Impact
were embedded in the Impact narrative, and were therefore more difficult
to discern from more quantifiable end-product Impacts. For the group,
*"The quantitative data really sold it ... I think the narratives got you half-
way. The quantitative data sort of pushed it into that three, four star realm"*
P3OutImp9(POST). This debate is not only about how to value quantitative and narrative-based claims, and declaring that quantifiable evidence
was favoured, but surrounds the expectations panels had regarding the
types of evidence underpinning different claims of Impact. Whereas the
narrative was important, in many situations Impact claims could have
been more convincing if quantitative evidence had been supplied, allowing for comparisons: *"so it's a way in which you have to look as to how would
you quantify impact in supplementation to the very real necessity from the
narrative" P0OutImp5(POST)*. However, panels were aware that different
Impact claims were supported with different types of evidence: *"different*

continuums". For claims of economic impact, quantitative evidence would be supplied as supporting evidence:

> *...so there's different continuums. And similarly with the diagnostics, if you develop a new diagnostic tool, test some microorganism in food or in blood or whatever, you'd then have to take that insight or that observation into that start-up and show that the start-up has a particular turnover and with a particular number of people and that would be the economic impact. P0OutImp3(POST)*

Here, public engagement was part of achieving Impact, playing a vital role in pushing it or as a productive interaction (Spaapen and Van Drooge 2011), but it was not valued highly if it was presented as the only Impact. As different types of evidence were expected from claims of policy influence, or changing ways of thinking, this altered how more nuanced claims, including those of public engagement, were valued in practice.

Finding that Linear Link

Linearity echoes in all associations with Impact assessment. In the pre-evaluation interviews, there was a risk of the evaluation scale (Derrick and Samuel 2016) tipping in favour of a group view that favoured a conceptualisation of Impact that was linear. As with other strategies of Impact valuation, the decision to adopt a rational approach was not concerned with questions regarding *what* is Impact but instead *how* to navigate it. This change of focus also influenced how the group navigated Impact.

By cross-referencing the pre- and post-evaluation interviews, the concerns of Derrick and Samuel (2016) were justified in that the group adopted a strategy favouring linearity. This worried one evaluator from the overarching Main Panel who, having reservations, did not approve this group-based decision. For this evaluator, the reason for the adoption of this group-level strategy was based on the type of evaluator within the panels who, as medics, *"didn't get that"*, and the group was *"lulled themselves into this sort of seduction that they did it really well and it all worked"*, which is a reflection of "happy talk" and therefore risks groupthink (Sunstein and Hastie 2015):

Societal impact is, by definition, a social process. And the medics don't get that because they only get anything that's medical. So they have not understood the very strong literature from the social sciences that research impact is not always linear. They've assumed that the research impact is linear. And that is problematic. And now they've lulled themselves into this sort of seduction that they did it really well and it all worked. But actually, they are blind to the biases and that worried me hugely. P0OutImp4(POST)

However, as the above evaluator continues, this group approach was adopted in opposition to their point of view regarding the linearity of Impact realisation, and also in response to how narratives within the ICSs were constructed. The group chose to adopt this approach as a way of making comparisons during the valuation process, and were lured by strong constructions that emphasised a linear approach to Impact:

And so I think people who presented highly organized ICSs saying first we did this and then we contacted the other and then the other, and showing this linear link, and particularly tying it to some kind of quantified metric, you know, they got a lot. But the people who did less well … are the ones that were saying things like, well, we promoted public debate. Even though they really did, and they gave quotes, it doesn't sound so good as we're on page 136 of NICE guideline 115. P0OutImp4(POST)

This also relates to the type of evidence that was preferred to make comparisons, and is therefore a natural extension of the previous strategy. However, from this evaluator's point of view, this *"…huge bias towards quantitative linear research or quantitative research that's got a linear link with practice … wasn't fair"*, and did not reflect an evidence-informed approach to the valuation of Impact. In this way, even though the majority of the panels actively shelved the more difficult discussions surrounding *"what is Impact"*, this evaluator described how the failure of the group to consider this question unfairly biased the evaluation outcomes.

Independent from the losing narrative of the above evaluator, other evaluators felt confident in explaining approaches that favoured constructions of linearity. For one evaluator, linearity was favoured because *"…if the Impact was clearly drawn and precise one could make the judgment with confidence" P4OutImp2(POST)*. The response from others clearly echoed the concerns of *P0OutImp4(POST)* that the overwhelming tendency for linearity to be constructed within case studies would "lull" evaluators towards a strategy that would directly favour these types of Impact:

> So I think—yeah, in the cases I can think about it was really looking for things like specific activities between the original output and the eventual Impact that suggested there was a chain of events between the two. P5OutImp4(POST)

This strategy was adopted across each panel's practice despite dissenting opinions (P0OutImp4), disapproval from the Main Panel, and academic literature supporting a non-linear perspective on Impact assessment: *"…the more difficult ones are where you simply do a piece of research and then kind of you feel that it may or may not trickle into practice. I think that's more difficult" P3OutImp6(POST)*. It is not my aim to judge the decisions made by the panel; however, I do question the process used to reach these decisions. As such, my concerns are in line with those of the Main Panel A evaluator described here, but are based not on an assertion of what Impact is and isn't, but a fear that the shelving of difficult questions, despite the peers and mechanics on offer during the evaluation, is an artefact of groupthink, and not robust deliberation.

Developing the Centricity Strategy

As a unique strategy developed in practice by panels, *Centricity* recognises Impact as a complex pathway and combination of contributors and organisational and political actors. In this strategy, if a smaller claim of Impact was considered by the panel as an essential pre-cursor (attributable) to another larger, more downstream Impact, then both Impacts were considered essential and valued equally. Centricity refers to how valuing Impact is made possible by the necessary step claimed as Impact. In other words, to assess its value, a counter-question is asked of the submission: Could the end-product (Impact) have been possible if this step described in the submission had not existed? This is not about assessing the value of the contribution in realising the Impact (a judgement that was shelved, Chap. 6), but instead identifying whether the claim could be reasonably associated with the final Impact claim:

> ...*was the research essential for that Impact? If that research was kept out and claimed by that particular institution, if that research was vital in order for that Impact to occur, then we would usually accept it even if other institutions had also contributed to it. P0P1OutImp1(POST)*

For the health sciences this was very useful when it came to assessing the value of research in screening programmes, or the influence of policy changes on health policy (it would certainly help the valuation for the example used in the introduction regarding Clare Oliver): *"so you got to measure every single outcome and it's almost impossible sometimes to say which piece of which activity helps us"* P2Imp2(POST). Centricity means that if the claim was perceived as making a contribution to the Impact as a final *"benefit or effect"*, then the panel would determine whether the submission represented a necessary step in achieving the Impact. If, in line with the definition of Centricity provided in the previous paragraph, the claim for Impact was determined to be a necessary contribution to the final Impact, then it was valued equally to all other necessary steps in achieving that final Impact. In other words, if the Impact could not have been achieved without this intermediary step, then the claim was valued by the panel in the same way as if it had been entirely and solely responsible for that Impact.

Centricity acknowledges that Impact is the accumulation of many interlocking steps, and not the result of any one piece of work, that in fact can be part of a *"large ecosystem"* of research ideas. This approach was surprising for some, who did not anticipate developing this type of strategy in vivo, and indeed, the potential for this strategy was not identified in evaluators' intended approaches to Impact in the pre-evaluation interviews. As the following evaluator describes, to treat all contributions equally acknowledged the way research built on *"other people's evidence and ideas"*:

> *...you know, we, we work with other people's evidence and ideas; that's how science moves forward and that's how we work in a large ecosystem with research ideas. So I don't think anyone was ever expecting that because we marked the case study as being four star that we said that everything that had been done was in that case study; it was all down to this, the other work of that professor or that research group. P1Imp1(POST)*

There was a tendency to value each contribution as individually attributable to the Impact, especially when the contribution was minor; however, the group decided to value each step in the "inverse tree" as equal provided that a reasonable case of a claims membership to the inverse tree towards Impact could be made. This was also a pragmatic decision, as valuing each contribution individually would have taken a lot of time, and was shelved by the panel:

> *an inverse tree, so it's like a family tree, the further back you go, the more and more research there is that contributed in some way to the Impact ... the difficulty is deciding where a piece of research appears to have a minor contribution to an Impact. P1Imp2(POST)*

At times, it was tempting to measure the value of the contribution, and some on the panel were in favour of this approach: *"some people were tempted to sort of downgrade it slightly if you didn't think the contribution was significant enough"* P1OutImp5(POST). But this decision was effectively shelved in favour of a binary decision about whether a contribution, even one *"somewhere in the middle"*, had been made towards the Impact:

> *Somebody described it before, they then did a little bit of work somewhere in the middle and then it got picked up by a pharma company or whatever and spun out as a drug. So you say, well, they weren't first—so they weren't the main driver of the novelty. And they didn't actually implement this in practice. They did a bit of research in the middle that contributed. P1OutImp5(POST)*

The strategy also allowed minor Impact claims to *"piggyback"* on the larger, more significant claims of others, a consideration of panels deciphering issues with authorship and contribution. Therefore, in line with the panel's experience of evaluating Outputs, a similar strategy was applied to Impact to ensure that the assessment process across all criteria remained logical, consistent and fair:

> *And it just comes back to the other point, where two institutes have both claimed the ICS and they claim different aspects of the research that went into it, and it's quite interesting how the weaker one often or the one that had less claim would be quite transparent about what they'd done and what the other institute had done or the research that the other institute had done. And they come up—so one of the cases I had was a test of Spina bifida. And it was quite clear that one of those institutes had a very minor role in what turned out to be big Impact. And that's quite a difficult one because they're on a paper, but you know, they probably didn't drive that piece of research. The research was at least two star so that it came within the criteria. So it was fine. But the contribution, they'd sort of piggybacked on a big Impact and that was hard to analyse in that case. P5OutImp1(POST)*

Centricity was also useful when valuing more nuanced claims of Impact less amenable to quantitative representation. Linking less tangible Impact claims with quantified outcomes, as Centricity allowed, such as the number of lives saved, profits, etc., made valuing Impact easier.

Adopting Centricity is more useful in less clinically focused sub-panels such as sub-panels 2 and 3 than for sub-panels 1 and 4, for example, but centricity was adopted by all panels regardless of their disciplinary focus. Specifically, the strategy allowed basic science discoveries further down the *"inverse tree"* and claimed in submissions from sub-panel 4 to be valued as highly as those from sub-panels 1 and 2, negating much of the criticism focused on the REF2014 Impact criteria, as well as the evaluation of Impact in general about how formalising the criterion would disadvantage and downplay the role of blue-sky research. Centricity allowed panels to remain immune to the narrative constructions by minimising any undue influence such constructions would have on the evaluation of the Impact. This was done by effectively removing the narrative from the consideration of Impact. By shelving an assessment of the value to focus on the Impact as an end-product, Centricity dismissed any value present in the ICSs through over-valuation and an *"embroidered version of the truth" P2OutImp8(POST).*

Adopting Centricity also allowed the panel to circumvent (but not shelve) many of the drawbacks associated with Impact assessment such as time-lag, causality and attribution. The strategy spoke to the pragmatic character of peer review driven by problem solving and satisficing (Lamont 2009) in practice, as Centricity allowed panels to bypass the problems associated with attribution (it wasn't an issue), as well as time-lags. For time-lag, the advantage is that some claims have more time to mature and are therefore more central to, and responsible for, achieving Impact. This would mean that they would be advantaged in an evaluation that focused solely on the *value* of this step in achieving the Impact end-product. However, by adopting Centricity, valuation at this step was dismissed in favour of determining if this step was essential for the Impact. This meant that older Impacts were on par with younger ones.

Centricity allowed the group to redefine the valuation process, and by doing so permitted basic research, occurring earlier in the inverse tree, to claim Impacts usually more easily attributable to applied research. However, as will be discussed in Chap. 6, adopting this binary approach to Impact contribution effectively shelved the essential step of making value judgements against Impact claims. The evaluator below described:

> I felt that our job was not simply a technical one of assessing whether research had had an Impact, and whether that Impact was well evidenced. I felt that to properly assess the reach and significance of that Impact, we would inevitably have to come to a view about values, about whether this particular type of Impact was really important or less important. P2OutImp1(POST)

As such, Centricity as a strategy was counter to his approach to peer review, which in effect was all about making value judgements about importance, rather than simply a technical exercise. Making a valuation judgement would have required more time and was not consistent with the time restrictions placed on the assessment, or a pragmatic approach to assessment.

Balancing Evidence, with Trust

A major difficulty facing the panel was how to sort through the variety of evidence underpinning the Impact claims made in the ICSs. Supporting evidence was crucial to justify and quantify (at times) the Reach and Significance of each case study by providing outside verification. Outside verification was seen as a procedural method to guard against gaming by submissions, and overselling the value of Impact through creative case study constructions. Without a more socialised experience of the concept of Impact either individually or as a group, this supporting evidence provided a sounding board for the valuation process and the development of the dominant definition. There was therefore a consideration of how much the group could trust the evidence supplied in the ICSs. However, as external sources of evidence of the Impact, rather than an assessment based on the opinions of experts, there was some "discomfort" in how to trust constructions as proof of Impact:

> *I think you'd probably get some consensus of some discomfort from a number of people about assessing them, and most of this discomfort came from the fact that how could they believe what was being told them without some additional proof. P0OutImp5(POST)*

This was also based on a pragmatic approach to Impact, as the time restrictions on the evaluation inhibited the ability to double-check every source of evidence: *"It wouldn't be true to say that we were in the position to check accuracy of every fact that was written. That would be an impossible task" P4OutImp4(POST)*. As a result, the panel was vulnerable to the influence of non-deliberation-based interpretations of the Impact's value: *"To note that really is true and again we are very dependent on what was written" P4OutImp4(POST)*. As an example of the types of evidence that were not immediately trustworthy, one evaluator reflected on how they doubted some *"wild claims"* made in the ICSs that were questionable, but accepted these because of the presence of a letter as part of the supporting documentation:

...there were things like wild claims; like for example, as a result of our programme deaths by fishermen at sea have decreased by 50 percent. And I am thinking I don't think that's true. That doesn't sound plausible to me and then there is a letter that's going, yeah, there were a lot of people that didn't die, and I was like, yeah. P4OutImp5(POST)

As a result, faced with the variety of evidence sources, as well as time restrictions on the evaluation process, the panel decided to adopt an approach to trust the evidence supplied in the case studies: *"we weren't doing this on kind of a court of law, evidential basis. There was a degree of trust"* P2OutImp8(POST). In some cases, panels *"were not allowed, of course, to go and do some background work on this. We were strictly instructed to deal with what was in front of us"*, and considering the limitations of the evaluation process, and the lack of experience of panellists, *"...I think sometimes people made a very good case that was very easy to accept"* P1OutImp7(POST).

Conclusion: Valuing Impact

In this chapter, I have started to paint the group as a powerful mediator of conflicting views around Impact (*what is Impact*). Although I cannot yet say how this negotiation occurred (Chaps. 5 and 6 will go into more detail), I show how negotiating differing evaluator notions around the object (Impact) prior to the evaluation process resolved into strategies that enabled the group to attribute a value around Impact, despite its ambiguity (*how to value Impact*). These strategies do not comply with any one model of Impact in particular, but rather are constructed, developed and applied in practice, by the group.

It is not the place of this book to question the outcomes, but it would be remiss of me not to question the potentially perverse effects of some of the strategies developed. Centricity as a strategy represents, to the best of my knowledge, a new and unique strategy that has not been considered previously. In addition, considering aspects of public engagement beyond the boundaries of the definition mechanic that implicitly dismiss its value as an Impact, point to the group developing in vivo strategies based on democratic deliberation and the group's ability to work around the confines of some mechanics. However, other strategies contained remnants of old, potentially dangerous approaches to valuation. In particular, Linearity as an approach may be the result of a pragmatic evaluative approach, but it can act to unconsciously downplay the value of some non-linear Impacts over others. An example of this might be in the way long-term, nuanced Impacts such as policy changes might be undervalued in preference to Impacts that naturally assume a more direct, linear realisation, such as commercialisation and forming spin-off companies.[4] However, such Impacts would be valued using a Centricity-focused strategy as long as a sufficiently strong submission constructed its role as essential to realising a more quantifiable, end-product Impact.

Adopting this strategy on the group level did have its share of opposition from individual evaluators, and yet despite this, it persisted as a group-wide strategy. This indicates that deliberation, as the foundation of group peer review, did occur and that despite individual-level mutiny, the group-wide strategy was developed, and that dissenting voices conformed. For this reason, I cannot fault peer review as a tool for valuing Impact, but in Chap. 6 I do investigate the extent to which this strategy was adopted as a result of deliberation, or as a method of avoiding further deliberation.

Notes

1. Tronnier, H. (1976). Solarium and Skin Cancer. Hautarzt, 27(1): 42.
2. For a literature review of all available research on the risk of melanoma and sunbed behaviour, please see Boniol, M., P. Autier, P. Boyle and S. Gandini (2012). "Cutaneous melanoma attributable to sunbed use: systematic review and meta-analysis." *BMJ* 345: e4757.
3. The 2016 Stern review, actually recommended that public engagement be included in impact assessments under the REF
4. Future research that involves analysing the characteristics of the case studies relative to the results will need to be performed to determine the extent that this is the case. Already there are a number of teams and research projects conducting research into this area.

References

Blau, P. 1964. *Exchange and power in social life*. New York: Wiley.

Collins, H., and R. Evans. 2007. *Rethinking expertise*. Chicago and London: University of Chicago Press.

Derrick, G.E., and G.N. Samuel. 2016. The evaluation scale: Exploring decisions about societal impact in peer review panels. *Minerva* 54 (1): 75–97.

———. 2017. The future of societal impact assessment using peer review: Pre-evaluation training, consensus building and inter-reviewer reliability. *Palgrave Communications*. https://doi.org/10.1057/palcomms.2017.40

Donovan, C. 2011. State of the art in assessing research impact: Introduction to a special issue. *Research Evaluation* 20 (3): 175–179.

Evans, Robert, and Harry Collins. 2010. Interactional expertise and the imitation game. In *Trading zones and interactional expertise*, ed. M. Gorman, 53–70. Cambridge: MIT Press.

Greenhalgh, T., J. Raftery, S. Hanney, and M. Glover. 2016. Research impact: A narrative review. *BMC Medicine* 14 (1): 78.

Huutoniemi, K. 2010. *Evaluating interdisciplinary research*. Oxford: Oxford University Press.

Lamont, M. 2009. *How professors think: Inside the curious world of academic judgement*. Cambridge, MA: Harvard University Press.

Luukkonen, T. 2012. Conservatism and risk-taking in peer review: Emerging ERC practices. *Research Evaluation* 21: 48–60.

Pier, E.L., J. Raclaw, A. Kaatz, M. Brauer, M. Carnes, M.J. Nathan, and C.E. Ford. 2017. 'Your comments are meaner than your score': Score calibration talk influence intra- and inter-panel variability during scientific grant peer review. *Research Evaluation* 26 (1): 1–14.

Samuel, G.N., and G.E. Derrick. 2015. Societal impact evaluation: Exploring evaluator perceptions of the characterization of impact under the REF2014. *Research Evaluation* 24 (3): 229–241.

Sinclair, C., and P. Foley. 2009. Skin cancer prevention in Australia. *British Journal of Dermatology* 161 (s3): 116–123.

Spaapen, J., and L. Van Drooge. 2011. Introducing 'productive interactions' in social impact assessment. *Research Evaluation* 20 (3): 211–218.

Sunstein, C.R., and R. Hastie. 2015. *Wiser: Getting beyond groupthink to make groups smarter*. Boston, MA: Harvard Business Review Press.

5

Peers, Experts and Impact

I'd see it as keeping the triangulation function, coming at it as different value sets. Equally able to judge but having a different value set. That's not just keeping us honest but having other points of discussion or other points of view.

Evaluation (Sub-panel 1), Pre-evaluation, Academic

Because all these people know each other as well, so they're pals. So you're an outsider socially, to a certain extent in those types of relationships. So how much weight they put on what you actually said when you said it, I don't know that you were given a reasonable hearing.

Evaluator (Sub-panel 5), Post-evaluation, User

So far this book has overlooked one vital mechanic of the evaluation process: the evaluators themselves. Just who is a suitable peer or expert for the assessment of Impact beyond academia?

Imagine you are a member of a large group assigned the task of deciding which is the best of three objects: an apple, a pear and a banana. You and your fellow group members have deliberated over this puzzle for some time, as some people are fans of apples, some of pears and some of

© The Author(s) 2018
G. Derrick, *The Evaluators' Eye*,
https://doi.org/10.1007/978-3-319-63627-6_5

bananas. To facilitate the task, a new member is introduced to the group: an expert in fruit, who brings with them new perspectives. In theory this may be beneficial, but in practice introducing a new member means that there is a period where the existing perspective of the group needs to be resolved with the new perspective introduced by the new member. As Lamont (2009) described, combining competing standards of disciplinary excellence "presents a greater challenge and creates the potential for double jeopardy … because expert and generalist criteria have to be met at the same time". This double jeopardy can distort discussions, polarise group opinions and, if nothing else, prolong the evaluation.

A major criticism of Lamont's (2009) book, from which this study draws much of its inspiration, is that it overlooks the role of expertise (contributory and interactional (Collins and Evans 2007)) in her study of panel operations (Collins 2004). For Collins and Evans (2007), the concept of interactional expertise, itself a form of tacit knowledge (Collins 2010) created in practice, underpinned the legitimacy of peer review to assess interdisciplinary research. The operationalisation of expertise within panels supports the concept of an evaluators' eye and the importance of the group when navigating an ambiguous criterion. However, this type of expertise is not sufficient to justify the use of peer review to assess Impact alone. It is arguable that evaluators can gain political capital if they rely on the existence (or not) of interactional expertise within the group so that they can bypass deliberation altogether.

Democratic deliberation models of evaluation are based on the strength that comes with bringing many differing, potentially dissenting voices together (Greene 2000), in an attempt to reach some common understanding around an evaluation object. Heterogeneous groups with complementary skills have been shown to make better group decisions than homogenous groups (Levi 2015). The decision of the REF2014 evaluation panels for Impact to comprise both academic- and user-evaluators centred on the basis that including dissenting, alternative voices would benefit the evaluation process. Indeed the change from peer review to one that emphasises "experts" extends the "delegated authority" (Jasanoff 1990, 2003) to include a wider range of democratic publics and their different modes of reasoning (Jasanoff 2012) to the deliberative process underpinning peer review. Of all the controversies surrounding the

REF2014, the decision to include non-academics, or user-evaluators, to assess Impact, has received the least backlash. It was assumed, along with similar evaluation models that encourage the inclusion of a variety of stakeholder perspectives (Mark and Shotland 1985; von Schomberg 2013), that the user-evaluators would not only enrich but also legitimise the peer review process surrounding Impact.

As Greene (2000) puts it, "voices that are not present, cannot speak".

For Impact, as with interdisciplinary research, there is no automatic "peer", and perspectives sought from experts within and "beyond academia" are therefore valid and essential. The underlying assertion for including outside, non-academic expertise is curious as it automatically places traditional academic-evaluators as incapable of appreciating wider research influence, by existing in a world parallel to the "real" world where everyone else exists. That is, by placing the evaluation object beyond the technocratic (Collins and Evans 2007) domain of traditional academic peers, their value to the assessment is reduced. Unfortunately, these assertions automatically demote the role of academics as in conflict with their perception of living, and taxpaying members of the public. They are therefore incapable of being both technocratic and democratic voices in the evaluation process. Voices beyond academia, as peers can potentially include everyone, regardless of their expertise, must then operate within a predominantly academic- led exercise, using a tool which is a strongly socialised part of academia. There is therefore no guarantee that voices that are present speak and, additionally, that they are heard (Greene 2000). The benefit of including users within peer review panels lies in their ability to navigate this academic environment, and to resist displays and in-group heuristic choices driven by the illusion of power. Indeed, there is little evidence to suggest that there is any additional value in including these user-evaluators, and much less to suggest that they can influence the evaluation outcomes. Indeed, we know from studies of behavioural economics that including experts does little to minimise the risk of group-level mistakes. Their inclusion therefore has less to do with ensuring that the group reaches the "right decision" and more to do with convincing outsiders that the decision was the right one. Experts are hence political tools towards promoting the legitimacy of the process, but are not necessarily active participants in the process.

In this chapter, I explore the concept of a "peer" for Impact around the central concepts of representation and expertise. I draw on notions of tacit knowledge and interactional expertise (Collins and Evans 2007; Collins 2010) to illustrate the importance of the group in navigating the evaluation of Impact. From this, and an in-depth exploration of how users were able to add value to the peer review process of Impact, I outline the ways in which peer review panels can be constructed for ambiguous criteria using membership as a political tool, as well as including outsiders as active participants in the evaluation. I am sensitive to the understanding that there are two sides to this chapter's story: that of the academics and that of the user-evaluators. The data shown here has been carefully separated to provide a continual comparison of views on opinions and practices around Impact. The premise for the chapter is that a user-evaluator's value to the evaluation process is dependent on their ability, and the group's willingness to allow them to become an effective and equal in-group member (Cooper et al. 2001) and participate fully in a robust deliberation underpinning peer review.

Why Are Panellists Chosen?

For Impact, finding suitable peers is difficult, as complete representation is an almost impossible task, and the level of desirable expertise around Impact is more diffuse and not necessarily commensurate with experience in the same way that it is for more traditional notions of research excellence. Expertise and representation as characteristics differ, as one is more relevant on the individual evaluator level (expertise), while the other (representation) is more of a group-level consideration.

Sufficient representation on the panel does not assume that a 50–50 divide between users and academics is necessary. In this study, academics dominated the sub-panels in number and at times outnumbered users 6:1 (sub-panel 5, Biological sciences). However, the extent to which the voices of user-evaluators were out-manoeuvred is not reflected through numbers alone. Despite the salient dominance of academics heavily influencing the standards executed in practice, there was no guarantee that the user-evaluators would remain passive participants.

The degree of representation of user and academic views also cannot be reduced to a clear "us and them" in-group conflict, since in many cases an evaluator could be both user and academic. In this study, participants self-categorised as either users or academics, and not all users were restricted to the evaluation of the Impact criterion. A minority of users were also involved in the evaluation of Outputs. Identification of user-evaluators and academic-evaluators was not as simple as labelling the Impact assessors as "users" and others as not. To counteract this, I asked evaluators to self-identify as a user or an academic-evaluator. Though many evaluators stressed that they were both, it became obvious through the use of "us and them" terminology which categories the evaluators felt most inclined. The majority of users entered the evaluation process after the evaluation of Outputs (Fig. 3.1), and substituted those on the panel who were restricted to evaluating Outputs only. This interchange of evaluators will become very important to consider as we start to focus on in-group dynamics.

Expertise as a characteristic is again more difficult to guarantee both at the individual and group level. For Lamont (2009), expertise and ensuring a panellist is a responsible professional are essential to trust panels with full sovereignty over the decision-making process and, by extension, the allocation of public funding: a step towards citizen participation in governing science (Jasanoff 2012). In this way peer reviewers act responsibly within their "delegated authority" (Jasanoff 1990) to exercise their "carefully circumscribed power to speak for the public on matters requiring specialised judgement" (Jasanoff 2003, 158). To ensure this, panel experts must be central to "the rule of cognitive contextualisation that requires that panellists use the criteria of evaluation most appropriate to the field or discipline of the proposal under review" (Lamont 2009, 106), although for some, the labelling of expertise is simple and refers to one who "knows the detail and can explain the reasons" (Mow 2010, 140). For Collins and Evans (2002), "expertise" extended beyond the appreciation of contributory knowledge and specialisation to types that value interactional, tacit and beer-mat knowledge. For Impact, insights into what constitutes sufficient expertise can be drawn from the standards expected from panellists within disciplines. One poignant example is from an analysis of how music and art researchers contemplate the level of expertise in peer review panels governing their field: "a non-expert may be moved by the music, but cannot peer review it". This disciplinary separation of expertise is similar to whether a physicist possesses sufficient expertise to evaluate history as a peer. For Impact, a level of disciplinary separation of expertise is more difficult to employ, and including users on the panel and representing specific stakeholder groups is seen as a bridge between specific and generalised expertise. Here, the issue is not centred on achieving a level of representation on the panel, since representing all different possible Impacts would be impossible, but rather on bringing to the panel sufficient expertise to value the object, in line with the rules of the panel, and of the field. This reflects the cognitive contextualisation that is essential for the functioning of peer review groups, and the legitimacy of these outcomes. Lamont (2009) again addressed this practical point and suggested that central expertise was not essential, but that expertise that has "a few degrees of separation" from the object would be sufficient. What this means for how users negotiate and promote an alternative form of expertise, in-group, is discussed below.

Balancing Representation with Expertise

Decisions are made by those who turn up, and the importance of what it means to be an academic "peer" has been overlooked in previous research, as has how the purposeful selection of peers influences the evaluation process and outcomes. Constructing panels for peer review balances issues relating to adequate *representation* and sufficient *expertise*. Here I explore how these issues were taken into account when constructing the REF Impact panels more generally, as well as how they pertain to evaluating the Impact criterion.

Addressing adequate representation meant that the panel needed to be inclusive of certain minority groups represented as peers, a sentiment that some evaluators were aware as being the basis for their nomination. However, representing minority groups in academia extended past gender, to also include non-research-intensive universities, as well as geopolitical considerations. One evaluator declared her membership as being based on this political representation: *"I am also a woman, I am at a new university... I am the sort of new university person"* P4OutImp6(PRE). Representation also included ensuring that voices representing certain interests (academic or political) in lines of research were physically represented. Having these views included, as one evaluator stated, would be *"valuable on the REF panels"*:

> *So we put forward our position which was that we thought someone with expertise in obesity could be valuable on the REF panels ... but we thought that there'd be at least one panel that could benefit from someone with expertise in obesity. P3Out1(PRE)*

Representation was viewed as important and thus *"at least one panel could benefit"* by having at least one peer on the panel who could voice these concerns and possibly frame the decision-making process. Where representation was limited in that panels needed to be a workable size (larger groups are more cumbersome and lead to reduced productivity and decreased efficiency (Levi 2015)), the concept of expertise would compensate for any loss of physical representation. Expertise, from the perspective of panel construction, refers to a combination of skills and experience. Although no panellist had experience with formal, ex-post impact evaluation (Samuel and Derrick 2015), their skills reflected the broader perspectives evaluators could bring to the evaluation relative to their disciplinary socialisation. Disciplinary specialisation was not a necessary component of expertise, and some evaluators considered their "open mind" as an advantage to the panel, indicating a willingness to compromise and negotiate: *"I'm more sort of generalist ... most academics, they lock themselves up in silos"* P0OutImp3(PRE). Expertise was also associated with their previous experience of panel dynamics. Panel chairs were permitted to nominate panellists outside of the formalised nomination process (2010), and in these decisions, past connections as well as a reputation of being "fair" were essential when making choices for the benefit of the panel: *"He [The Chair] presumably nominated me because he knows that I'm a fair person on panels"* P5OutImp2(PRE). Another evaluator described this aspect of expertise with panel dynamics, and the choice to include them, as understanding how "hawks and doves" work within the panel: *"...I am known to be a fair assessor. I am not a hawk, I am not a dove, and that's what I think that I bring to the process" P2OutImp8(PRE).* When considering how to construct panels for assessing the Impact criterion, both concepts of representation and expertise are shifted to consider a wider range of perspectives deemed necessary to navigate the new evaluation object. Here, the definition of a "peer" also broadened. In asking academic-evaluators prior to the evaluation about their value to the Impact assessment process as a peer, they still echoed sentiments of representation of certain disciplinary and political interests on the panel vital for considering Impact, especially health impact: *"I think this idea of gauging the Impact from a clinical perspective, it is important that we have some doctors in the process" P1OutImp3(PRE).* Expertise was more nuanced, as many researchers had experience engaging in Impact activities (public engagement included), but their experience evaluating it was limited ex-post. Indications of their expertise, and their sentiments of worth in assessing Impact, were heavily tied to recollections of their own experience engaging with Impact, and would potentially limit their ability to join deliberations that included Impacts beyond their sphere of experience and conceptualisation: *"I'm hard-core developments. I know how to get a medicine basically into a product into a patient, so people" P3OutImp7(PRE).* Evaluators were also aware of their own skills relative to the skills brought by others, and how this would substitute for gaps in expertise and representation, as well as complement other skills within the panel: *"well certainly my understanding of randomised clinical trials is probably greater than anybody else on the neuroscience panel" P4OutImp4(PRE).*

Including users in the evaluation was perceived as a way of combatting any perceived deficit in representation of the panel for Impact, as well as also broadening the expertise base available. Many academic-evaluators did not perceive themselves to be deficient in the expertise necessary to evaluate Impact, despite the range of strong views about its nature and the value of some Impacts over others. There were even doubts expressed over the purpose of including users on the panel, and the problems their presence might present for the evaluation outcomes. These included a non-professional and haphazard approach to assessment that would be immune to a more academically socialised approach to assessment that would understand *"…the more sophisticated arguments that an academic might put forward to defend themselves in that context"* P6OutImp2(PRE). The source of these almost tribal concerns was notions of identification as an academic, and non-representation of the concerns facing the academic. Additionally, by representing non-academic organisations and interests, academics were concerned that their presence would negatively alter the panel dynamics by introducing untrustworthy, external sources counter to the concerns of the academy: *"we do have people on there who are not necessarily dedicated researchers. They are representing other bodies"* P3OutImp1(PRE). Although the value of user-evaluators' expertise was rarely questioned, as there was widespread support for the "fresh perspectives" anticipated from the user-evaluators, these "fresh perspectives" were not expected to *"cause trouble"* if they were in line with those of the academically led consensus: *"I don't know whether we may come to a big divide between stakeholders and us but even in panels where we have a large lay representation the consensus has usually been quite clear"* P1OutImp2(PRE). As such, there was an assumption that users not only represent user interests and organisations, but that they demonstrate expertise by being able to *"understand the research process well"* and that *"depending on how much experience they've got of strictly academic things as opposed to the rest of the working things, it would be a challenge for some and there would be things that need a lot of explanation"* P3OutImp2(PRE). Through this, it was clear that academics felt that users would be entering into their world, the peer review panel, rather than having a sense that both perspectives were entering the process equally. By entering this world, it was assumed that users would submit to the academically led practices underpinning the panel's behaviour.

From the user point of view, they faced unique challenges based on the expectations their fellow academic evaluators had about their worth to the panel and to the assessment of Impact. As a way of comparing the perspectives, it is important to also consider the users' perspectives. Academics were already confident with being nominated as a peer and anticipated problems with users only if they consciously admitted that there was a deficit in their knowledge or approach. Contrary to academic concerns, users did not see their ability to provide a fresh perspective as evidence of a deficit in understanding of the academic community. As one user put it, *"my brain is academic"* P1Imp1(PRE), and this only strengthened their resolve when it came to negotiating them in practice: *"I am not going to challenge the academics on their view of academic assessment, and it would be interesting to see if the academics challenge my commercial judgement"* P1Imp1(PRE). However, despite users being conscious of the potential value of their perspectives: *("[I am] bringing in more about what value this has to us and for wider society"* P3Imp1(PRE)), they were also conscious of a need to operate according to the academically led rules of peer review. Nonetheless, users saw themselves as equal participants prior to the evaluation process regardless of whether they were viewed as such by the academic-evaluators. The main challenge faced by the users was how to ensure that their perspectives were considered as equal during democratic panel deliberations. Their success in penetrating this group and behaving within the group-generated norms of panel behaviour would determine the extent to which these "fresh perspectives" would penetrate the group's dominant definition and influence the evaluation outcomes.

Why Include Users?

For Impact, everyone is a peer and everyone is an expert.

Theoretically, the person in the street could be considered an Impact peer, and they would certainly be capable of providing the "fresh perspective" that is "beyond academia" expected of the Impact users. Including them, however, would risk losing the sense of professional and delegated responsibility (Jasanoff 1990) essential for trusting evaluation panels with the level of sovereignty given to them to make decisions about public funding distribution (Chubin and Hackett 1990; Lamont 2009). Within peer review, experts are given a bit of a free pass with public funding decisions. In fact it is the last remaining decision about public funding that is made by individuals with no accountability for those decisions, increasing the validity of deferring the responsibility for these decisions from the individual level to a group level. The justification for these decisions when it comes to Impact is stronger if reasonable, non-academic professionals are represented within that group; however, our users were not completely devoid of the academic socialisation necessary to operate within these panels: *"We were not really external people, we were not really completely separate from the university setup"* P3Imp6(POST). Our theoretical person in the street would find it difficult to have their opinions heard and considered valid by the panel.

Achieving a politically desirable level of user representation was limited both by the workable size of the panel and by the variety of Impacts under consideration. Adequate user representation, or at least the appearance of it, may work to legitimise the evaluation outcomes, but it is not always practical. In contrast, there was an effort to include users as a way to *"rebalance the system"* P6OutImp2(POST). The question of who is a user for an assessment of Impact that uses peer review is answered not only by considering their ability to "represent" non-academic interests, but also how they would behave and operate within the group. However, this level of interaction towards a group consensus would need to ensure that users were actively involved in the evaluation process, and not just passively acknowledged. Therefore, their influence on the panel and value to Impact requires a more detailed examination of the in-group interactions and heuristics.

The Political Value of User-Evaluators

Aside from the obvious recommendation that Impact evaluation should include users, the value of including them is linked to the political strength of the process, the Impact as a criterion, peer review as an assessment tool and the legitimacy of the outcomes. Its success, or appearance of success through adequate representation independent of considering how users worked with the panel, was essential: *"I think that if it was just academic lead, I don't think it would have as much credibility"* P4OutImp3(PRE). Members of the Main Panel noted how including users was used to deflect criticism that an assessment of Impact as "beyond academia" would represent views that are non-academic: *"I think there is obviously the question of sort of credibility of the exercise, if you're claiming Impact outside the academic domain, then I guess the credibility of it would be less if all the judgements are made by academics"* POP1OutImp1(POST).

The absence of users would also mean that the validity of the outcomes would not be convincing to the public: *"I think it's the same with the Impact if there were no users, in the public domain would not sound quite so convincing" P0P1OutImp1(POST).*

The political value was also based on the assumption that users are closer to the value of the Impact, and therefore the level and type of expertise of users afforded the panel would be different provided by academics who are also *"clinicians and sort of public health doctors and health practice researchers" P0P2OutImp1.* Another evaluator describes this as users being able to understand the *"realities of translating the basic information into something that is practical and useful" P0OutImp5(POST).* Later in the interview an evaluator linked the proximity of users to the *"realities of research that is practical and useful"* to the legitimacy of the outcomes but doubted that, excluding the appearance of legitimacy, users improved the process: *"I think they just lent legitimacy to what we're doing. I don't think they improved it… I wouldn't say that they improved the process" P0P2OutImp1(POST).* On a group level, there was recognition that by including users, the collective responsibility for the Impact assessment outcomes was shared more convincingly, and that within the group, deficits in understandings and conceptualisation of Impact value of both users and academics were used together, and that for Impact, *"both judgements"* were needed:

> *I think it's extremely important that users and academics are both part of the process because the emphasis of one and the other are different, and you need both judgments. You need a judgment from the user on the societal evidence, which is not the judgment that the academic community comes with. And you need judgment from the academic as to how big this is as a scientific figure.*
> *P0OutImp3(POST)*

This type of teamwork, that defers certain aspects of the evaluation process to different types of experts, may work in theory, but a more robust consideration of who a valuable user is for the assessment of Impact is seen by cross-referencing evaluator interactions that occurred within the panel and between evaluators and considering how this influenced panel group behaviour. Only through considering the group's approach to Impact, and the influence users had on this direction, is the risk of groupthink examined. I mention groupthink here as users represented the provision of an organised external perspective offered to the panel that, when implemented in practice, can be used as a powerful antidote to overly pragmatic, simplistic groupthink-based decision making.

Users Value to Impact Evaluation or Valuation?

During panel deliberations, the perspectives provided by the user-evaluators did not directly influence the group's dominant definition, adopting instead a role that was passively acknowledged by the academic, although they did directly influence the valuation of Impact and there-fore the evaluation outcomes. Once the dominant definition had been developed, the panel concentrated on the process of valuing each Impact claim relative to the 1-4-star Impact rating scale provided as a mechanic (HEFCE 2010).

The influence of users was not related to their role as a political tool in representing the non-academic perspective about Impact, and their influence was not a factor in having a large number of users on the panel sup-porting a particular view. Indeed, users were outnumbered on the panel, but to assume that this would disadvantage user-based perspectives in practice is to overlook the importance of the group. As one user put it, the evaluation is not about the collected opinions of individuals, but instead a negotiated group-level decision that is characteristic of expert-driven evaluations:

> *I think that people are looking from the outside and people who wish to critique the REF might say oh, you know, you haven't got lay members; it's not very democratic, which I think is to misunderstand what's going on here… It's an expert assessment of Impact and it does require people to understand the process that's involved in research leading to Impact. P1Imp2(POST)*

And although users were perhaps not the leaders in driving a consensus towards the evaluation of Impact, as many of the challenges thrown their way prevented them from taking this lead role actively (*"Well, they were* *certainly listened to respectfully, shall I say, and it was definitely useful to have a strong voice saying, look, this is important, but … they made up 20 percent of the assessors … they do only have a weak voice, of course"* P0P2OutImp1(POST))*, as one academic-evaluator put it *"there were certain aspects where the user perspective was helpful, genuinely helpful in terms of reaching conclusions and where the opinions of the users influenced also the opinions of the academics"* P0P1OutImp1(POST).

Their first influence on the panel was to act as a guard against the very worst academic behaviour in peer review. Prior to starting the Impact evaluation, the majority of the panel had recently completed evaluating the Outputs criterion, which had required a different approach than was required of Impact, one that was less critical: *"…they tended to look at these applications a bit more like peer review article submission and would be quite critical … so it's a slightly different sort of frame of mind to set themselves in."* P1OutImp1(POST). Such an approach was not consistent with the approach required of Impact. In this situation the users played an important role in preventing the academic-evaluators from getting *"sunk into the research mode again"* P0OutImp6(PRE), when it came to Impact. Users noted how an evaluation hangover from evaluating Outputs influenced the initial approach adopted by the academic-evaluators. Consequently, users had to adopt the role of the societal conscience for academics, reminding academics that *"although it's important to have a Lancet paper, actually what they all want to do is treat patients"* P1Imp1(POST), defend the relevance of the Impact criterion against academics who were *"disdainful of Impact"* P2Imp3(POST), and limit the level of academic-based criticisms used to value Impacts. One academic-evaluator noted how users influenced his behaviour in evaluating Impact:

> *…they brought a different perspective to the table and were able to override quite often the natural tendency of the academics in the subpanels to be extremely judgmental of each other and rather talk each other down.* P0OutImp2(POST)

Users also encouraged a generous approach to valuing Impact, and their influence can be seen in the evaluation outcomes. In Chap. 3, I showed that the scoring of Impact tended towards the 3- and 4-stars end of the rating scale, compared to the scoring for Outputs which was more discriminant across the star-ratings. This tendency towards a culture of generous marking influenced by the input of the users was noted in the interviews, from both academics and users alike. Additionally, in Chap. 4 we saw how the panel adopted a strategy of generosity around valuing Impact, which as we examine below was the influence of the *"intimate knowledge" P0P2OutImp1(POST)* provided by the user-evaluators. As the group had access to this knowledge, and a different perspective of the Impact through the users, academic-evaluators felt more comfortable in making valuations that were, on average, more generous: *"I mean something like a guideline, something that's straightforward, sometimes they added value that we didn't appreciate as academics" P0OutImp6(POST)*. Academics labelled users as the *"voice of moderation [upwards]"*; *"…we listened to them and they were actually, if you like, the voice of moderation but moderation usually in the direction of upwards, rather than downwards" P1OutImp4(POST)*, as well as convincing the group to adopt a *"glass half full approach"*:

> *…people should be looking for the half full glass, not the half empty glass. And what you see with scientists is that they sometimes are very critical and do not see the positives and focus on the negative small issues and not the big benefits. P0OutImp3(POST)*

As an example of this practice, one user recalls a moment when they questioned the direction in which the group consensus was travelling and actively worked towards changing the evaluation approach and resultant star-level scoring:

> *…why on earth are you picking holes in this? If you stand back from it and look at it from my perspective as a drug industry person, or somebody out there in public health this is having enormous impact and you are hell bent on finding problems with it. P2Imp3(POST)*

Users do more for panel deliberation around Impact than simply through representing particular interests or organisations; they can also influence the group's evaluation strategy. Although their presence as users did not give their views any added value: *"I don't think there was necessarily additional weight given to their comments but I do think that their comments were absolutely taken into account alongside those of the academic panel members"* P5OutImp3(POST). Their ability to provide additional perspectives about the value of Impact, rather than the nature of Impact, allowed panels greater confidence in awarding higher scores for Impact. By providing a real-world perspective, users could re-orientate panel scoring behaviour, and ensure that deliberations around the Impact criterion were not confused by carry-over behaviours that were dominant in associating value with the more traditional Outputs criterion.

The Challenge for Users

To influence the development of the dominant definition and influence the valuation strategies listed in Chap. 4, the users faced challenges that unconsciously excluded them from an academically led evaluation process. If a mechanism against groupthink is that groups utilise all resources available (including the users), then overcoming these challenges to participate in deliberations was of paramount importance. This was a daunting task.

Users already faced high expectations from academics about the value of their contribution as a *"fresh perspective"*. A lot of stress was placed on these users to provide this rich, alternative position, and yet the ability of users to do this was completely dependent on their ability to permeate an already established group that had already developed, as one user indicated, *"a very strong culture"* P1Imp1(POST). Academics were aware of this challenge facing the users *("But I think it's going back to that point about making sure people are really well prepared and making sure they're well integrated P3OutImp5(POST))*, and how important it was that new members of the group were *"integrated"* sufficiently that they shared the *"panel ethos"* P4OutImp2(POST). I explore two of these challenges and how they reflect on the value of different experts as peers in this evaluation construct around Impact. By exploring the challenges faced by users to extend the peer community and the ability to overcome them, I examine the relevance of academic peer review to assess societal impact. To do this, I combine user reports of these difficulties with a consideration of how the evaluation mechanics limited or facilitated their inclusion.

Cultural Differences

Ask any academic about their world and they will tell you of one dictated by conflicting rules, tensions, egos and politics. Academia is competitive, exclusive and, above all, elitist. For users, some of whom were acknowledged for their research backgrounds, entering and operating in this world was intimidating, and in many cases, their lack of experience was obvious to academics (*"I think the other thing that I noticed in the user evaluators is that not having much experience of what the academic environment is really like is a negative"* P4OutImp2(POST)), and their contributions at times resulted in academics questioning their role in dictating the direction of a highly ingrained part of academic governance: *"once a researcher, are you always a researcher?"* P3OutImp8(PRE). Indeed, for some academics, the contribution of users who were divorced from the experience of academic life devalued their contribution because of their inexperience in academic peer review:

> *It was a lot of work for them. I think academics are used to that type of work. I think it is hard work for people who are not used to it.* P2OutImp9(POST)

Users needed to work against the deeply ingrained cultural practices surrounding the operation of academic peer review, as well as the socially constructed group culture that was dominated by academics. Here, the emphasis was on the users adapting to the academically dominant peer review group, and not the group altering its working practices to incorporate them. Users needed a strategy to navigate the panel's existing evaluation approaches and culture.

What did not help this integration process were notions from both academics and users of their differences in professional approach and overt comments on physical and cognitive differences: *"I think that they [the academics] were dressed fairly casually ... at senior NHS management meetings you wouldn't go in a jumper"* P3Imp6(POST). This unconsciously polarised panel culture on differences between academic and user views, rather than constructing a committee culture representative of one cohesive group (the evaluators' eye). Gaining direct evidence of unconscious bias behaviour is difficult, and yet these judgements betrayed this polarisation between evaluator types and also, potentially, their influence in deliberations. As such, users felt polarised and outnumbered on panels and, more importantly, they felt unprepared for the *"strong culture" P1Imp1(POST)* that dictated panel behaviour. Encountering culturally embedded norms of behaviour and professional conduct (*"I was at some meetings, the only person who was wearing a tie" P3Imp6(POST)*) was confronting for users who approached the evaluation with their own belief of professionalisation that wasn't suitable for the environment.

The influence of the cultural boundaries that dictated practice within these panels raised concerns that users were passively acknowledged on the panel, but not necessarily actively engaged in deliberations. As outsiders to the panel, active engagement of users was not automatic but wholly dependent on the strength of the users' voice, and their ability to work within academically dominated peer review panel cultures and submit to these culturally based rules of engagement (Lamont and Huutoniemi 2011): *"Even though there was only one of her, I think she made a really important contribution and she had a good, strong voice. And that's not easy when you've got a bunch of mostly professors [Laughter]" P3OutImp5(POST)*. As passive side-lining of users by panels echoes a risk of developing groupthink, the prospect of balancing the alternative, pre-evaluation lauded prospects of *"fresh perspectives"* around attributing value to Impact was considered too difficult for the group to achieve. On the other hand, considering the lack of experience of the academics around evaluating Impact, and the lack of peer review experience of the users, this may simply be reflective of the group adopting a pragmatic approach to the evaluation. For the time being, I will consider these two possibilities separately.

By examining user experiences of contributing to deliberations, a sense of how these cultural norms favoured academic views in practice was reported in how users were *"browbeaten by their academic counterparts"*. One user-evaluator recalled how he had *"...tried to explain to them about how their culture could be seen from the outside" P1Imp1(POST)*, as an attempt to make academics conscious of the cultural barriers faced by users. This conflict wasn't personal, but for users who were unaccustomed to these rules, at times it could be intimidating, especially how notions of excellence are debated between experts through critique and how disciplinary standards of value are negotiated. As one user reflects:

...the academic environment in which the discussions is held is quite an intimidating one. It's not intended to be a criticism of an academic context. And actually I think it was—it's good because it does enable, you know, allow quite a frank exchange of directly conflicting views without, you know, emotion coming into it. So you know, I sometimes found myself completely at odds with somebody over marking with their scoring or something. But there was never any sort of emotional context to it. It was an academic, if you like, or an intellectual debate. And I think that's quite an important characteristic. There was nobody getting all sort of heads up or getting the hump because they weren't getting their way. It was in the spirit of a you know, I think quite open, quite frank and quite candid and quite rapid fire, pacy discussion of lots of different case studies. And that's an important characteristic of the people who were in there. P3Imp2(POST)

Indeed, academics also reflected how the *"rapid fire, pacy discussion"*, academic-deliberation-dominated nature of the group seemed difficult for users to become accustomed to, and this indirectly affected how users were able to influence deliberations. Nonetheless, the user also acknowledged that there was a level of professionalism ingrained in how ideas were played out in practice. In addition, when conflict of opinion occurred within panels it wasn't personal, but was *"candid"* and *"intellectual"*. Nor was the decision so easily swayed by individuals: *"there was nobody getting all sort of heads up or getting the hump because they weren't getting their way…"*, but instead was based on the interplay of ideas between people within a group of which users were, at least figuratively, a member. Users gained an appreciation of the culture of academically led group interplay that negotiates the value of objects:

I think it was a very—it was an interesting process to go through, because I think we all learnt about cultural norms and how we become—because we work within groups, to have the same cultural norms and if you work in a completely different group it can be quite difficult. And I think it's that—if you're expecting someone to come in who hasn't got the confidence or doesn't know that they are allowed to express a different opinion, they'd have to work within the cultural norm. It can be a bit of a challenge. But I think it's so worthwhile because what you get is a richer group at the end of it all. P1Imp1(POST)

As this user reflects, *"…it's so worthwhile because what you get in a richer group at the end of it all"*, but again, this user clearly acknowledges that their ability to influence deliberations about Impact was dependent on their ability to work within the panel culture already established, thereby acknowledging themselves as an academic outsider.

The type of exclusion discussed here was not explicitly excluding users from panel deliberations. Instead academics unconsciously diminished the value of dissenting user views by adhering to the academically led norms of the peer review environment. As P3Imp2 above reflects, their value is dependent on users knowing *"how to contribute in that kind of environment"*, and that means *"a bit more attention given to how you acclimatize them to the subpanel environment"*. Peer review is a pillar of academic autonomy, and academics are automatically habituated to its norms that dictate practice, behaviour and modes of professionalism within these panels. The extent to which these norms diminish the ability of users to democratically contribute to deliberations also diminishes their relevance as a tool to assess Impact. However, as I explore below, there are ways in which the cultural divide can be minimised in practice and through the strategic application of evaluation mechanics.

Evaluation Mechanics Working Against Users in Practice

You may remember from Chap. 3 how I discussed the different evaluation mechanics that were offered to panels and how these can have unintended and intended effects that ultimately influence the valuation of the object. Here I discuss how one mechanic, the evaluation structure, specifically the order the evaluation of each criterion took place, amplified the cultural divide between users and academics.

The Impact criterion was assessed after the evaluation of the Outputs criterion and in the period between the completion of the Outputs evaluation and the calibration exercise there was an interchange of evaluators. At this time, the academics who were only responsible for the Outputs evaluation (Outputs-only) exited the panel group, while the new users (Impact-only) assessors entered the group. This change of guard at the group level was noted by panellists, and for the academics who had already been *"fairly battered by the hundreds of thousands of papers...."* that they had just completed evaluating under the Outputs criterion, the introduction of new group members who were not tarnished by this prior-group experience was a shock that *"may lead to trouble"*:

> *I think the users felt as if they were—so they didn't play any part in the assessment of Outputs. So by the time the panel members were sort of fairly battered by the hundreds of thousands of papers they had gone through. The users, if you like, were sort of raring to go on the first day. That—so I think—and I think they commented, but actually there was a feeling that this—amongst the panel this may lead to trouble. P1OutImp7(POST)*

The users also felt that joining the group at this stage was difficult, and that if they had been introduced to the panel earlier it would have allowed the group to utilise the expertise brought by the user-evaluators more efficiently:

> *...it would be something useful to think about how you build a sort of a group perspective or a group sense which would reinforce impact expertise of bringing Impact assessors together at the beginning of the process rather than letting them develop a relationship to mature toward the end of the process. P3Imp2(POST)*

The academics also felt that this would be important and *"easily corrected"* P0OutImp6(POST) but, interestingly, there was an assumption that this change in evaluation structure would allow the users to become more used to *"working with academics"* P0OutImp6(POST), and not necessarily for the academics and the group to alter their working methods to better utilise the users as group members. This would also allow users to become accustomed to the cultural norms underpinning the *"alien environment"* of the academically led peer review panel:

> *So I think for impact assessors coming into what is virtually a completely alien environment with all the kind of subtleties about behaviour and dress …. They would have used a different set of abbreviations and they would have had different assumptions about how things were done in a sense. P3OutImp6(POST)*

For users, being able to navigate the subtleties about behaviour and dress that had been developed within the group during the evaluation of the previous Outputs criterion is important to actively participate in the group deliberations for Impact. The reference to the *"set of abbreviations"* showed a use of language that users were not sufficiently socialised to use within the group. This translated to how the group approached their assessment and scoring behaviour, relevant to the language of the mechanics:

> *And I think it's challenging if you've come in and you're not working in academia, to come in and be part of an existing group who were already working together and are kind of confident about discussing and scoring and assessing. … And I think there is probably more work that needed doing on how those people are getting involved and have a voice and their time and knowledge is used effectively I think. P3OutImp5(POST)*

This change in membership was noted by the academics, who described it as disruptive to their working style and approaches to assessment: *"… people who are jumping in and out because it's slightly disruptive"* *P4OutImp1(POST)*. One academic explained how introducing users late was *"holding us back"* by having to re-explain previously discussed concepts, and reach new group-based understanding as to their use in valuing the object:

> *For example they [users] would come in an afternoon on the third day of a four-day meeting, and our chair would be talking over things and some of the users would say "Sorry, we don't understand what's that acronym?" and we'd think,*

"Oh for goodness sake," we knew it, they didn't but yet they were holding us back. We were on three days of meetings and had just felt like they just haven't quite grasped some of the things that we have. How could they, because they haven't been at the [previous] meetings. P4OutImp1(POST)

Indeed, the verbs used by the academics to reflect this change of evaluators between the Outputs and Impact criteria assessment process reflect the extent to which this event was disruptive. In these examples, users were "catapulted in" *("I'm not entirely sure if all of that worked because the impact assessors kind of got catapulted in" P3OutImp9(POST))*, "parachuted in" *("I think the other purely impact assessors found it difficult being sort of parachuted in when everyone else knew everyone else and they didn't" P3OutImp10(POST))*, and even referred to as being "shoehorned in" *("And I think the ones that came in kind of halfway through the process were sort of shoehorned in" P3OutImp5(POST))*. Overall, this disruption influenced the extent to which users were able to both enter the group seamlessly and utilise all group behaviours and subtle signs with the same level of understanding and finesse as the already established members.

Users, who were effectively novices within their own panels, were also sensitive to this disadvantage. This reinforced to all evaluators the perception that users were "outsiders" who had *"infiltrated" P3OutImp9(POST)* the process. This affected the ability of users to *"place things in context"* and *"get a feel for how we [the panel] worked"*, and introduce them to the panel dynamics:

But because they hadn't worked with the panel for so long, so they didn't have the feel for how we worked and they were sort of coming inside and so it was a bit more difficult for them to place things in context. P5OutImp2(POST)

This required the panel to start again and to develop new methods of assessment that incorporated the alternative and *"fresh perspectives"* of the new user panel members. The period required by the panel to re-calibrate took time away from deliberating Impact, tempting the panel to adopt pragmatic simplifications and risking groupthink. If a group adopts a pragmatic evaluation strategy (Chap. 6) in light of restricted time, and a large panel of conflicting views, then the mechanics need to allow for informal in-group re-calibration independent of formal assessment process.

Conclusion: How to Incorporate Outsiders

Influence in a group is not necessarily achieved by having an equal number of allies on each end of a tug-of-war (representation), and nor does it mean that you lead an argument or evaluation process. Group decision making can benefit from diverse membership only if this diversity is evident to everyone on the panel (van Arensbergen et al. 2014), and if all voices are able to speak, be heard and be listened to by other members. In this way, the influence of perceptions of expertise, as well as considerations of the professional and personal conflicts that may occur between people possessing different expertise types, is an important precursor to determining how a panel will work, if it will work well and the generation of results. We know that if group members are aware of who the experts are in reference to a specific task, then members will adjust their group decision to that of the experts (Bonner and Baumann 2012). However, this influence of expertise only works if group members are respectful of the type of expertise brought to the panel, and if they consider it above or even equal to their own.

In this chapter, I have shown how academics saw the role of users (pre- and to a lesser extent post-evaluation) as a political tool necessary to legitimise the outcomes of evaluating an object that existed "beyond academia". The loci of the value naturally decreased the level of expertise academic-evaluators could contribute towards producing legitimate evaluation outcomes, and also distanced them as reasonable peers for its valuation. The inclusion of user-evaluators and the promise of their *"fresh perspectives"* on Impact meant that their value to the process prior to the evaluation was based on their contribution to the legitimacy of the outcomes, and not their contribution to the process of valuation. Users were activity acknowledged, but not expected to be actively engaged in the peer review process. Indeed, the users experienced in-group cultural barriers that worked against their active engagement of the peer review process, some of which were unconscious and expected in a deeply academically ingrained peer review process. Other barriers were unexpected and yet more obviously executed and re-enforced by the evaluation mechanics. If users had a difficult time ensuring that their voice was heard in the group, in many ways the architecture of the evaluation actively worked against this by not allowing users to understand and utilise the already developed in-group interactional expertise (Collins and Evans 2002) used by the panel as an alternative to specialised contributory expertise normally demonstrated in the peer review of more socialised notions of research excellence. Since the value of users to the evaluation process is contingent on the group's willingness and ability to become effective and equal in-group members, these barriers only served to reinforce the previously developed committee culture and to actively resist infiltration by outsiders. Instead, by not allowing the temporal and intellectual space necessary to re-establish the group's identity (Langfeldt 2001), the evaluation structures prevented these outsiders from having a pronounced influence on the valuation process around Impact. However, the users were able to provide enough input to influence the group's consideration of the value of Impact, rather than to extend the debate surrounding its nature as anticipated in the pre-evaluation interviews. Specifically, the users provided a sounding board for academic approaches to valuation, holding a mirror up to the academic-evaluators' own behaviour around scoring. This had the effect of encouraging a more generous approach to valuing the Impact, as compared to the *"grant-mode"* where many evaluators tend to be more discriminant in their scoring behaviour for traditional notions of academic excellence. This tendency is reflected in how the panel scored Impact higher than the Outputs criterion where users were not as represented, nor was their expertise of "beyond academia" relevant. The opportunity lost here is the type of expertise expected from users by the evaluation designers and by the academic-evaluators prior to the evaluation about the "fresh perspectives" on the nature of Impact. To work well, democratic deliberation models must allow for these debates to occur between different stakeholder groups around the object, rather than allowing a pragmatic approach to be adopted that prioritises consensus over and above the dissenting views presented by these outsider stakeholder groups. This is an interesting point to keep in mind as we move to the next chapter on groupthink.

References

Bonner, B.L., and M.R. Baumann. 2012. Leveraging members expertise to improve knowledge transfer and demonstrability in groups. *Journal of Personality and Social Psychology* 102 (2): 337–350.

Chubin, D.E., and E.J. Hackett. 1990. *Peerless science: Peer review and US science policy.* Albany: State University of New York Press.

Collins, H. 2004. Interactional expertise as a third kind of knowledge. *Phenomenology and the Cognitive Sciences* 3: 125–143.

———. 2010. Interdisciplinary peer review and interactional expertise. *Sociologica* 3. https://doi.org/10.2383/33638.

Collins, H., and R. Evans. 2007. *Rethinking expertise.* Chicago and London: University of Chicago Press.

Cooper, J., K.A. Kelly, and K. Weaver. 2001. Attitudes, norms, and social groups. In *Blackwell Handbook of social psychology: Group processes*, ed. M.A. Hogg and R.S. Tindale, 259–282. Oxford: Blackwell.

Greene, J.C. 2000. Challenges in practicing deliberative democratic evaluation. *New Directions for Evaluation* 2000 (85): 13–26.

HEFCE. 2010. REF2014: Panel criteria and working methods. http://www.ref. ac.uk/media/ref/content/pub/panelcriteriaandworkingmethods/01_12.pdf. Accessed 1 Mar 2016.

Jasanoff, S. 1990. *The fifth branch: Science advisors as policymakers.* Cambridge, MA: Harvard University Press.

———. 2003. (No?) Accounting for expertise. *Science and Public Policy* 30 (3): 157–162.

———. 2012. *Science and public reason.* London and New York: Routledge (Taylor & Francis Group).

Lamont, M. 2009. *How professors think: Inside the curious world of academic judgement.* Cambridge, MA: Harvard University Press.

Lamont, M., and K. Huutoniemi. 2011. Comparing customary rules of fairness: Evaluative practices in various types of peer review panels. In *Social knowledge in the making*, ed. C. Camie, N. Gross, and M. Lamont, 209–232. Chicago, IL: University of Chicago.

Langfeldt, L. 2001. The decision-making constraints and processes of grant peer review, and their effects on the review outcome. *Social Studies of Science* 31 (6): 820–841.

Levi, D. 2015. *Group dynamics for teams*. London: Sage Publications.

Mark, M.M., and R.L. Shotland. 1985. Stakeholder-based evaluation and value judgments. *Evaluation Review* 9 (5): 605–626.

Mow, K.E. 2010. *Inside the black box: Research grant funding and peer review in Australian research councils*. Saarbrücken: Lambert Academic Publishing.

Samuel, G.N., and G.E. Derrick. 2015. Societal impact evaluation: Exploring evaluator perceptions of the characterization of impact under the REF2014. *Research Evaluation* 24 (3): 229–241.

van Arensbergen, P., I. van der Weijden, and P. van den Besselaar. 2014. The selection of talent as a group process. A literature review on the social dynamics of decision making in grant panels. *Research Evaluation* 23 (4): 298–311.

von Schomberg, R. 2013. A vision of responsible innovation. In *Responsible innovation*, ed. R. Owen, M. Heintz, and J. Bessant. London: John Wiley.

6

Risking Groupthink in Impact Assessment

You know, I think it was a team effort, in the end actually. And the panel
could be quite proud of what it achieved
P2Imp1(POST)

...it's not until you are faced with the job of having to do this, that these
things come alive
P2OutImp1(POST)

The entire premise for this research was the, perhaps naïve, assumption
that when charged with the formalised duty to assess Impact, and when
decisions had financial implications, peer review groups would resolve all
the issues currently debated concerning its assessment. The ongoing
tensions of how best to measure Impact, and also how to compensate for
the drawbacks associated with Impact evaluation with the application of
expertise and appropriate evidence, would be resolved by these groups of
experts in practice, through peer review. As a result, the panel would
emerge suitably enlightened and armed with new avenues of previously
inconceivable methods and strategies of Impact valuation.

© The Author(s) 2018
G. Derrick, *The Evaluators' Eye*,
https://doi.org/10.1007/978-3-319-63627-6_6

By shifting the focus of evaluation to the valuation of Impact, I have shown how understanding Impact is best done when we understand how academic evaluation groups transpose the concept, reach a consensus and define it among themselves. The importance of this process is independent of whether or not the problems associated with Impact assessment are resolved or not, as they certainly place no barrier to reaching an outcome. As such, call it socially constructed, mutual learning, social practice whatever, the key is that we can't separate characteristics of Impact from the processes imposed on value and recognise it as such.

Evaluating any concept within a group comes with its share of risks, and in this chapter I examine the risk of groupthink and other group drawbacks associated with the approach to evaluating societal impact. By bringing it all together, I investigate the process of valuing Impact purely as a group process. I therefore only consider the themes analysed in the post-evaluation interviews if they were encountered and resolved by groups of evaluators, rather than by comparing individual responses.

Group Behaviours Around Impact

In pursuit of a democratic deliberation that would eventually guide the group's committee culture and the evaluation process, Lamont and Huutoniemi's (2011) "customary rules of fairness" play a large role in qualifying knowledge claims. As a process dependent on a very human interpretation of academic "scholarship", executing these conventions in peer review panels enables certain types of knowledge, and limits the influence of others. In an ideal world, knowledge limited in practice would be that stemming from unwelcome, undemocratic sources and would include those personal, unconscious or intrinsic biases that threaten to infiltrate the evaluation process and jeopardise its reputation as "fair". The uniqueness of these biases, and hence possibly their influence, is that they guide panel deliberations without the need to be formally written down and hence are used to mobilise the dominant definition. Panellists often take them for granted—although they are more explicitly referred to when reflecting on inappropriate behaviour of other panellists, as we will see later in this chapter. In Chap. 5, I showed how the cultural norms exercised within panels could unconsciously downplay contributions from users, relating to how these customary rules of fairness are employed, as well as their influence on panel culture. Although academics are never formally taught these rules, nor can they describe them explicitly, they form an important part of their professional socialisation identified when conflicting concepts of excellence are at play. Further, the applications of these rules are constructed within peer review panels and dictate how individuals deal with and weigh up competing forms of expertise, excellence and value in practice. Lamont and Huutoniemi (2011) worked to document these customary rules believing that, although the evaluation site will differ according to their purpose, object, focus and disciplinary perspective, certain underlying factors transcend these differences to play a vital role in the socialisation of expertise within peer review.

In the case of Impact, and the REF2014, considering the lack of experience panellists had with the evaluation object, and how the panel was broadened in both representation and expertise, the execution of these rules may seem even more important as evaluators wrestle with the criterion and its mechanics. These rules may be more pronounced in light of this inexperience, but also due to the need to reach a solution within strict time limits. We might therefore expect that evaluators become more reliant on these rules to govern correct behaviour as they wrestle with their own tendencies to resort to a *"grant mode"* approach.

Underpinning the execution of these rules was a process of deliberation, whether fully democratic or more structured and involving champions to present a case before the panel. Within this deliberation, ideas are aired by each evaluator and considered equally by others. Of course, in reality considerations of implicit and explicit power, as well as the manifestation of bias (cognitive, etc.) interfere with this rather idealised belief that open deliberation underpins good peer review. As an extension, when I refer to evaluation as a product of the group, rather than solely of individual values and defects, I refer to how deliberation acts as the precursor to the formation of the dominant definition. During deliberation, ideas are open and all evaluators *("good panel members actually"*

P1Imp1(POST)) consider the merits of concepts shared by colleagues independently from the power of the alliances and personality clashes which facilitate their valuation:

> *I thought the subpanel I was on was excellent because people were prepared to challenge each other but it was done in a very mature way. People would discuss the issues; I won't use the word robustly, because that implies, you know, it was uncomfortable. It wasn't at all. It was good challenge, good discussion, consensus quickly reached. P1Imp2(POST)*

In this quote specifically, the evaluator referred to how during the deliberation stage, panellists challenged each other. As a dynamic exercise, this provided the necessary condition for the panel to *"discuss the issues"* whether *"in a very mature way"*, *"robustly"* or not, and allowed the panel to move towards a *"consensus quickly reached"*. There is also a whisper of disciplinary respect for expertise in this quote and in others from user-evaluators *("...I think we were all quite confident to express ourselves and also comfortable to listen to what others were saying" P1Imp1 (POST))*, and also in reflections of the process of deliberation being *"collegial" P3OutImp9(POST)* and that evaluators *"disagreed in a friendly way" P3OutImp7(POST)*. This respect also echoes Lamont's (2009) customary rules of fairness, and for Impact similar customs were at play that, *"despite personality differences"*, allowed a *"well managed"* deliberation necessary for individual evaluators to orientate themselves around Impact as an evaluation object. Deliberation gave the object meaning and moved it beyond the ambiguity which underpinned their *"nervousness"* about the evaluation described in the preceding chapters.

Through challenging opinions, the group started to form alliances to underpin the dominant definition. Challenging opinions during this deliberation allowed for people to shift alliances and to cede their own views in preference to those of fellow panellists who were more convincing: *"And I think people were very good at keeping open and listening to each other and shifting and acknowledging when they had shifted their view" P3OutImp5(POST)*. Despite customary rules of fairness being less investigated for the assessment of non-traditional and more ambiguous notions of research excellence, this does not imply that they don't exist. It does suggest, however, that in light of new challenges, individual evaluators are amenable to abandoning pre-conceived ideas for new ones (especially when the basis of the argument for doing so is more emotive than it is evidence-informed), and also that evaluators defer to expertise, respecting disciplinary sovereignty around the object where expertise is more nuanced. It also suggests that for evaluators, attempting to limit idiosyncrasies in their evaluative behaviour is more difficult if the evaluation is based more on a *"gut feeling" P2OutImp6(POST)* than stemming from experience. Indeed, there are evaluation conditions that are both favourable and unfavourable to their identified customary rules of fairness (Lamont and Huutoniemi 2011). In panels considering a topic which is of interest to non-academic audiences, as well as consisting of generalists employing the rules associated with deferring to expertise and respecting disciplinary sovereignty, as well as methodological pluralism, cognitive contextualism is considered unfavourable. Customary rules become more important if the objective of the evaluation is less about reaching the "right outcome", and more about ensuring that the process of reaching the outcome was perceived as fair or that evaluators were *"…all trying to do a job, responsible job as best we could" P2OutImp5(POST)*. Indeed, achieving *"fairness"* was a desirable goal for many evaluators and was associated with a peer review process that is objective, constructive and mutually amicable between evaluators:

> So, I generally think that the process was fair. I didn't get a sense that there was any—you know, people who were dominating a particular case study, one way or the other. So I think it was all amicable and respectful and constructive. P4OutImp3(POST)

In the pursuit of this fairness, investing time in the execution of these rules, especially around perceptions of expertise, while respecting the disciplinary sovereignty of fellow panellists (i.e. not to ruffle anyone's feathers or to hurt their feelings) is vitally important in considerations of panel culture: *"…and we respected each other's expertise, and people respected my expertise. And that was great when you are working with a group" (P1OutImp6(POST))*. The ability to defer to the expertise of another is perhaps, theoretically speaking, not expected by Lamont (2009), and

Lamont and Huutoniemi (2011), but in cases of Impact, as in assessments with more overlap in disciplinary perspectives of submissions, the tendency to defer to expertise is reduced, and there is more explicit reference to the role of intuition in grounding evaluation decisions. For the REF panels, where there was very little specialist Impact expertise available among panellists, and everyone was essentially a novice; this intuition was described as a *"gut feeling"*. The reliance on one's gut to drive the valuation of Impact proposals is understandable considering Impact's ambiguity, but it does little to resolve the issue relating to more explicit reflections about the nature of the object itself. It also does little to ensure that the evaluation is expert-driven and more than driven by *"…senior grumpy old men which a lot of us were" P2OutImp5(POST)*, unless it specifically refers to a gut, rather than a head/mind as a marker of expertise.

Exhibiting other customary practices around Impact was a variation on the rule of methodological pluralism (Lamont 2009; Lamont and Huutoniemi 2011). In considerations of traditional notions of excellence, this rule relates to approaching a submission on the standard of the applicant, rather than relying on personal preferences and lenses of different locations of production. This is usually related to the ongoing qualitative-quantitative divide, and the differing norms of different disciplines, but in the case of Impact it relates to setting the boundaries of Impact valuation as *"an academic pursuit"* and is not applicable to how Impact is achieved in other settings:

> *But that was few and far between any of the discordance on scores; there was always openness in discussion. And the discussions revolved around the fact that this was an academic pursuit; it was the basis, this was not set out as a drug discovery platform as it would be in industry, for example, but rather an academic institution. The basic question is followed up by the drug being developed, and that may or may not involve a pharmaceutical company taking it out into practice. But that was only one or two areas in which people may have been expecting to see something more for an impact evaluation, as opposed to just sitting down and seeing what the person was trying to tell them.* P0OutImp5(POST)

The consideration that the Impact was the product of *"an academic institution"* and not a pharmaceutical company *("set out as a drug discov-*

ery platform as it would be in industry") means that it was considered through an academic lens, and not based on the norms that exist beyond it. This was a pragmatic decision, and one that acknowledged that the dominant lens of expertise within the panel came from academics. Despite the content of some of the submissions existing beyond the academically grounded expertise of the majority of evaluators, this methodological pluralism is also reflected in an explicit *"trust"* that panellists decided to have in the majority of the content of the submissions as a strategy around Impact valuation. Other rules and their operationalisation were reflected in how panellists were desirous to reach a consensus and how limiting personal idiosyncrasies were accepted towards achieving that goal. In the absence of precedent or experience of evaluation on behalf of the evaluators, I have previously alluded to the dominance of personal opinion or even bias in orientating the evaluation. Although in previous chapters I stressed that the application of these personal lenses (idiosyncrasies) may be unconscious, in line with the customary rule of limiting their influence, evaluators actively applied this rule (*"There are panel members who work very hard to reach consensus and others who don't" POP2OutImp1(POST)*), as their influence (undue or not) was seen as countering the desire to reach a consensus. In these cases, evaluators needed to be willing to cede ground and limit their idiosyncratic tastes, as the panel would eventually run out of time: *"...I guess we probably would have agreed to disagree but also agreed that the process was to come to a conclusion" P2Imp2(POST).*

Here it is important to reflect on a point in Chap. 5 about the role of doves and hawks in panel constructions, and the willingness of some to compromise more than others: *"Well, some people have strong opinions, I suppose. Others try and explore other people's views and they're happy to adjust" POP2OutImp1(POST).* Within the panel, having a hawk can be important not just to lead consensus and convince others to cede their position (gain allies), but also because their presence is a way of ensuring that your peer review panel uses democratic deliberation as a tool for consensus building. Considering how customary rules of fairness work to limit the influence of hawks (limiting idiosyncrasies, methodological pluralism), and to ensure that doves are heard (democratic deliberation and deferring to expertise), alliances and strategic voting were used to facilitate consensus building. In this way, hawks and doves would be resolved in practice:

> *...there would be large differences in the assessors in these gradings. Often people would agree to meeting half way so if you had a four star or a two star, it would end up as a three star unless someone was really adamant about their own score. P1OutImp1(POST)*

These customary rules are employed towards the development of the dominant definition, but they are not reflective of the group's decisions around Impact as they are employed unconsciously and do not benefit the deliberation process. The extent to which they can inhibit the process is discussed below.

Building a Consensus Around Impact

Customary rules, as described by Lamont and Huutoniemi (2011), provide the social conditions necessary for panels to build a consensus around an evaluation object, as well as the foundation necessary for panellists to feel that the process was fair. A sense of ownership was expressed by individual evaluators indicating not only that a consensus was formed, but also a strong identity associated with the evaluation process and its outcomes. I saw this group strength and identity in how evaluators gave their accounts of the Impact evaluation process:

> *...But I mean, that I think, gradually that became understood and everybody understood that that's the way it is and that's the way we have to do it. And I think everybody actually acted correctly, accordingly, in that way. P0P1OutImp1(POST)*

However, in keeping with the purpose of this chapter, I focus not on how unconsciously employed rules influenced the interplay between evaluators, but how panellists consciously aligned themselves with particular viewpoints about Impact. This consensus formed the basis for each of the valuation strategies around Impact discussed in Chap. 4. For Impact, and its ambiguous web of valuation, this unconscious application of customary rules is less assured (and its boundaries, by definition, broader) as evaluators are far less confident with the meaning of the object under investigation and how their experience relates to its valuation. Instead, more conscious acts in order to reach a consensus are required on behalf of individual evaluators. In this chapter I explore the explicit strategies employed by individuals to ensure that a consensus is reached around Impact. In addition, having user-evaluators within the panel means that the power of unconsciously employing customary rules is diminished as evaluators are not necessarily sensitive to their importance in group processes. As I explored in Chap. 5, academics regarded the late addition of users to the panel as *"disruptive"*. Their influence was significantly reduced, and more conscious choices towards building a group consensus are required. As one user described it:

> *I think all I can say is that by the end of the discussions a consensus had been reached. You know, I think everybody starts this sort of thing from a slightly different position which is inevitable and part of the reason you have panels is if people discussed to reach a consensus then that's fine, nothing wrong with that. P1Imp2(POST)*

To reach a consensus, evaluators orientate themselves consciously and are therefore able to explicitly favour more convincing narratives of fellow panellists, as well as refuse the influence of unconvincing and/or opposing narratives. A tug-of-war situation is easily pictured here where narratives that have more influence on the dominant definition are those that garner the most support in group situations, by attracting and therefore recruiting other evaluators as allies. So whereas the act of building a consensus requires conscious decisions individually, the construction of the dominant definition occurs and is applied unconsciously on a group level. The dominant definition is the result of group members developing and agreeing to support a decision that will be in the best interest of the whole (being the entire panel).

Despite the evaluators' relative inexperience with Impact, reaching a consensus was *"much easier than we all thought it might be"* P0OutImp2(POST), and *"surprising"*. *"You know, in the end there was a high consensus which was surprising considering we'd never done it before"*

P1OutImp2(POST). Additionally, all identified references to a consensus being reached elicited the idea that, despite the plethora of differing views about the object, the group came together as one, through one consensus which became the evaluators' eye. This group consensus acknowledged that they *"didn't end up having huge disappointments" P1OutImp4(POST)*, and that the pursuit of a consensus became a *"workable process"*:

> *Despite the fact that we all went in, I think, saying, how are we ever going to get this right, how are we going to judge what is a one, two, three or four with these rather vague written cases. But when it came to it, it wasn't nearly as hard. And therefore, as I said in a previous answer, I think we've all ended up actually thinking that this is a workable process. P1OutImp4(POST)*

On their own, the references above do not indicate the process of consensus building, but when combined with recollections of how these decisions guided the process and how, with time, the evaluation process became easier, the act of building consensus and the dominant definition became two separate but dependent concepts dictating the group evaluation process. As the quote below illustrates, participants discussed this consensus as guiding decisions that were, *"...in the end ... unanimous"*:

> *In the end most decisions were unanimous, when we had fours; I don't remember a single scuffle. I'm sure there were some debates around scores, where scores were put down, P3OutImp9(POST)*

Through recollections of how the process became easier towards the end, we understand that the consensus was clear and the dominant definition was operationalised clearly within the group. Although from a group dynamics point of view, a consensus being reached without *"...a single scuffle"* is worrisome as it risks a process influenced more by groupthink than the democratic airing and valuing of ideas through deliberation. As Bailer (2011) noted, *"too much agreement is in fact a sign that the review process is not working well, that reviewers are not properly selected for diversity, and that some are redundant"* (Bailar 2011). According to (Langfeldt 2001), deliberation is vital to the development of a committee culture that guides the evaluation; therefore, when too many evaluators agree, or a consensus is reached *"easily"* or *"quickly"*, the quality of the deliberation is questioned.

A quality deliberation is, ideally speaking, one where numerous, opposing viewpoints are aired and then negotiated in practice, and the group actively considers the value of each viewpoint, before reaching a consensus regarding which narratives are more convincing to a greater number of panellists (Eckberg 1991). Peer review as a tool depends on this. However, an easily obtained consensus may just reflect a high level of competence of individual panellists, rather than a poor deliberation during assessment (Langfeldt 2001). Therefore, for peer review panel decisions, a certain level of disagreement between panellists is to be expected even for traditional notions of research excellence. I would expect that this level of disagreement would be amplified as evaluators endeavour to deal with new and uncertain criteria (Derrick and Samuel 2014), as well as with a greater diversity of panel membership. With this in mind, I explored how this consensus was reached, rather than solely focus on a binary consideration of whether a consensus was reached or not.

Strategic Voting to Combat Resistance

Evaluators told me that, in line with previous research, the ability to deliberate openly within panels and with other panellists was a vital factor underlying the group's ability to reach a consensus: *"...if there was any discrepancy, we all discussed it ... there were a lot of discussions and a lot of disagreements, but we did agree in the end" P1OutImp2(POST).* Through these deliberations, the group focused on the necessity of reaching a common language around Impact. This was essential considering that the mechanic provided that defined Impact was so broad that reaching a disciplinary-specific understanding of the concept (Main Panel A was one discipline perspective around Impact) would be difficult if the language of the mechanics were adopted alone. What transpired was *"…a good balance, I think, in terms of people's views and the eventual outcome" P4OutImp3(POST)*. However, there were times when discussion, in triads or in group sessions, was not sufficient to form a consensus. In these cases, open, strategic voting (Lamont 2009; Lamont and Huutoniemi 2011) was used to identify those evaluators who were resisting the formation of a consensus. The use of strategic voting shifted the focus from a discussion where competing ideas about the Impact's values were in contention, to one that focused on individual evaluators who were out of line with the group's desire to reach a consensus:

> *And we had sort of fairly lengthy discussions about the case studies, this was quite a time-consuming part of our work. And at the end the leads were asked to propose if they could form a consensus. Where the consequence either of the discussion and/or the leads was disagreement about the scores then it was put to vote. P2OutImp3(POST)*

At this point, conscious individual strategies were employed to ensure that a consensus was reached and in many cases, *"…getting that conception equally accepted across the whole panel probably took some time" P3OutImp2(POST)*. In some panels that were more multidisciplinary in nature and a consensus more difficult to achieve (Cole et al. 1981), it was more common to see these conscious consensus-building strategies employed by individual evaluators. As an example, Panel 3, which was previously discussed as more multidisciplinary in focus, reported a challenge in reaching a consensus through deliberation alone:

> *…it was a very multi-disciplinary panel with people from very different backgrounds in terms of from biomedical science through to people who were much more social scientists. So very unusual concentration I think. And that was some of the challenges sometimes about getting an agreement. And we had to sit and listen to each other. P3OutImp5(POST)*

Forming a Common Identity

Having to *"sit and listen to each other"* was an essential ingredient in reaching a consensus in Panel 3, but, instead of being an unconscious customary rule, it required a conscious effort on the individual's behalf to listen and therefore democratically participate in deliberation. This also meant that individuals were consciously required to negotiate evaluation narratives that were contrary to their own, and ally themselves with another. Evaluators from Panel 3 described that one of the main obstacles in forming a consensus was the lack of, as the evaluator below described, a *"common understanding"* and *"common identity"* related to the disciplinary diversity of the panel. This meant that at times evaluators needed to defend their points of view in an effort to recruit allies within the panel, and risk failing to recruit sufficient allies towards a consensus that supported this narrative as the dominant definition. A winning narrative, indicated through the reaching of a consensus, meant that for some evaluators its price was their own independently held ideals around the value of Impact.

> *I had one where somebody all of us would think it was a three or something like that, you get one person that would think it was a one because it's probably more fundamental. That they may well have been right about them, trying to think of examples and they can't, where there was instances, where there would be one person with the kind of extreme view. In general almost always people said, you know, if you got into a group of eight or ten people would say, you know, yeah well, okay, I would change that. There was once or twice where people have said no, I am prepared to change that. P3OutImp6(POST)*

The inevitability of reaching a group consensus was that some individual evaluators and their viewpoints would need to lose arguments, be out-voted or simply had to give in to other lines of reasoning.

Conscious Consensus-Building Behaviour

From the individual evaluator's perspective, there were two conscious behaviours identified from the interviews that were used within the panels in the pursuit of a group consensus: (1) giving in, or externally sacrificing one's ideals; and (2) internally self-calibrating. When an evaluator "gave in" it was because the individual's ideals around the object were overpowered by the group, either through open deliberation or strategic voting where they *"grudgingly conceded"* (*"And in the end in some cases there were strong feelings in which one person, you know, finally made, you know, somewhat grudgingly conceded to the other"* P4OutImp2(POST)), or through direct intervention (peer pressure) from other panellists who had allied themselves with an opposing narrative or saw an individual's behaviour as counterproductive to the group reaching a consensus:

> *I remember challenging him and saying I don't know that's true. And he said— well, it's got to be, and he was really tricky rather difficult—I thought bloody hell. How do we recruit this guy? And anyway, as we went on, he mellowed. He at one time said, oh, I think I have been too hawkish in these scores. I need to rethink what I'm doing and so on.* P2OutImp5(POST)

When a consensus was closer to being achieved, at times it required *"the whole panel"* of panellists who had aligned themselves in more dominant locations within the tug-of-war to pressure others to join them by telling them directly that they were *"wrong"*: *"Well, I mean, one of these had to be resolved by basically the whole panel, subpanel and telling the assessors that they were wrong. It was quite a straightforward way of doing it"* P5OutImp4(POST). On the other hand, self-calibrating was a way that evaluators would internally sacrifice their ideals, for more dominant narratives, in order to reach a consensus. However, unlike the "giving in" of the previous strategy, this one was done internally, without the need for input from other group members or voting in order to over-rule their perspective. At times, self-calibration echoed the mutual learning process that panels went through together around Impact, which required individuals to *"recalibrate their scores"* as the evaluation progressed:

> *So some people almost began to recalibrate their scores. This is all, I've given it a three but probably in view of what's just been discussed over the previous hour, this is probably really a four. So there was learning going on as we went through it.* P2OutImp5(POST)

Employed consciously, each evaluator would get *"…a feeling for where it sat"* and they re-evaluated their scores and valuation process accordingly. By and large, this was a more peaceful process than giving in, as it did not require any active intervention by the group (through voting) or by other evaluators from competing narratives (recruiting allies). As such, the motivation underpinning the tendency to self-recalibrate was to maintain a consistency in approach across evaluations, as much as reaching and preserving a group-based consensus:

> *But what tended to happen is you read it and very soon got a feeling for where it sat. And then you self-calibrated. So you know, I did my analysis, I did my sort of my review and then I went back through everything and just checked to see you know, do they look the same. P1Imp1(POST)*

My panellists acknowledged how this group consensus, once formed, resulted in the evaluation process becoming easier and more fluid: *"We had a lot of discussion early on and then once we'd reach a consensus about where we were going then we didn't have a lot of those discussions later on"* *P2OutImp6(POST)*. This supports this book's emphasis on investigating how the group reaches a consensus around its dominant definition, which then, in turn, provides the evaluators' eye with which the group values each submission. Once a consensus is formed through debate, and the dominant definition is widely understood and continually applied by group members, there is little need for further deliberation.

However, during the exploration of how these strategies worked, what was missing was a consideration by the evaluators about how the ways in which a consensus was reached were different in the case of Impact. Although reaching a consensus is a vital prerequisite for identifying and applying the dominant definition, it was surprising that despite the newness of the criterion, panels did not reach a consensus around aspects of Impact that were perceived to be of more value compared to others. Instead, panels were focused more on constructing meaning around the evaluation mechanics provided than on constructing an independent meaning of the value of Impact. To examine how this developed in committees and how it would influence the evaluation outcomes, I examine below the formation of the group committee culture around Impact.

Forming a Committee Culture Around Impact

The committee culture is the main important by-product of the group peer review process. The stronger the culture, the lighter the evaluation burden for the individuals. Forming a strong committee culture not only embodies the dominant definition, but also the way in which this dominant definition is applied, fairly and equally across submissions. A strong committee culture is essential when dealing with large panels, a large volume of submissions, a diverse panel membership and ambiguous objects, all of which characterise the tasks faced by the REF panels. It is based on the development of mutual respect between reviewers that reflects how individuals acknowledge and utilise the strengths, weaknesses, biases, preferences and perception of expertise of other evaluators during the evaluation process.

> So that meant that the panel had worked together for some months and I think it's fair to say that a considerable degree of mutual respect, trust had drawn up as a consequence of working together. P4OutImp2(POST)

The committee culture also encompasses how the group applies the dominant definition to develop valuation strategies, and the decisions that they have made (explicitly and implicitly) about how they utilise the tools available to them including expertise (mechanics), and what the outcomes will look like. As a result, the valuation process becomes *"almost formulaic"*, as *"...the issues that came up were very similar issues in each of the subpanels, so it was not as if they were looking at every different case study with a different set of issues, some common issues had an almost formulaic way of being resolved"* P0OutImp6(POST). Remaining sensitive to how the committee develops its relationship between members is also an indicator of the success of the dominant definition in practice. A successful dominant definition is the result of a more socialised and confident group that is, as a result, more efficient in practice.

The Influence of Power

The committee culture of peer review panels is sensitive to perceptions of power (Langfeldt 2004; Lamont and Huutoniemi 2011; Langfeldt and Kyvik 2011), and influences how the panel orientates itself around the level of expertise within the group: "*It was more of a cultural contention than an individual contention*" *P1OutImp5(POST)*. The group sessions are also sensitive to overt display of power during deliberations, which results in "*hawks*" having louder, more dominant voices. At times, the panel may be more sensitive to the influence of these louder voices, irrespective of whether they are hand-in-hand with the more dominant narratives surrounding Impact. It is also sensitive to conscious and unconscious biases, especially if combined with other displays of power in practice. Within the group, the existence of dominant narratives from voices considered by the group as more influential (power) can legitimise viewpoints that encompass these biases and embed them into the committee culture and hence the dominant definition and valuation strategies. Such biases might act against certain applicants (gender bias, halo effect (Marsh et al. 2008; Kadar 2010; Lee et al. 2013)) or may act on certain submissions by side-lining divergent views about Impact that are voiced by less influential "*doves*" during the evaluation. Too much attention to power and not enough to deliberation as a democratic process risks conservatism, as in the case of interdisciplinary research (Laudel 2006; Huutoniemi 2010), or groupthink. If too much power is attributed to one or a small minority of individuals then the benefits of group decision making, the mutual responsibility of outcomes and therefore the advantage of peer review as a tool are lost.

From the previous chapter, we saw an example of a power discrepancy between the academic- and user-evaluators. Here, despite all evaluators being positive about incorporating user-evaluator viewpoints into the evaluation, in practice, users were "*browbeaten by their academic colleagues*", and displays of power manifested themselves in how academics actively brought users back into line: "*So there were more than a few occasions where the user was outside, somewhat out of line from the other assessors who were academics*" *P2OutImp8(POST)*. This also related to how competing views were negotiated with the views of academics "*trumping the lay assessor with scientific expertise, if you like, but in the nicest possible way"*. User views were, in practice, viewed as if they had originated from a less powerful expert base:

> *I got a feeling that occasionally we'd stick out for a study with Impact which was clearly really good. It's such a really important Impact, and this user says that in their experience cystic fibrosis is not very important or something. I'm sorry, this is an important study. I know you've got to give this a four. So there was a little bit of that—saying that slightly trumping the lay assessor with scientific expertise, if you like but in the nicest possible way. P2OutImp5(POST)*

This is not to suggest that user-evaluators were all compliant "doves" sensitive to displays of academic power (in Chap. 5 we discussed how they had been influential in developing valuation strategies). In fact, Panel 3 (multidisciplinary panel) users reported how they developed their own alliances around Impact specifically to challenge the dominant group rhetoric: *"…we had as a group of impact assessors developed a sort of a cohort confidence or a sort of peer group support network, if that makes sense" P3Imp2(POST)*. However, in this and other panels, despite taking the lead on evaluation deliberations in their smaller sub-groups, the users reported being more likely to "give way" to the more dominant narratives from academics, as a way to reach a consensus within the panel: *"We ended up generally—on the whole, they were nice people and we kind of tended to give way actually" P2Imp2(POST)*. Academic-evaluators were aware of the power of their narratives over those originating from the users: *"…sometimes they [users] might have felt like they were a little bit sort of an—almost pushed into a corner" P3OutImp9(POST)*. Despite being a process concerned with competing narratives, academics were advantaged by the fact that *"…there were more of us than them actually" P4OutImp5(POST)*, even though at times academics found that it was *"…very hard to knock them off their perch" P3OutImp2(POST)*.

By and large, the greatest display of power within the panel was yielded by the Chair(s) of the panel (also a member of the Main Panel), who had the responsibility for ensuring that the panel worked efficiently and consistently and that the resultant dominant definition was applied equally across submissions. In this way, even though many evaluators worked together to form a single eye, it was the duty of the Chair to ensure that this eye was applied consistently:

> *Say that I have to censor that, but sometimes in a general discussion they [users] sort of missed the point and the Chair was sort of patient with them and brought them back to why we're here, what we were doing and thinking. P2OutImp5(POST)*

The Chair also worked to side-line divergent views if they stemmed from anything other than acceptable evaluative practice of individuals (customary rules): *"And I think we would have jumped on anybody both the Chair and the group would have jumped on anybody who got a bit stuck up"* *P2OutImp5(POST)*. They unconsciously enforced the panel culture and became the figurehead for in-group cultural power. One member of the overarching Main Panel relayed how the Chair of a sub-panel had actively involved them in a group discussion as a way of aiding the formation of a consensus:

> *...by discussion and the Chairs got involved by adding in other evaluators into the fray, [such as by] bringing in some of the main panel individuals to help us and balance it out. So in the end, it was all a unanimous evaluation after the points were discussed, [that is] what individuals thought, and why one person was ranking it very highly and another person was ranking it very low. P0OutImp5(POST)*

In this example, the Chair served to actively guard the group from the conscious risk of groupthink, and a tendency to adopt conservatism. In this way, at least, the use of the conscious power of the panel Chair was employed appropriately to ensure that the peer review panel worked effectively.

The Risk of Groupthink

Instances of groupthink are difficult to pinpoint in practice, especially using only recollections from individuals about the process. For peer review, mutually constructed responsibility for the outcomes (committee culture) and the pride taken in the evaluation by individual evaluators (Sunstein and Hastie 2015) make it difficult to capture admissions of shortcomings or a consideration of the benefit of alternative evaluation strategies. Too much explicit demonstration of pride has been suggested to reflect "happy talk" is an indicator for groupthink.

Impact is at risk of groupthink due to the nuanced level and types of expertise, the lack of experienced evaluators' hand in valuing the object, and the consequences of an extended peer community. Peer review is a logical choice for valuing this object, as it allows for competing views to be aired and negotiated by a large panel of experts. This results in deliberation being used as a weapon against the development of groupthink, assuming that the deliberative process does not reinforce dangerous proxies, or skewed tendencies towards valuing the object. In this way, more deliberation is not necessarily a negative precursor to the development of groupthink (Solomon 2006), as deliberation influenced by groupthink cannot be described as rational. Instead, the open appreciation of dissent if it occurs is epistemologically valuable to the decision-making process as it can introduce new ideas and potentially recruit its own allies that would otherwise be silent. Groupthink as behaviour does not seek to consider the value of dissenting viewpoints to the deliberative process, but instead seeks to silence or avoid their influence. As such, the examples discussed in this chapter were identified in the data by the way that they limited the choice, or actively avoided the need for further deliberation to resolve in-group conflicts around the object.

An incident of dissent from within the group, all things including influence of power remaining equal, is valuable as it can provoke further deliberation and a consideration of alternative approaches to the object. However, pressure to reach a consensus, usually within restricted timescales, can impede rational deliberation, silence dissenting voices and increase the risk of groupthink (Janis 1982; Aldag and Fuller 1993; Baron 2005; Solomon 2006). Groupthink is difficult to pinpoint methodologically, and is usually identified through the various shortcuts taken by groups during a decision-making process in preference to engaging in robust deliberation to solve problems, by either a non-intervening observer or a post hoc reflection. The very nature of groupthink means that during the evaluation the group is unaware of the cost of these shortcuts, that their adopted strategy is not robustly considered and that they are unaware of how their decisions influence the outcomes.

I have already briefly discussed a number of situations during the evaluation process when the risk of groupthink was theoretically higher—in the way that dissenting perspectives from users were only adopted when they contributed to the group's narrow interpretation of their value to the evaluation (Chap. 5), and how easily panellists would refer to the REF guidance to resolve issues, rather than to resolve it through robust (and potentially time-consuming) deliberation (Chap. 3). In this chapter, I explore specific instances of groupthink as well as other group-based errors in decision making including instances of social loafing, shelving, over-pragmatism and satisficing. I hesitate to make, unless it is specifically referred to by the evaluation group, unsupported conclusions as to whether these group dynamics led to the group making a wrong or bad decision. This book is not about evaluating whether the group made the right decision, as this implies that it made the wrong decision. An evaluation by peer review, by definition, cannot make the wrong decision as the outcomes already hold strong social and political capital. Instead, I question the process with which the group reached the decision and, more holistically, whether there is room for improvement in these decision-making processes around Impact.

Social Loafing and Ambiguous Objects

Social loafing in groups has been described as *"a kind of social disease … it has negative consequences for individuals, social institutions and societies"* (Latane et al. 1979, 831). It was first observed in 1913 by Ringlemann (1913) who noted that when a group of people collectively pulled on a rope, the output was less than when group members pulled individually (Ringlemann 1913; Kravitz and Martin 1986). This was termed "social loafing" (when individuals in a group work less than they would if they worked individually) and deemed to have a detrimental effect on organisations and decision-making processes (including on cognitive tasks (Petty et al. 1977)), when it was shown that individual effort decreases in a curvilinear fashion when people work as a group (Ingham et al. 1974).

It is difficult to separate social loafing from a more general sharing of expertise (mutual construction) within a panel. However social loafing can be distinguished through acknowledgement of deferring decisions to others in the group, as well as placing far more weight on some opinions than others because of a perceived lack of expertise: *"If somebody knew the area really well, then you, of course, put more weight on their opinion ... and by and large, people who were more expert, more weight was put on their opinion" P1OutImp2(POST).* Social loafing is not the same as sharing expertise, but is instead the act of not weighing in on debates outside the evaluator's area of expertise and relying on others to make the judgement for you. In one example, an evaluator described how, at times they relied on others to make a decision on assigning star-ratings (valuation) on their behalf, and vice versa deferring to a perceived deficit of expertise:

> *But it was probably the odd member of the panel who was less familiar with the breadth of methods. And so when I was negotiating with them, they were a bit more unsure and I said, it's all right. "This is a three, don't worry". So and the same with me, you know, somebody would say, "oh, this is definitely three. I know this area". I said okay, I said three or whatever. So there tended to be a bit of that going on where we deferred to the other person. P2OutImp5(POST)*

Whereas an ideal model of peer review would have these two evaluators deliberate over their differences to reach a mutual understanding, social loafing effectively bypasses this stage in favour of using another panellist's already established decision in place of a reasoned conclusion of their own. Effectively, this allows one panellist to loaf from the expertise of the other.

Why is this a problem for groups and, more importantly, why is it a problem for Impact? As discussed in Chap. 5, there is no exact understanding of who is an expert for Impact. Loafing, when the perception of "expertise" is fluid, is actually pointless. Academics felt *"further away"* from the evaluation of Impact than they did for more traditional aspects of research evaluation (*"...it just illustrates how that [Impact] was further away from what I felt really happy to be able to quantify and assess" P5OutImp3(POST)*), and therefore more likely to loaf from a perceived expert within the group. Here, as with many dynamics within groups, power plays a large role, with the "hawks" assuming a higher level of power than the "doves", and their level of confidence gives the illusion of, but not the benefit, expertise. Instead, evaluator confidence as a proxy for power in the way they express their opinions (hawks) becomes an additional dangerous false proxy for expertise. This risks the tendency for individuals to loaf from dominant voices and illusions, arriving at decisions based on false pretenses:

If you get loud people who contribute strongly in their own area they bias the assessment of their own area but then they contribute across the piece; that's quite helpful. And other people who are very, very good in their own area but never say anything about anybody else's area. P1OutImp5(POST)

Since a peer review group cannot develop a dominant definition around a view of Impact that they have not been exposed to and therefore not considered, the link between social loafing and groupthink becomes clear. Indeed, the ability to "hide in the crowd" seems to be a main motivation to loaf, as when individual rewards are associated with effort (Harkins et al. 1980), or when individual effort is being monitored (Williams et al. 1981), individuals are less likely to loaf. In peer review groups, the main benefit associated with a group evaluation process is that the Outputs are attributed to a group level, and so one would imagine that in these situations social loafing behaviour would increase. As the evaluator below described, loafers are to be expected, and so when engaging in the evaluation it is about *"getting the balance of contribution correct"*:

So for me being a good panel member has to be somebody who contributes appropriately and we all know that there are people who don't say enough and there are people who say too much. So it's about getting the balance of contribution correct. P4OutImp5(POST)

Considering the variety of ways that research can generate Impact, and the even greater number of ways in which these pathways can be valued, the tendency to loaf in Impact evaluation would be more pronounced. In addition, since Impact for our panellists would be a first, and therefore either more arduous or interesting, the tendency to loaf is amplified as panellists as individuals have less knowledge or fewer skills in general: "*if it was a topic area that was not in your field, I mean I would have—speaking for myself, I would gladly have deferred. It probably happened more often than that*" *P2OutImp7(POST)*. It is therefore even more important that all perspectives of individuals are considered when developing a dominant definition, and so all individuals need to exert as much effort, influence and confidence in their opinions as if they were working alone.

This was not the case for all panellists. Users, for example, were specifically introduced to the panel to bring an alternative perspective to the evaluation process, and the tendency to loaf is decreased if they feel the contribution that they make is unique and no other group member can contribute the same skills (Harkins and Petty 1982). We would therefore not expect users to decrease their productivity towards the task, and more so, because they were introduced to the panel later, and were less likely to be fatigued from the evaluation of Outputs. Indeed, when speaking with academic-evaluators, there was a tendency to loaf from the perceived "expertise" provided to the evaluation of Impact by the users:

> *I think there's that element, and I suspect that the discussions about Impact were made easier by having users involved because they dispelled myths and educated the panel members about what is and is not important from a user's perspective.* *P1OutImp5(POST)*

However, as seen in Chap. 5, the influence of Users was normalised, and so the loafing described here is disproportionate to the level of power given to them over the evaluation. It also appears vastly unfair, with users suckered into (Kerr 1983) providing ideas in deliberations but without the power to influence the group's final dominant definition. From a group perspective, and even more from a perspective that considers situations where the risk of groupthink is enhanced, this is problematic. It is too easy for the panel to adopt a groupthink approach, in the light of the perceived expertise, and therefore burden users with a disproportionate load of Impact to assess, as opposed to engaging in a more idealised democratic discussion. In fact, the tendency for the majority of evaluators to loaf is increased in situations where members over-participate (Simms and Nichols 2014). Further, it echoes the sucker effect (Kerr 1983), if this strategy develops into one shared by the group, especially in peer review situations where the outcomes are attributed to the group, and not on the individual level. One evaluator described this sucker effect as an idealised model of Impact evaluation, where academics provided the legitimacy of the process and yet the users shouldered the burden during the evaluation process as a social compensatory approach:

> *So I think that a slight flaw in the process is that the genuine users need to feel that they have sufficient understanding and awareness of possible Impact so that they don't defer to those who are from within academia at all. P3OutImp8(POST)*

When we turn our attention away from the motivations of the individual panellists to one that considers the structure of the evaluation around Impact, the question remains whether social loafing occurs due to a deficit in coordination or motivation. An important characteristic of the REF2014 Impact evaluation panels, apart from their large size, which is also associated with an increased likelihood to loaf (Sorkin et al. 2001), was the interchange of panellists after the evaluation of the Outputs (Outputs-only out and Impact-only in) and before the Impact evaluation process. This is important as group cohesiveness is associated with an increased risk of social loafing (Williams and Sommer 1997; Karau and Hart 1998), and as we explored in Chap. 5, many panellists noted how this interruption influenced the group's culture and sense of cohesiveness. However, social loafing can also be beneficial to the group, effectively reducing stress placed on the individual for the completion of the task. For the REF2014 Impact assessment panels, evaluator fatigue was indeed an issue when, especially after the evaluation of the Outputs criteria, the academic-evaluators had already endured a long assessment process. This level of evaluation fatigue upon beginning the valuation of the Impact criterion contributed to a larger burden on user-evaluators to "lead" discussions pertaining to Impact, effectively permitting academics to loaf.

One exception was when the temptation to loaf risked conflict with the group's dominant definition or strategies around assessing Impact. A prominent example is when the group's need for "expertise" as a loafing object ran counter to their decision to be generous, and value and trust the information contained in the submission about the Impact. It was acknowledged that many evaluators possessed "insider knowledge" regarding the submission that would lead to a *"more critical" P1OutImp7(POST)* approach. When the desire to loaf would have resulted in an approach that contradicted the group's dominant definition, and evaluation strategy, the dominant definition would reign. In the example below, the group decided against loafing from the expertise provided by the evaluator with "insider knowledge", and instead based their assessment on the evidence supplied in the submission (constructions):

> *They tended to be more judgmental and harsher about this and saying, well, actually, I know full well that the story you have here, although true, leaves out a lot and it isn't actually as strong a case as it looks as if it is here. And I think fairly early on in the process, although we were prone to listen to things like that and in fact we did several times, our chairman was fairly clear that we should not take that into account and we ended up being, if you like, subservient or well behaved. And we said, okay, we can't take this into account. We're going to judge what we've got in front of us. Okay, we hear what you say, but we shouldn't actually take your specialist knowledge into account because we're told not to, so we don't. So that's the way we did it. P1OutImp4(POST)*

Loafing as an individual behaviour within a group deserves more attention, especially within peer review groups addressing unknown or unique criteria where the object of loafing is difficult to extract from illusions of perceived expertise by group members. Whereas prior research has shown that peer review groups are more likely to favour conservative outcomes when faced with ambiguous criteria, I hesitate to assume that these are natural responses to the criteria, over and above the influence of behaviours such as social loafing. Certainly, the concept of social loafing fits this book's eye analogy perfectly where individuals reduce their hold on a particular conceptualisation of Impact, in favour of joining forces with more dominant views represented by the evaluators' eye. For Impact, however, which is an object of importance for the future of research, loafing is disappointing, and questions the authority of peer review as a choice of evaluation tool.

Pragmatic Evaluation

Pragmatic evaluation refers to a tendency by evaluators and panels to take shortcuts during the evaluation process due to time constraints. Time is, in general, a very under-researched motivator of evaluation panels and is also the reason why funding bodies try to regulate the evaluation through the use of various mechanics. Maintaining a level of control of an evaluation for a funding and/or government body is a way of ensuring that the evaluation progresses efficiently, and this indirectly refers to how the evaluation results are perceived as fair and legitimate to the academic community. Additionally, the longer an evaluation takes, the more expensive the process becomes, reducing the political value of outcomes and of assessment frameworks in general. It is in the best interests of the funders that the evaluation is completed in a timely fashion, lest the trade-off between the cost of the evaluation and the amount of funding distributed become untenable. On an individual evaluator level, time and cost are again intertwined variables. For an expert, the time spent in a closed room (think black box) arguing with other experts is time better spent doing research or being away from other professional and personal activities. There are therefore both personal and professional motivations for individual evaluators to ensure that the process is completed "efficiently". However, as with groupthink, when time constraints become the principle motivator behind the evaluation in exchange for a more robust approach, the legitimacy of the process is jeopardised, as too is the relevance of the results. And again, the effects on the evaluation of Impact, especially when the evaluators have little or no experience to fall back on and push the evaluation process towards a speedy completion, are expected to be amplified.

The influence of time was a frequently mentioned factor when panellists referred to the obstacles facing the evaluation, or when trying to explain away shortcomings that were present in the evaluation process. In these examples, they mentioned how they had to keep moving in order to process a large number of submissions (*"I think we had about 200 Impact case studies to look at, so we had to keep moving" P2OutImp9(POST)*), and how the time constraints resulted in shortcuts being taken with the impact case studies. These shortcuts, as one evaluator reflects, could have been avoided if the panel was permitted more time:

> *...individual impact case studies could have been a bit roughly treated just because of the speed at which decisions had to be made. There would have been no better way to do it than we did it, unless more time were devoted to it.* P3OutImp2(POST)

As a consequence of these shortcuts, a more democratic approach to peer review that favours a mutual construction of an evaluation strategy based on deliberation is not possible. Instead, adopting a pragmatic approach leads to evaluations *"signing off wherever agreed"*, rather than being able to engage in a more robust deliberation, taking into account rises and falls in the strength of an argument and leading to a group approach to the assessment: *"And most of our time was just spent trying to get together to discuss difference in points of view or, you know, just signing off wherever agreed"* P5OutImp4(POST). In the case of the REF2014 panels, the pragmatic approach was a necessary reaction to the structure of the evaluation where a shifting panel membership at the end of the Outputs evaluation, and prior to the Impact criterion evaluation, also disrupted the already established committee culture. This required the newly formulated panel to re-establish a committee culture through mutual consideration of views, leaving less time for deliberation.

Time, and its limitations, also influenced the group's choice of strategy when it came to the assessment of Impact. As such, any strategy that would require a significant time investment in order to implement in practice was not supported at the group level. For example, one evaluator explained how *"...we became pretty pragmatic in the end, just to get through the business"* P2OutImp8(POST), and how this influenced the choice of evaluation strategy, and/or factors in the dominant definition. The choice to trust the information contained within the submissions about the Impact was, at least in part, a pragmatic one as engaging in a more robust strategy of checking outside information or the information received from evaluators who had insider information (above) would have been more time consuming: *"…to some extent the limiting factor was our own time and energy. I don't think there was any difficulty if you wanted to go into reading up the background literature cited [but] most people didn't have the time to do that"* P4OutImp4(POST). Another choice, which was at least in part a pragmatic one, was the group's adoption of a linear perspective of Impact. Although the panellists were aware of the drawbacks to this approach, especially when it came to valuing Impact in practice these concerns were side-lined in order to *"get on with the job at hand"*: *"And you know, even if you felt there were, as I did about the model of Impact, the linear model of Impact, one then suspends that critique in order to get on with the job at hand"* P2Imp1(POST). Finally, the generous approach to scoring Impact broadly adopted by the panels was also partially a pragmatic choice. It reflected not only the limited time of the panels, but also the lack of socialisation professionally panellists had towards the Impact criterion. The tendency to *"force the scores upward slightly"* was a reaction against an approach which would have required the group to engage in longer, more detailed deliberations about a variable they did not feel comfortable. The choice to favour the higher end of the scale was an acceptable *"compromise"*:

…it was okay to compromise, but I do think perhaps the speed with which the process, these compromises had to be made in what was effectively a one or two-day workshop of speed-dating. I think that did rather force the scores upward slightly. Just people tired of trying to hold the position downwards and they could compromise somewhat. So probably more time needs to be devoted to the speed dating and—just call it dating. P3OutImp2(POST)

However, as with the above choices, the evaluator reflected that such a compromise would not have necessarily been chosen if the panel was permitted more time to "date" both the criterion of Impact and competing convictions within the panel about its characteristics as an evaluation object. As pragmatic choices, these strategies reflect groupthink as they favoured an approach that minimised the group's need to consider potentially conflicting views beyond the frame of the already mutually developed dominant definition.

Satisficing to Evaluation Mechanics

Described as a sub-optimal decision-making strategy (Barge and Gehlbach 2012), satisficing is making a choice or judgement that is "good enough" and not the "best" (Simon 1957, 1972; Schwartz et al. 2002; Byron 2005), which usually optimises benefits from the decision (Simon 1972), given cognitive and situational constraints. Barge and Gehlback (2012) identified a number of ways that satisficing can manifest in how individuals can respond in surveys, and others have focused on the approach of medical professionals when evaluating patient records (Kadar 2010). In both these examples, individuals satisfice by choosing the same response every time, rushing through the instrument or quitting early, all of which can be seen at the group, peer review level. The option to satisfice is usually chosen to conserve cognitive effort (Simon 1957; Simon and Stedry 1968) and, as with social loafing, is usually pronounced in groups simply because outcomes are attributable to the group and not the individual. Lamont (2009) saw satisficing as an organisational logic and part of a pragmatic approach adopted by panels and, when adopted, it can risk the integrity of the decisions made, as it is not an optimal model which combines the best of all expert views. For Impact, a certain level of satisficing is to be expected, where the decisions made might not be optimal, but are good enough in that they are made in light of obvious limitations of knowledge and experience (on the individual's behalf) and the restrictions of the evaluation structure, as well as in line with the rules that govern the evaluation process (evaluation mechanics). For this reason, although satisficing in groups for traditional forms of academic excellence is part of adopting a pragmatic, more linear approach to evaluation, for Impact it deserves separation from the pragmatism described above.

The tendency to satisfice is usually circumvented by saturation, or in other words, when panellists stop searching for new information or perspectives on the object, but this too can be jeopardised through bias, as individuals are motivated to find new information only to satisfy their needs (Wilson 2005). The decision to stop searching, and to make a decision based on a perception that the information obtained is sufficient, is in itself subjective. The group must choose between the benefits of obtaining more information and the cost of continuing to search (Schmid 2004). In other words, a group must decide whether their dominant definition is sufficiently enhanced by the potential of further information. For Impact and the REF2014 Impact evaluation panels, this is a difficult decision to make as there is no standard by which the concept of "best" can be judged, and Impact is continually evolving and socially determined: *"I worry about it I think because it's such a baggy concept, however hard we might try you are genuinely comparing apples with grapes" P2Imp2(POST)*. For groups, the decision to stop searching for information is also a collective construction stemming from a sufficiently large majority exerting influence on the minority's need for further information (Abercrombie et al. 1994, 360) and, for the REF2014 panels, one that was restricted by the evaluation mechanics on offer. Satisficing is in this way related to the risk of groupthink as it focuses on producing "good enough" results, and was, in the case of the REF2014 Impact evaluation panels, more contingent on the mechanics and a tendency to stick to the rules, rather than leading the evaluation through discussion and deliberation.

Satisficing was seen when, against the best intentions of the panel to explore the value of the Impact through deliberation, the evaluation process was halted in favour of adopting good enough results reflected in the HEFCE evaluation guidelines ("the rules"): *"So we stuck to the script, I have to say" P2OutImp7(POST)*. Here, evaluators described how when deliberation *"drifted away"* during the evaluation, the evaluation mechanics were used as a strong tool to judge the submission over and above continuing the peer-based deliberation:

> *It was entirely through discussion and often it was matters of just reverting back to what the rules of engagement were because people often drifted away from what was actually said in the document about how well they should be assessed. Some of them could be relatively easily addressed by just saying "well actually the rules are very clear on this". You can't argue both ways, you can only argue one way on this. P0OutImp2(POST)*

Even though the mechanics were *"useful tools"* which provided *"a better understanding of exactly what the REF guidance says about things like clinical trials, or about influence on governmental and regulatory policies"* P3Imp2(POST), I was concerned with the way that they shadowed the evaluation process in favour of deliberation. To continue the discussion started by P0OutImp2(POST) above, the evaluator who was a member of the Main Panel that oversaw the evaluation process on each of the sub-panels recalled how the mechanics were used to prevent panels from *"heading towards not only the wrong conclusion but partly the wrong conclusion we had to default to had they obeyed the rules and done what they'd been asked to do"* P0OutImp2(POST). Maybe the use of the words "wrong conclusions" was a slip of the tongue by this evaluator; however, this same trend was translated onto other panels overseen by the Main Panel, where evaluators changed their decision based on the influence of the mechanics:

> *There was very little area where we had major problems in disparity, and if we did we looked at the definitions again and had conversations about it, at times you changed your score because you would say ok I got that wrong that did happen, and at other times you compromised in between. That's how you—that's how we worked it in the end. P3OutImp7(POST)*

Despite the influence of the mechanics, evaluators were aware that their decisions were not "optimal" or best and that obeying the mechanics was a behaviour adopted in favour of the more time-consuming deliberation-based approach: *"We felt comfortable to rely generally on the REF Impact guidance"* P3Imp2(POST). This did not, however, stop the evaluators from reflecting on how satisficing to the mechanics required them to *"grit their teeth"*: *"But according to the rules, I mean, actually send it back to HEFCE and according to the rules we were instructed that that was appropriate. And we did not agree but you know we had to accept that"* P1OutImp2(POST). At times, this led the evaluator to reflect on the role these mechanics played in dictating the evaluation process and minimising their contribution by permitting some members of the group to satisfice (*"I think some panel members got slightly irritated that there was this political steer from above" P3OutImp2(POST)*) rather than participate in a democratic expert-based deliberation on Impact.

Shelving Evaluation Limitations

Shelving is the group decision to address shortcomings of evaluating an object, by effectively avoiding them. This was a new behaviour identified in this study. As frequently mentioned, Impact is a particularly ambiguous evaluation object with shortcomings associated with causality, attribution and time-lag. An underlying ambition of this book was that by examining Impact assessment in practice, new strategies for overcoming these inevitable shortcomings would be highlighted. Instead, the panels adopted a number of strategies surrounding the object (Chap. 4) as well as a number of group-based behaviours during the process that echoed an overly pragmatic approach to evaluation, and facilitated the completion of the evaluation, by avoiding deliberation as a problem-solving tool and as a basis for developing in-group heuristics around Impact.

Whereas some group behaviours have little or no influence on the legitimacy of the process as they are acknowledged drawbacks and seen to have a negligible influence on the evaluation outcomes, others are more dangerous. Shelving as a new group behaviour is one dangerous example of this latter group, because in comparison to a pragmatic approach which still focuses on the evaluation object, shelving diverts the attention from the nature of the object, focusing it elsewhere. This indirectly allowed panellists to adopt overly simplistic, pragmatic approaches towards Impact, especially when it came to scoring: *"…if we didn't know how to deal with it, you put a three on it. If you thought it was fantastic, you put a four on it"* P3OutImp2(POST).

For Impact, using proxies for its evaluation has been a focus of much of the criticism regarding its formal evaluation, and so seeing these proxies adopted through evaluative practice, and more so as the result of a group-based peer review system, is worrying. Further, this is problematic for the Impact criterion as avoiding the complexity of the evaluation object as a group limits the ability of individuals to apply their experience in future evaluation processes. As the first formalised ex-post evaluation of Impact, there was a big opportunity for these panels to address these drawbacks and to directly form navigation and valuation strategies based on their experiences. Shelving difficulties during the evaluation does the

Impact agenda no favours, and actually further questions the legitimacy of using Peer review to evaluate Impact by risking groupthink.

Shelving was a common strategy adopted by panellists when it came to addressing shortcomings in the nature of Impact and their evaluation practice towards it: *"So I think you're raising some issues that were not always totally 100 percent resolved" P0OutImp3(POST)*. In particular, the issue of attribution where it was unclear whether the evaluation outcome should reflect the Impact, but also the submission's contribution to that Impact, was effectively shelved: *"So I think these are really troubling things about impact and contribution, which perhaps everybody just had to shelve , which was a shame" P3OutImp2(POST)*. To be fair, the evaluation mechanics also provided a vehicle by which this behaviour was permitted by directing panels to focus on the final *"effect or benefit"* as the Impact, rather than the value of the pathway (Derrick and Samuel 2014; Samuel and Derrick 2015). As one of the evaluators describes below, in the case of Impact of smoking cessation legislation, the difficulty with the evaluation at first was to identify and reward the main contributors. There is a sense that the panel initially adopted an approach to valuing Impact as an effect or benefit, contingent on the Impact definition mechanic, and awarded star-ratings based on the submission's value in contributing to this final product. However, valuing the contribution directed the focus of the evaluation away from the object (Impact) and based it on a subjective judgement of whether *"the contribution was significant enough"*. This refocusing the evaluation away from the object onto a different aspect and then being *"told very clearly"* to *"park that and assess [it]"* is evidence of shelving by the group:

> *...a significant number of medical schools put in case studies that said we were instrumental in the success of the smoking cessation legislation. And of course, everybody played a part probably. But you know, who were the main drivers and who really drove that forward? And you know, the Impact of smoking cessation is obviously 4 stars, probably 10 stars. So then it becomes a threshold issue of is there enough underpinning research from this institution to qualify this impact? And that was very difficult; sometimes, some people were tempted to sort of downgrade it slightly if you didn't think the contribution was significant enough. But that's a bit like the assessment of Outputs because I know that last time there was a bit of iteration of the scoring based on what you thought*

the contribution was. But this time we were told very clearly that if you think somebody's made a significant contribution to a paper, you then park that and assess the paper and give it a score. And in a way that's what we did with Impact. So once the—once you accept the contribution was appropriate then you scored the Impact. And there's no doubt that the contribution to the Impact varied. I don't know how you pull that all apart. P1OutImp5(POST)

Although shelving issues to avoid further deliberation around an object is a pragmatic approach that is familiar to all peer review scholars, when it comes to Impact it has worrying implications. Even the evaluators acknowledged the overly simplistic approach taken when it came to attributing value to Impact: *"I think most of us feel that although it's a pragmatic way of doing it, it kind of works, it isn't really an accurate reflection of what we've been striving to measure" P1OutImp4(POST).* There is little benefit in using experience from the REF2014 Impact evaluation panels to inform future peer review valuation surrounding impact if, as part of that process, evaluators are permitted to completely duck the issues. However, on the flip side, it is important to be aware of these pitfalls when assessing the legitimacy of using peer review as the tool to assess Impact. Although peer review may be the gold standard for traditional modes of research outputs, this is not to say that it must remain a gold standard for all types of criteria.

Conclusion: The Benefit of Groups Evaluating Impact

There are obvious benefits associated with evaluating ambiguous objects through groups, politically as well as individually. However, with the benefit of group expert decision making comes the risk of group behaviours jeopardising the decision-making process as well as risking the legitimacy of the outcomes. In this chapter, I have shown the behaviours that bring groups together, but also the behaviours that question how the outcomes were generated. These include the group's tendency to avoid deliberation as the primary problem-solving tool, thereby overlooking the importance of debating the nature of Impact, as well as valuing it.

This chapter has shown how the panel used group-level heuristics to negotiate around the Impact criterion, develop the dominant definition and employ strategies for its valuation. It has also identified four in-group behaviours that were employed for the evaluation of Impact and that mimic groupthink, by avoiding deliberation as a consensus-building and problem-solving tool. You may ask why this is a problem since similar studies of peer review have identified pragmatic approaches to evaluation as acceptable limitations of employing peer review (Lamont 2009). The problem lies not in the peer review process itself but in its assumed legitimacy as a gold standard tool for evaluating ambiguous objects such as Impact. Many previous studies have argued that it is impossible to design an evaluation system that adequately reflects the variety of ways in which research can have Impact. By highlighting the drawbacks of its evaluation, where the evaluation is not governed by a robust, expert-driven appreciation of Impact, but rather by a series of approaches that are deemed *"good enough"*, we add fuel to the debate over whether Impact can be and therefore should be evaluated at all. The extent to which the community acknowledges and accepts these in-group heuristics as negligible in the face of potentially adopting a metric-driven approach as an alternative will determine the suitability of peer review as the evaluation tool of choice.

References

Abercrombie, N., S. Hill, and B. Turner. 1994. *The Penguin dictionary of sociology*. 3rd ed. New York: Penguin Group.

Aldag, R.J., and S.R. Fuller. 1993. Beyond fiasco: A reappraisal of the groupthink phenomenon and a new model of group decision processes. *Psychological Bulletin* 113 (3): 533.

Bailar, J. 2011. Reliability, fairness, objectivity and other inappropriate goals in peer review. *Behavioral and Brain Sciences* 14 (01): 137–138.

Barge, S., and H. Gehlbach. 2012. Using the theory of satisficing to evaluate the quality of survey data. *Research in Higher Education* 53 (2): 182–200.

Baron, R.S. 2005. So right it's wrong: Groupthink and the ubiquitous nature of polarised group decision making. *Advances in Experimental Social Psychology* 37: 219–253.

Byron, M. 2005. Simon's revenge: Or, incommensurability and satisficing. *Analysis* 65 (4): 311–315.

Cole, S., J.R. Cole, and G.A. Simon. 1981. Chance and consensus in peer review. *Science* 214 (4523): 881–886.

Derrick, G.E., and G.N. Samuel. 2014. The impact evaluation scale: Group panel processes and outcomes in societal impact evaluation. *Social Science and Medicine*, in press.

Eckberg, D.L. 1991. When nonreliability of reviews indicates solid science. *Behavioural and Brain Sciences* 14 (1): 145–146.

Harkins, S., B. Latane, and K. Williams. 1980. Social loafing: Allocating effort or taking it easy? *Journal of Experimental Social Psychology* 16: 457–465.

Harkins, S., and R.E. Petty. 1982. Effects of task difficulty and task uniqueness on social loafing. *Journal of Personality and Social Psychology* 43: 1214–1229.

Huutoniemi, K. 2010. *Evaluating interdisciplinary research*. Oxford: Oxford University Press.

Ingham, A., G. Levinger, J. Graves, and v. Peckham. 1974. The Ringelmann effect: Studies of group size and group performance. *Journal of Experimental Social Psychology* 10: 371–384.

Janis, I.L. 1982. *Groupthink: Psychological studies of policy decisions and fiascoes*. Boston, MA: Houghton Mifflin Company.

Kadar, N. 2010. Systemic bias in peer review: Suggested causes, potential remedies. *Journal of Laparoendoscopic & Advanced Surgical Techniques* 20 (2): 123–128.

Karau, S.J., and J.W. Hart. 1998. Group cohesiveness and social loafing: Effects of social interaction manipulation on individual motivation within groups. *Group Dynamics: Theory, Research, and Practice* 2 (3): 185–191.

Kerr, N.L. 1983. Motivation losses in small groups: A social dilenma analysis. *Journal of Personality and Social Psychology* 45 (4): 819–828.

Kravitz, D.A., and B. Martin. 1986. Ringelmann rediscovered: The original article. *Journal of Personality and Social Psychology* 50 (5): 936–941.

Lamont, M. 2009. *How professors think: Inside the curious world of academic judgement*. Cambridge, MA: Harvard University Press.

Lamont, M., and K. Huutoniemi. 2011. Comparing customary rules of fairness: Evaluative practices in various types of peer review panels. In *Social knowledge in the making*, ed. Charles Camic, Neil Gross, and Michèle Lamont, 209–232. Chicago: University of Chicago Press.

Langfeldt, L. 2001. The decision-making constraints and processes of grant peer review, and their effects on the review outcome. *Social Studies of Science* 31 (6): 820–841.

————. 2004. Expert panels evaluating research: Decision-making and sources of bias. *Research Evaluation* 13 (1): 51–62.

Langfeldt, L., and S. Kyvik. 2011. Researchers as evaluators: Tasks, tensions and politics. *Higher Education* 62: 199–212.

Latane, B., K. Williams, and S. Harkins. 1979. Many hands make light the work: The causes and consequences of social loafing. *Journal of Personality and Social Psychology* 37 (6): 822–832.

Laudel, G. 2006. Conclave in the Tower of Babel: How peers review interdisciplinary research proposals. *Research Evaluation* 15 (1): 57–68.

Lee, C.J., C.R. Sugimoto, G. Zhang, and B. Cronin. 2013. Bias in peer review. *Journal of the American Society for Information Science and Technology* 64 (1): 2–17.

Marsh, H.W., U.W. Jayasinghe, and N.W. Bond. 2008. Improving the peer-review process for grant applications: Reliability, validity, bias and generalizability. *American Psychologist* 63 (3): 160–168.

Petty, R.E., S.G. Harkins, K. Williams, and B. Latane. 1977. The effects of group size on cognitive effort and evaluation. *Personality and Social Psychology Bulletin* 3: 579–582.

Ringlemann, M. 1913. Recherches sur les moteurs animes: Travail de l'homme. *Annales de l'Institut National Agronomique* 12 (1): 1–40.

Samuel, G.N., and G.E. Derrick. 2015. Societal impact evaluation: Exploring evaluator perceptions of the characterization of impact under the REF2014. *Research Evaluation* 24 (3): 229–241.

Schmid, A.A. 2004. *Conflict and cooperation: Institutional and behavioural economics*. Malden, MA: Blackwell.

Schwartz, B., A. Ward, J. Monterosso, S. Lyubomirsky, K. White, and D.R. Lehman. 2002. Maximizing versus satisficing: Happiness is a matter of choice. *Journal of Personality and Social Psychology* 83 (5): 1178.

Simms, A., and T. Nichols. 2014. Social loafing: A review of the literature. *Journal of Management Policy and Practice* 15 (1): 58.

Simon, H.A. 1957. *Models of man*. New York: Wiley.

————. 1972. Theories of bounded rationality. *Decision and Organization* 1 (1): 161–176.

Simon, H.A., and A.C. Stedry. 1968. Psychology and economics. In *Handbook of social psychology*, ed. G. Lindzey and E. Aronson. Reading, MA: Addision-Wesley.

Solomon, M. 2006. Groupthink versus the wisdom of crowds: The social epistemology of deliberation and dissent. *The Southern Journal of Philosophy* 44 (S1): 28–42.

Sorkin, R.D., S. Luan, and J. Itzkowitz. 2001. *Rational models of social conformity and social loafing. Subjective probability, utility and decision making conference.* Amsterdam: Netherlands.

Sunstein, C.R., and R. Hastie. 2015. *Wiser: Getting beyond groupthink to make groups smarter.* Boston, MA: Harvard Business Review Press.

Williams, K., S. Harkins, and B. Latane. 1981. Identifiability as a deterrent to social loafing: Two cheering experiments. *Journal of Experimental Social Psychology* 40: 303–311.

Williams, K.D., and K.L. Sommer. 1997. Social ostracism by coworkers: Does rejection lead to loafing or compensation? *Personality and Social Psychology Bulletin* 23 (7): 693–706.

Wilson, T.D. 2005. Evolution in information behavior modelling: Wilson's model. In *Theories of Information behavior*, ed. K.E. Fisher, S. Erdelez, and L. McKechnie. Medford, NJ: Information Today.

7

Working Smarter with Multiple Impacts and One Eye

> And so there was the view that look, we mustn't do harm, first rule of medicine.
> *P2OutImp5(POST)*

The worldwide Impact agenda continues to and will continue to grow. All countries with a sufficiently robust university and research system are increasingly looking to cash in on their innovation investment by incentivising and formally rewarding success in research that occurs beyond academic realms. This redefinition of the science-society relationship to one that formally ties the interests of one to the future of the other is seductive to policymakers and funding organisations alike. It is also a relationship that is not going away any time soon, regardless of any academic dissent. In the UK, the future of the Impact criterion as part of the REF2014 has also been assured through numerous post-REF2014 evaluations of the process. The Stern report, released during 2016, recommended that the Impact criterion continue and be evaluated using peer review, but with very few recommendations on how to improve the evaluation process itself. Likewise, initial decisions for the structure of the

© The Author(s) 2018
G. Derrick, *The Evaluators' Eye,*
https://doi.org/10.1007/978-3-319-63627-6_7

next Research Excellence Framework, REF2021, have confirmed that the value of Impact will increase from 20% to 25% of the overall evaluation.[1]

Other countries are also actively seeking to implement Impact-like criteria and similarly ambiguous objects albeit under the various guises of valorization (The Netherlands); Broader Impacts (the US); Engagement (Australia) and societal benefits (the EU). However, there is little consideration of the process of valuation of any future ambiguous criteria that include research excellence beyond academia, apart from the tedious and repetitive debates about the potential role for metrics. In these debates, metrics are considered only if peer review is seen to be lacking or too sensitive to bias or other externally pervasive influences. In this way, this book makes a reluctant contribution.

This book provides an alternative perspective to the Impact agenda, one that sees the evaluation of Impact as a dynamic process sensitive to a mixture of harvesting, capitalising and leveraging multiple notions of expertise, available evaluation resources and mechanics for the construction of a dominant definition around this ambiguous object. In peer review panels especially, individual panellists' standards must be calibrated and tensions among other panellists and their differing conceptualisations of Impact value are carefully managed in balancing acts of ongoing tugs-of-war requiring negotiation and compromise to reach a consensus. Although this kind of dynamic is not new for considerations of how peer review panels or groups reach a common identity with which to facilitate their tasks, for notions of Impact and similar ambiguous objects, appreciating this interplay is vital to interpret the evaluation outcomes, and also to understand how peer review as a tool can be better utilised in future evaluations. By extension, this book offers recommendations for evaluating other ambiguous objects, be that under Impact's various guises (valorization, broader impacts, societal value, etc.) or other non-traditional criteria (Interdisciplinarity, etc.).

For Impact, too many pieces of research concentrate on analysis of the thousands of Impact case studies as evidence of the nature of Impact. This is a short-sighted and all too easy way to understand Impact's nature. It also neglects to consider the choices and strategies adopted by the panel as an active participant in its valuation. In other words, by neglecting to identify and consider the evaluators' eye, the appreciation of Impact and the myriad of ways that it can be realised is only part of the story. This book also shows that interpreting the evaluation outcomes cannot and should not be divorced from understanding how these decisions or an attribution of value was made. What emerges is a totally different focus on how to understand Impact—one that considers the dynamism of the democratic deliberation model of evaluation underpinning peer review, with new group-led strategies that navigate its inherent shortcomings as an evaluation object. This is all done along with a political guarantee that the outcomes will be perceived as robust, fair and legitimate, simply because they were delivered through the gold-plated black box of peer review. In addition, viewing the challenges facing Impact evaluation on the group level, rather than at the individual evaluator or individual case study level changes (for the better) the types of recommendations that are available for future peer review panels and assessment processes.

There are some obvious drawbacks associated with this study. These include that appreciating panel dynamics would be and will always be better understood using an ethnographic approach, rather than the in vitro approach used here. Although we can assume, from an analysis of the outcomes, that the panel adopted certain strategies for valuation, we cannot say with certainty why this was the case and why a strategy was adopted by the entire group, rather than just being favoured by a handful of individual panellists. An ethnographic approach would, at least in part, provide more definitive insights to these questions. The concentration of the study on one panel concerned with Health, Medical and Biomedical research is another obvious drawback. Drawing on debates from wider, more diverse panels would perhaps uncover other, previously unconsidered strategies from Impact valuation. In addition, whereas in my panels deliberations over the nature of Impact were scarce in favour of strategies for its valuation, other panels may have debated its nature more robustly, simply because an appreciation of Impact is more tacit for health research than it is for fields such as the humanities and social sciences.

None of these drawbacks, however, dilute this book's central premise that understanding the nature of Impact and evaluating Impact are two separate questions. Drawing conclusions about the nature of Impact based on its evaluation outcomes is a false proxy and can only ever produce recommendations that are applicable to one specific evaluation process, ex post. In addition, as this book debated, these recommendations risk being based on the nature of the mechanics, whether Type I or III, rather than the true nature of Impact. Such recommendations made in the past do not acknowledge the social interplay necessary where evaluator personalities and the clashing of social and political ideas about Impact enrich the evaluation process and develop the evaluators' eye. If nothing else, this book provides evidence that cautions this overly simplistic, outcome-centred analysis of Impact.

Is Peer Review the Tool for Impact?

Yes it can be, but only if panels work smarter.

In the opening chapter of this book, I stressed that peer review was a game that could be played, and won; however, the extent to which this game can be won for Impact was less certain as the evaluators themselves were uncertain of how to approach this elusive object. Debates continue regarding the nature of Impact, its pathways, its predictors, how to "fast track" it and how to monitor it. These debates overshadow a more important focus on its evaluation as a tool for determining its value. Lamont (2009) called it a social view of peer review, one where the nature and value of the object were inescapably intertwined with the panel's culture and interaction between panellists, where the tendency to do "good enough" betrayed neither the integrity of the individual nor of the outcome. There was political and intellectual safety in assuring that the outcome was based on the conflicting opinions of experts, and this underpinned peer review as the tool of choice for evaluating traditional notions of excellence.

As a concept, the value of Impact and how Impact plays out is located beyond the domains of the academy and also beyond the domains of regular peer reviewers' expertise. To appreciate its value for assessing Impact, an ambiguous object, we must dig deeper into the theoretical and conceptual foundations of peer review as an evaluation tool. On the surface, there is strength in adopting an evaluation stance that encourages deliberation as a problem-solving mechanism between different and often dissenting expert voices around the object. As a result peer review appears to be a widely appropriate tool for assessing Impact, however unconsciously this choice is made. However, as with all group dynamics, there are drawbacks that are accepted as normal practice in many evaluations, but for Impact they have potentially perverse effects.

Throughout this book I have shown that, similar to all group peer review processes, the interplay of evaluators, their personalities and the clashing social and political ideas about Impact act to stimulate deliberation and enrich the evaluation. There are obvious advantages to a group approach to assessing Impact that is akin to many hands make light work. This is especially the case if those hands come with conflicting and potentially dissenting views about the object based on a wide range of preferences and experiences. In this study, there was disagreement around the group's choice of Impact valuation strategies, but this personal dissent was relinquished in favour of a group approach. However, the extent to which this choice was driven by proxies of power and expertise within the group, or else motivated by groupthink, remains an important consideration when regarding whether peer review is an appropriate tool to evaluate Impact.

How to combine all these hands, or voices, into the evaluators' eye in the spirit of democratic deliberation models is a strength underpinning the application of peer review. However, ensuring that all these voices and hands are listened to equally, as well as considered equal in their dissent as well as their cooperation, remains a challenge. Voices cannot be heard unless they are present, and so ensuring that the panel is sufficiently representative is one major consideration, but, conversely, silenced voices present cannot be heard and this is a major challenge for peer review panels, and even more for ambiguous objects such as Impact. Therefore, how to get panel groups to work smarter is unequivocally tied to the notion of how to get as many of these voices aired, contributing to the deliberation and considered in a balanced, democratic approach. This may be over-idealised, but ensuring smart Impact evaluation through voicing, sharing and solving differing notions of value in peer review panels is crucial to guaranteeing its legitimate role in future assessment strategies, as well as a desirable end-goal for all research. This also means that the socialised norms of what constitutes Impact excellence will be shared with the wider academic community both by publicising results and by re-absorbing panellists into academia and communicating these norms among their peers. Working smarter therefore leads us to ensuring the future of the Impact agenda.

Is Over-Pragmatism Dangerous for Impact?

Most academics take the peer review process, and the legitimacy of its outcomes, for granted. It is assumed to be led by and wholly dependent on expert judgement. This judgement is valid because it is seen as stemming from those experts who are also our peers and therefore best placed to robustly comment on the merit of our research plans and achievements. Hence, there is academic community-wide faith in the peer review process that automatically minimises the influence of how the types of social interplay discussed in this book drive the evaluation process.

If peer review fails as a tool, an alternative is needed. At the moment an alternative is offered by metrics and this is, however inappropriate and underdeveloped at the moment, seemingly void of unwanted, and non-expert based social and political factors. Metrics also offer a significantly cheaper and potentially more efficient tool than peer review, which is grounded in strategies that are deemed good enough rather than ideal. However, automatically assuming that metrics provide the only available alternative because the REF2014 peer review assessment of Impact was sensitive to pragmatism is dangerous. Metrics cannot and will never provide the kind of robust, deliberative evaluation that is necessary for ambiguous objects such as Impact and so metrics will never substitute for peer review. A number of reports already attest to this fact (see Wilsdon 2016). Pragmatism as a group approach in normal situations is not damaging but when adopting it serves as a gateway to groupthink by actively avoiding deliberation as the primary consensus- building and problem-solving tool, it risks the future of the criterion as a valuable aspect of research excellence.

Varying levels of pragmatism is found in all peer review panels. For Impact, especially early in the evolution of the Impact agenda, ensuring that the panel behaviour does not resort to overly pragmatic or groupthink-driven choices is vitally important to ensure that the consideration of the criterion is legitimised and widely recognised as important by the academic community. The key to Impact, as well as other similarly ambiguous objects, is for panels as a group to effectively utilise all resources made available to them, and to employ sufficient intellectual and temporal space to utilise deliberation as a tool for resolving differences and reaching a consensus.

Over-pragmatism, in this book, acts to dampen deliberation as a consensus-building and problem-solving tool within panels by permitting (in the case of mechanics, providing) seemingly viable "outs" that can push the evaluation towards completion, within allotted time frames. At the moment, Impact needs deliberation about its nature relative to assessments of value simply because of the myriad of ways in which research can have an influence on society. This book shows that debates regarding its nature and value are two distinct avenues of consideration; one that is left for debates outside the evaluation room, and the other deeply embedded in panel dynamics and pragmatic strategies developed to navigate its evaluation. Over-pragmatism makes it too easy for panels to sidestep this difficult debate, in favour of assigning similar values to all Impacts, such as was seen in the panel electing to adopt a strategy that favoured a generous approach. This approach is evident in the evaluation outcomes and does not reflect a more discriminative approach that is necessary for evaluations of excellence. This conservative approach is common for ambiguous criteria, but here the conservative approach was to "do no harm" rather than to employ a greater level of scrutiny based on a community-wide consensus about what natures of Impact are important and valuable.

Getting impact evaluation right does not imply coming up with a "right" outcome, or an outcome that is different from the ones generated by the REF2014 panels. Analysing how panels should evaluate Impact better is not the focus of the book, although one can be forgiven for drawing such a conclusion. Concluding that there is a preferred method of valuation assumes that a better decision could be made independent of the expert advice available during panel deliberations. It would also imply that the REF2014 peer review panels came up with the wrong outcomes, and no one outside the panels is in a position to conclude this unless they possess some type of normative stance that is unhelpful in debates surrounding Impact evaluation. The outcomes of all peer review processes are automatically the right decisions, since they were based on the combined judgement of peers, regardless of the drawbacks associated with group heuristics. However, getting the Impact evaluation process right using peer review is about ensuring that the panel works smarter. My focus is therefore to ensure that the smart behaviour desired of panels also guarantees a legitimate and robust exercise based on sufficient expert-level deliberation in groups, rather than on changing the outcomes.

I don't want this to read as a manifesto, or a call to arms. It is not. Research impact is important to value and be formally acknowledged if not only to reward those who achieve Impact success but who fail to be rewarded by systems that neglect Impact in favour of more traditional research excellence—the "recognition deficit" as I refer to it. Ensuring that Impact is firmly embedded in the research and evaluation cultures also implies that evaluation is appropriate and shares a common belief about what is excellent and what is important to reward. Manifestos protesting that the application of metrics as a tool in research evaluation all echo calls that evaluations must be appropriate and faithful to the aims of the evaluation, and to the future of research (Cagan 2013; Hicks 2015). The peer review of Impact should be no different. Adopting overly pragmatic approaches to its evaluation threatens Impact, and the recommendations offered below are constructed around measures that discourage groups from adopting potentially damaging in-group evaluation heuristics.

The Next Step

Towards working smarter, Impact assessment by peer review faces three main challenges. The first challenge is around how peer review groups navigate ambiguous evaluation objects and avoid conservatism due to overly pragmatic and groupthink-driven approaches. The second challenge to working smarter implies that all voices are heard within the panel. These "voices" do not directly relate to different types of evaluators, although including user-evaluators as central and equal partners in the evaluation process is vital, but more broadly to the different opinions open for consideration by the group. Finally, in the face of an unknown, unconditioned criterion and a range of new actors as evaluators, and against a tendency towards conservatism, peer review groups must avoid the temptation of groupthink, by adopting overly pragmatic approaches (i.e. cutting corners) that comes from avoiding deliberation to solve problems around Impact.

All recommendations stem from the importance of utilising tools and approaches that provide greater intellectual and temporal space for deliberation as a consensus-building and problem-solving tool. This also implies minimising the potentially perverse influence evaluation mechanics play on re-enforcing any in-group biases against different ideas or voices. Specifically, the evaluation mechanics should not work against new, conflicting or dissenting voices being aired freely within panels, or minimise the influence of such voices by culturally based illusions of power or hierarchy.

Working Smarter

On the basis of the results offered by this book, the following are recommendations to encourage peer review groups to work smarter around Impact. The recommendations are also applicable to other, similarly ambiguous criteria that are beyond the academically habituated notion of research excellence. These recommendations are applicable not only to the Impact criterion in future REF exercises, but also to other countries and organisations looking to implement a consideration of Impact, or other similarly ambiguous criteria, in assessments employing peer review.

First, the evaluation should aim to provide the panel with enough temporal and intellectual space for the development of a strong committee culture around the criterion. This implies that the structure of the evaluation and, in particular, the order in which the criteria is evaluated are vital. Ideally, I recommend that ambiguous criteria be evaluated before traditional criteria to give the panel an opportunity to build their culture around the trials and tribulations regarding this new, untested object.

This means that for REF-like exercises, Impact should be evaluated first. Assessing Impact first also minimises the potentially pervasive influence of experiences of evaluating previously completed criteria feeding into the strategies adopted by the panel for Impact, in other words the influence of *"grant mode[s]"* of evaluation. User-evaluators found existing panel culture reminiscent of the experiences underpinning the evaluation of the Outputs criterion previously. For users, this was difficult to penetrate due to implications in the way they were able to participate equally and the value of deliberation as a problem-solving tool for panels. Assessing Impact first would have allowed a committee culture to be built around the object's ambiguity, automatically including users within that culture. This would not completely bypass the effect of in-group appreciations of academic power and hierarchy, but it would serve to minimise their influence. As the voices of user-evaluators are central to democratic deliberation evaluation models, as well as to the legitimacy of peer review as an assessment tool, it is essential that there is no disadvantage attributed to introducing these user-evaluators later.

This leads to the next recommendation, which relates to how evaluation mechanics can be used to facilitate an evaluation of Impact and similarly ambiguous objects. This goes beyond the above recommendation of altering the evaluation structure to focus on the influence individual mechanics have on framing the evaluation process, whether intended or not. Akin to ensuring that panels work smarter, smarter evaluation mechanics must also be designed and made available to the panel. Smarter mechanics are those which are focused on facilitating the evaluation regardless of whether their effects are intended or not (ideally Type I and Type III). In this way, smart mechanics do not act to inhibit deliberation or allow panels an escape route to avoid deliberation and instead adopt overly pragmatic or groupthink- driven valuation strategies. Instead, by facilitating the evaluation, mechanics should act to ensure that the evaluation is based on expert deliberation and not the mechanics, lest artefacts be identified in evaluation outcomes. Designing smart mechanics implies a role for panellists, as much as it does the mechanic designers and providers. As an example, the 2016 Stern report recommended that the REF2014 Impact definition be broadened to explicitly include how research impacts public understanding, cultural impacts and impacts on curricula/pedagogy (Stern 2016). In addition recent decisions made in preparation for REF2021 point towards an even broader definition for Impact. This is a reasonable recommendation that echoes how this study identified how panels worked around the mechanics to extend the definition to include notions of public engagement as an Impact. However, broadening the definition of mechanic also implies a larger role for deliberation, as more Impact types are to be considered. This necessitates a large deliberation of the nature of Impact relative to its value, something the current study identified as lacking. Therefore, a broader definition of mechanic must also be accompanied by the necessary space for deliberation and consideration of dissent within the panel. In addition, the role of the sub-criterion (Significance and Reach) as mechanics should also be minimised in light of this broader definition to allow panellists to make the types of value judgements necessary for a large variety of Impacts. Another recommendation may be to restrict the panel size, but given the large number of submissions, this is not practical.

Hand in hand with the above recommendation is the third and final recommendation: to evaluate Impact types together, rather than under a single disciplinary grouping (the REF2014 used "Units of Assessment"). If a debate about the nature of Impact relative to its value is not possible, then such an association can be avoided by evaluating groups of similar Impacts (groups of Impact types), rather than a range of Impacts through one disciplinary lens. This avoids a potentially never-ending deliberation around the value of one type of Impact over another within panels. For example, evaluation of Impacts by type, and not by discipline, implies that all Impact-generating commercial outcomes should be assessed together and separate from Impacts that occur on policy. Separating Impact assessment by type would make it easier for panels to operationalise sub-criteria such as the Significance and Reach. It would also allow for more directly relevant stakeholders to be represented within the peer review panels, increase their power during panel deliberations, and ensure that the level of expertise of the panels was more central and relevant to the criterion's assessment process.

Implementing these three recommendations is not mutually inclusive, although they are linked, and organisations may wish to implement other changes that are based on this book's overarching theme of ensuring that peer review panels work smarter. Peer review remains the ultimate, however idealised, tool for assessing research excellence, and will remain so in the future. Working smarter with the evaluation tool rather than changing it ensures that the evaluators' eye is clear, bright and focused on the horizon as well as the combination of many conflicting colours.

Notes

1. UK Government. (2017). REF2021: Research Excellence Framework. Initial Decisions on the Research Excellence Framework 2021. REF2021/01. 01 September 2017.

References

Cagan, R. 2013. The San Francisco declaration on research assessment. *Disease Models and Mechanisms* 6: 869–870.

Hicks, D., P.F. Wouters, L. Waltman, S. De Rijcke, and I. Rafols. 2015. The Leiden Manifesto for research metrics. *Nature* 520 (7548): 429.

Lamont, M. 2009. *How professors think: Inside the curious world of academic judgement.* Cambridge, MA: Harvard University Press.

Stern, N. 2016. *Building on success and learning from experience: An independent review of the Research Excellence Framework.* Department for Business, Energy & Industrial Strategy.

Wilsdon, J. 2016. *The metric tide: Independent review of the role of metrics in research assessment and management.* London: SAGE.

References

Abercrombie, N., S. Hill, and B. Turner. 1994. *The Penguin dictionary of sociology*. 3rd ed. New York: Penguin Group.

Abramo, G., C.A. D'Angelo, and F. Rosati. 2015. Selection committees for academic recruitment: Does gender matter? *Research Evaluation* 24 (4): 392–404.

Aksnes, D.W., and R.E. Taxt. 2004. Peer reviews and bibliometric indicators: A comparative study at a Norwegian University. *Research Evaluation* 13 (1): 33–41.

Aldag, R.J., and S.R. Fuller. 1993. Beyond fiasco: A reappraisal of the groupthink phenomenon and a new model of group decision processes. *Psychological Bulletin* 113 (3): 533.

Andersen, L.B., and T. Pallesen. 2008. "Not just for the money?" How financial incentives affect the number of publications at Danish research institutions. *International Public Management Journal* 11 (1): 28–47.

Arribas-Ayllon, M., and V. Walkerdine. 2008. Foucauldian discourse analysis. In *The Sage Handbook of qualitative research in psychology*, ed. Carla Willig and Wendy Stainton-Rogers, 91–108. London: Sage.

Aubé, C., V. Rousseau, and S. Tremblay. 2011. Team size and quality of group experience: The more the merrier? *Group Dynamics: Theory, Research, and Practice* 15 (4): 357.

© The Author(s) 2018
G. Derrick, *The Evaluators' Eye*,
https://doi.org/10.1007/978-3-319-63627-6

Auranen, O., and M. Nieminen. 2010. University research funding and publication performance—An international comparison. *Research Policy* 39 (6): 822–834.

Australian Technology Network of Universities. 2015. Innovate and prosper: Ensuring Australia's future competitiveness through university–industry collaboration.

Bailar, J. 2011. Reliability, fairness, objectivity and other inappropriate goals in peer review. *Behavioral and Brain Sciences* 14 (01): 137–138.

Barge, S., and H. Gehlbach. 2012. Using the theory of satisficing to evaluate the quality of survey data. *Research in Higher Education* 53 (2): 182–200.

Baron, R.S. 2005. So right it's wrong: Groupthink and the ubiquitous nature of polarised group decision making. *Advances in Experimental Social Psychology* 37: 219–253.

Bence, V., and C. Oppenhein. 2005. The evolution of the UK's research assessment exercise: Publications, performance and perceptions. *Journal of Educational Administration and History* 37 (2): 137–155.

Bernardin, H.J., H. Hennessey, and J. Peyrefitte. 1995. Age, racial, and gender bias as a function criterion specificity: A test of expert testimony. *Human Resource Management Review* 5 (1): 63–77.

Blau, P. 1964. *Exchange and power in social life.* New York: Wiley.

Boniol, M., P. Autier, P. Boyle, and S. Gandini. 2012. Cutaneous melanoma attributable to sunbed use: Systematic review and meta-analysis. *BMJ* 345: e4757.

Bonner, B.L., and M.R. Baumann. 2012. Leveraging members expertise to improve knowledge transfer and demonstrability in groups. *Journal of Personality and Social Psychology* 102 (2): 337–350.

Bornmann, L. 2012. Measuring the societal impact of research. *EMBO Reports* 13 (8): 673–676.

———. 2013. What is the societal impact of research and how can it be assessed? A literature survey. *Journal of the American Society of Information Science and Technology* 64 (2): 217–233.

Bornmann, L., and H.-D. Daniel. 2005. Committee peer review at an international research foundation: Predictive validity and fairness of selection decisions on post-graduate fellowship applications. *Research Evaluation* 14 (1): 15–20.

Bornmann, L., and W. Marx. 2014. How should the societal impact of research be generated and measured? A proposal for a simple and practicable approach to allow interdisciplinary comparisons. *Scientometrics* 98 (1): 211–219.

Bornmann, L., G. Wallon, and A. Ledin. 2008. Does the committee peer review select the best applicants for funding? An investigation of the selection process for two european molecular biology organization programmes. *PLoSOne* 3 (10): e3480.

Bourdieu, P. 1975. The specificity of the scientific field and the social conditions of the progress of reason. *Information (International Social Science Council)* 14 (6): 19–47.

———. 1984. *Distinction: A social critique of the judgement of taste*. Cambridge, MA: Harvard University Press.

Bourdieu, Pierre. 1997. Capital cultural, escuela y espacio social. *Siglo* xxi.

Buxton, M., and S. Hanney. 1996. How can payback from health services research be assessed? *Journal of Health Services Research* 1 (1): 35–43.

Byron, M. 2005. Simon's revenge: Or, incommensurability and satisficing. *Analysis* 65 (4): 311–315.

Cagan, R. 2013. The San Francisco declaration on research assessment. *Disease Models and Mechanisms* 6: 869–870.

Cetina, K.K., J. Clark, C. Modgil, S. Modgil, I.B. Cohen, K. Duffin, S. Strickland, R. Feldhay, Y. Elkana, and R.K. Merton. 1991. Merton's sociology of science: The first and the last sociology of science? *JSTOR* 20 (4): 522–526.

Chubb, J., and R. Watermeyer. 2016. Artifice or integrity in the marketization of research impact? Investigating the moral economy of (pathways to) impact statements within research funding proposals in the UK and Australia. *Studies in Higher Education* 1–13. https://doi.org/10.1080/03075079.2016.1144182.

Chubin, D.E. 1994. Grants peer review in theory and practice. *Evaluation Review* 18 (1): 20–30.

Chubin, D.E., and E.J. Hackett. 1990. *Peerless science: Peer review and US science policy*. Albany: State University of New York Press.

Cole, S., J.R. Cole, and G.A. Simon. 1981. Chance and consensus in peer review. *Science* 214 (4523): 881–886.

Collins, H. 2004. Interactional expertise as a third kind of knowledge. *Phenomenology and the Cognitive Sciences* 3: 125–143.

———. 2010a. *Tacit and explicit knowledge*. Chicago and London: University of Chicago Press.

———. 2010b. Interdisciplinary peer review and interactional expertise. *Sociologica* 3. https://doi.org/10.2383/33638.

———. 2014. *Are we all scientific experts now?* Cambridge: Polity Press.

Collins, H.M., and R. Evans. 2002. The third wave of science studies: Studies of expertise and experience. *Social Studies of Science* 32 (2): 235–296.

Collins, H., and R. Evans. 2007. *Rethinking expertise*. Chicago and London: University of Chicago Press.

Comer, D.R. 1995. A model of social loafing in real work groups. *Human Relations* 48 (6): 647–667.

Cooper, J., K.A. Kelly, and K. Weaver. 2001. Attitudes, norms, and social groups. In *Blackwell Handbook of social psychology: Group processes*, ed. M.A. Hogg and R.S. Tindale, 259–282. Oxford: Blackwell.

Dahler-Larsen, P. 2007. Evaluation and public management. In *The Oxford Handbook of public management*, ed. E. Ferlie, L.E. Lynn Jr., and C. Pollitt. Oxford: Oxford University Press.

———. 2011. *The evaluation society*. Palo Alto, CA: Stanford University Press.

———. 2012. Constitutive effects as a social accomplishment: A qualitative study of the political in testing. *Education Inquiry* 3 (2): 171–186.

———. 2014. Constitutive effects of performance indicators: Getting beyond unintended consequences. *Public Management Review* 16 (7): 969–986.

de Jong, S.P., J. Smit, and L. van Drooge. 2015. Scientists' response to societal impact policies: A policy paradox. *Science and Public Policy* 43 (1): 102–114.

De Rijcke, S., P.F. Wouters, A.D. Rushforth, T.P. Franssen, and B. Hammarfelt. 2016. Evaluation practices and effects of indicator use—A literature review. *Research Evaluation* 25 (2): 161–169.

Deem, R., S. Hillyard, and M. Reed. 2007. *Knowledge, higher education, and the new managerialism: The changing management of UK universities*. Oxford: Oxford University Press.

Derrick, G., I. Meijer, and E. van Wijk. 2014. Unwrapping "impact" for evaluation: A co-word analysis of the UK REF2014 policy documents using VOSviewer. *Proceedings of the Science and Technology Indicators Conference*.

Derrick, G.E., A.S. Haynes, S. Chapman, and W.D. Hall. 2011. The association between four citation metrics and peer rankings of research influence of Australia researchers in six fields of public health. *PLoSOne* 6: e18521.

Derrick, G.E., and V. Pavone. 2013. Democratising research evaluation: Achieving greater public engagement with bibliometrics-informed peer review. *Science and Public Policy* 40 (5): 563–575.

Derrick, G.E., and G.N. Samuel. 2014. The impact evaluation scale: Group panel processes and outcomes in societal impact evaluation. *Social Science and Medicine*, in press.

———. 2016. The evaluation scale: Exploring decisions about societal impact in peer review panels. *Minerva* 54 (1): 75–97.

———— 2017. The future of societal impact assessment using peer review: Pre-evaluation training, consensus building and inter-reviewer reliability. *Palgrave Communications.* https://doi.org/10.1057/palcomms.2017.40.

Donovan, C. 2011. State of the art in assessing research impact: Introduction to a special issue. *Research Evaluation* 20 (3): 175–179.

Donovan, C., L. Butler, A.J. Butt, T.H. Jones, and S.R. Hanney. 2014. Evaluation of the impact of National Breast Cancer Foundation-funded research. *The Medical Journal of Australia* 200 (4): 214–218.

Eckberg, D.L. 1991. When nonreliability of reviews indicates solid science. *Behavioural and Brain Sciences* 14 (1): 145–146.

Epley, N., and T. Gilovich. 2006. The anchoring-and-adjustment heuristic: Why the adjustments are insufficient. *Psychological Science* 17 (4): 311–318.

Epley, N., B. Keysar, L. Van Boven, and T. Gilovich. 2004. Perspective taking as egocentric anchoring and adjustment. *Journal of Personality and Social Psychology* 87 (3): 327.

Esser, J. 1998. Alive and well after 25 years: A review of groupthink research. *Organizational Behavior and Human Decision Processes* 73 (2/3): 116–141.

Evans, Robert, and Harry Collins. 2010. Interactional expertise and the imitation game. In *Trading zones and interactional expertise,* ed. M. Gorman, 53–70. Cambridge: MIT Press.

Faigman, D.L., J. Monahan, and C. Slobogin. 2014. Group to individual (G2i) inference in scientific expert testimony. *The University of Chicago Law Review* 81 (2): 417–480.

Fernández-Zubieta, A., A. Geuna, and C. Lawson. 2015. Mobility and productivity of research scientists1. *Global Mobility of Research Scientists: The Economics of Who Goes Where and Why* 105.

Finkel, A. 2015. Research Engagement for Australia (REA): Measuring research engagement between universities and end users. Presentation to Universities Australia.

Fogelholm, M., S. Leppinen, A. Auvinen, J. Raitanen, A. Nuutinen, and K. Väänänen. 2012. Panel discussion does not improve reliability of peer review for medical research grant proposals. *Journal of Clinical Epidemiology* 65 (1): 47–52.

Franceschet, M., and A. Costantini. 2011. The first Italian research assessment exercise: A bibliometric perspective. *Journal of Informetrics* 5 (2): 275–291.

Frodeman, R., and J. Parker. 2009. Intellectual merit and broader impact: The National Science Foundation's broader impacts criterion and the question of peer review. *Social Epistemology* 23 (3–4): 337–345.

Gallo, S.A., J.H. Sullivan, and S.R. Glisson. 2016. The influence of peer reviewer expertise on the evaluation of research funding applications. *PLoS One* 11 (10): e0165147.

Geuna, A., and M. Piolatto. 2016. Research assessment in the UK and Italy: Costly and difficult, but probably worth it (at least for a while). *Research Policy* 45 (1): 260–271.

Gibbons, M., C. Limoges, H. Nowotny, S. Schwartzman, and P. Scott. 1994. *The new production of knowledge: The dynamics of science and research in contemporary societies.* London: SAGE.

Giraudeau, B., C. Leyrat, A. Le Gouge, J. Leger, and A. Caille. 2011. Peer review of grant applications: A simple method to identify proposals with discordant reviews. *PLoSOne* 6 (11): e27557.

Grant, J., P.-B. Brutscher, S. Kirk, L. Butler, and S. Wooding. 2010. *Capturing research impacts: A review of International practice.* Documented briefing. RAND Corporation.

Greene, J.C. 1997. Evaluation as advocacy. *Evaluation Practice* 18: 25–36.

———. 2000. Challenges in practicing deliberative democratic evaluation. *New Directions for Evaluation* 2000 (85): 13–26.

Greenhalgh, T., J. Raftery, S. Hanney, and M. Glover. 2016. Research impact: A narrative review. *BMC Medicine* 14 (1): 78.

Hackett, E.J., and D. E. Chubin. 2003. *Peer review for the 21st century: Applications to education research.* Ed. National Research Council. Washington, DC.

Hall, D., and S. Buzwell. 2013. The problem of free-riding in group projects: Looking beyond social loafing as reason for non-contribution. *Active Learning in Higher Education* 14 (1): 37–49.

Harkins, S., B. Latane, and K. Williams. 1980. Social loafing: Allocating effort or taking it easy? *Journal of Experimental Social Psychology* 16: 457–465.

Harkins, S., and R.E. Petty. 1982. Effects of task difficulty and task uniqueness on social loafing. *Journal of Personality and Social Psychology* 43: 1214–1229.

Harnad, S. 1985. Rational disagreement in peer review. *Science, Technology, & Human Values* 10 (3): 55–62.

Haynes, A.S., G.E. Derrick, S. Chapman, S. Redman, W.D. Hall, J. Gillespie, and H. Sturk. 2011. From "our world" to the "real world": Exploring the views and behaviour of policy-influential Australian public health researchers. *Social Science & Medicine* 72: 1047–1055.

HEFCE. 2010a. REF2014: Panel criteria and working methods. http://www.ref.ac.uk/media/ref/content/pub/panelcriteriaandworkingmethods/01_12.pdf. Accessed 1 Mar 2016.

———. 2010b. Research Excellence Framework impact pilot exercise: Finding of the expert panels. H. E. F. C. f. E. (HEFCE).

———. 2010c. Units of assessment and recruitment of expert panels. REF 2014.

———. 2011. Assessment framework and guidance on submissions. REF 2014.

Hemlin, S., and S.B. Rasmussen. 2006. The shift in academic quality control. *Science, Technology, & Human Values* 31 (2): 173–198.

Herbst, M. 2007. *Financing public universities.* New York: Springer.

Hicks, D. 2012. Performance-based university research funding systems. *Research policy* 41 (2): 251–261.

Hicks, D., P.F. Wouters, L. Waltman, S. De Rijcke, and I. Rafols. 2015. The Leiden Manifesto for research metrics. *Nature* 520 (7548): 429.

Holbrook, J.B. 2010. The use of societal impacts considerations in grant proposal peer review: A comparison of five models. *Technology & Innovation* 12 (3): 213–224.

Holbrook, J.B., and R. Frodeman. 2011. Peer review and the exante assessment of societal impacts. *Research Evaluation* 20 (3): 239–246.

Holbrook, J.B., and S. Hrotic. 2013. Blue skies, impacts, and peer review. *A Journal on Research Policy & Evaluation.* https://doi.org/10.13130/2282-5398/2914.

Huutoniemi, K. 2010. *Evaluating interdisciplinary research.* Oxford: Oxford University Press.

———. 2012. Communicating and compromising on disciplinary expertise in the peer review of research proposals. *Social Studies of Science* 42 (6): 897–921.

Ingham, A., G. Levinger, J. Graves, and v. Peckham. 1974. The Ringelmann effect: Studies of group size and group performance. *Journal of Experimental Social Psychology* 10: 371–384.

Ingwersen, P., and B. Larsen. 2014. Influence of a performance indicator on Danish research production and citation impact 2000–12. *Scientometrics* 101 (2): 1325–1344.

Janis, I.L. 1982. *Groupthink: Psychological studies of policy decisions and fiascoes.* Boston, MA: Houghton Mifflin Company.

Jasanoff, S. 1990. *The fifth branch: Science advisors as policymakers.* Cambridge, MA: Harvard University Press.

———. 2003. (No?) Accounting for expertise. *Science and Public Policy* 30 (3): 157–162.

———. 2012. *Science and public reason.* London and New York: Routledge (Taylor & Francis Group).

Johnston, S.C., J.D. Rootenberg, S. Katrak, W.S. Smith, and J.S. Elkins. 2006. Effect of a US National Institutes of Health programme of clinical trials on public health and costs. *Lancet* 367 (9519): 1319–1327.

Kadar, N. 2010. Systemic bias in peer review: Suggested causes, potential remedies. *Journal of Laparoendoscopic & Advanced Surgical Techniques* 20 (2): 123–128.

Karau, S.J., and J.W. Hart. 1998. Group cohesiveness and social loafing: Effects of social interaction manipulation on individual motivation within groups. *Group Dynamics: Theory, Research, and Practice* 2 (3): 185–191.

Kerr, N.L. 1983. Motivation losses in small groups: A social dilemma analysis. *Journal of Personality and Social Psychology* 45 (4): 819–828.

Kerr, N.L., R.J. MacCoun, and G.P. Kramer. 1996. Bias in judgement: Comparing individuals and groups. *Psychological Review* 103: 687–719.

King's College London and Digital Science. 2015. *The nature, scale and beneficiaries of research impact: An initial analysis of Research Excellence Framework (REF) 2014 impact case studies.* King's College London and Digital Science.

Knorr-Cetina, K.D. 1983. *The ethnographic study of scientific work: Towards a constructivist interpretation of science.* London: Sage.

———. 1991. Epistemic cultures: Forms of reason in science. *History of Political Economy* 23 (1): 105–122.

Knott, M. 2015. *Academic publications to become less important when funding university research.* Sydney: Sydney Morning Herald.

Kravitz, D.A., and B. Martin. 1986. Ringelmann rediscovered: The original article. *Journal of Personality and Social Psychology* 50 (5): 936–941.

Kuruvilla, S., N. Mays, and G. Walt. 2007. Describing the impact of health services and policy research. *Journal of Health Services Research & Policy* 12 (suppl 1): 23–31.

Lamont, M. 2009. *How professors think: Inside the curious world of academic judgement.* Cambridge, MA: Harvard University Press.

Lamont, M., and K. Huutoniemi. 2011a. Comparing customary rules of fairness: Evaluative practices in various types of peer review panels. In *Social knowledge in the making*, ed. C. Camie, N. Gross, and M. Lamont, 209–232. Chicago, IL: University of Chicago.

———. 2011b. Opening the black box of evaluation: How quality is recognized by peer review panels. *Bulletin SAGW* 2: 47–49.

Langfeldt, L. 2001. The decision-making constraints and processes of grant peer review, and their effects on the review outcome. *Social Studies of Science* 31 (6): 820–841.

————. 2004. Expert panels evaluating research: Decision-making and sources of bias. *Research Evaluation* 13 (1): 51–62.

————. 2006. The policy challenges of peer review: Managing bias, conflict of interests and multidisciplinary assessments. *Research Evaluation* 15 (1): 31–41.

Langfeldt, L., and S. Kyvik. 2011. Researchers as evaluators: Tasks, tensions and politics. *Higher Education* 62: 199–212.

Latane, B., K. Williams, and S. Harkins. 1979. Many hands make light the work: The causes and consequences of social loafing. *Journal of Personality and Social Psychology* 37 (6): 822–832.

Laudel, G. 2006. Conclave in the Tower of Babel: How peers review interdisciplinary research proposals. *Research Evaluation* 15 (1): 57–68.

Laudel, G., and G. Origgi. 2006. *Introduction to a special issue on the assessment of interdisciplinary research*. Oxford: Oxford University Press.

Lee, C.J. 2012. A Kuhnian critique of psychometric research on peer review. *Philosophy of Science* 79 (5): 859–870.

Lee, C.J., C.R. Sugimoto, G. Zhang, and B. Cronin. 2013. Bias in peer review. *Journal of the American Society for Information Science and Technology* 64 (1): 2–17.

Leisyte, L., and J.R. Dee. 2012. Understanding academic work in a changing institutional environment. In *Higher education: Handbook of theory and research*, ed. J.D. Smart, 123–206. New York: Springer.

Levi, D. 2015. *Group dynamics for teams*. London: Sage Publications.

Luukkonen, T. 2012. Conservatism and risk-taking in peer review: Emerging ERC practices. *Research Evaluation* 21: 48–60.

Manville, C., S. Guthrie, M.-L. Henham, B. Garrod, S. Sousa, A. Kirtkey, S. Castle-Clarke, and T. Ling. 2015. *Assessing impact submissions for REF2014: An evaluation*. Cambridge: RAND Europe.

Mark, M.M., G.T. Henry, and G. Julnes. 2000. *Evaluation: An integrated framework for understanding, guiding and improving policies and programs*. San Francisco, CA: Jossey-Bass.

Mark, M.M., and R.L. Shotland. 1985. Stakeholder-based evaluation and value judgments. *Evaluation Review* 9 (5): 605–626.

Marsh, H.W., U.W. Jayasinghe, and N.W. Bond. 2008. Improving the peer-review process for grant applications: Reliability, validity, bias and generalizability. *American Psychologist* 63 (3): 160–168.

Martin, B.R. 2011. The Research Excellence Framework and the 'impact agenda': Are we creating a Frankenstein monster? *Research Evaluation* 20 (3): 247–254.

Mayo, N.E., J. Brophy, M.S. Goldberg, M.B. Klein, S. Miller, R.W. Platt, and J. Ritchie. 2006. Peering at peer review revealed high degree of chance associated with funding of grant applications. *Journal of Clinical Epidemiology* 59 (8): 842–848.

Merton, R.K. 1973. *The sociology of science: Theoretical and empirical investigations*. Chicago: University of Chicago press.

Molas-Gallart, J., and P. Tang. 2011. Tracing 'productive interactions' to identify social impacts: An example from the social sciences. *Research Evaluation* 20 (3): 219–226.

Mollick, E., and R. Nanda. 2015. Wisdom or madness? Comparing crowds with expert evaluation in funding the arts. *Management Science* 62 (6): 1533–1553.

Mow, K.E. 2010. *Inside the black box: Research grant funding and peer review in Australian research councils*. Saarbrücken: Lambert Academic Publishing.

Norman, R. 2002. Managing through measurement or meaning? Lessons from experience with New Zealand's public sector performance management systems. *International Review of Administrative Sciences* 68 (4): 619–628.

Nowotny, H., P. Scott, and M. Gibbons. 2001. *Re-thinking science: Knowledge and the public in an age of uncertainty*. Argentina: SciELO.

Olbrecht, M., and L. Bornmann. 2010. Panel peer review of grant applications: What do we know from research in social psychology on judgement and decision making in groups? *Research Evaluation* 19 (4): 293–304.

Oortwijn, W.J., S.R. Hanney, A. Ligtvoet, S. Hoorens, S. Wooding, J. Grant, M.J. Buxton, and L.M. Bouter. 2008. Assessing the impact of health technology assessment in the Netherlands. *International Journal of Technology Assessment in Health Care* 24 (03): 259–269.

Petty, R.E., S.G. Harkins, K. Williams, and B. Latane. 1977. The effects of group size on cognitive effort and evaluation. *Personality and Social Psychology Bulletin* 3: 579–582.

Pielke, R.A., and R. Byerly. 1998. Beyond basic and applied. *Physics Today* 51 (2): 42–46.

Pier, E.L., J. Raclaw, A. Kaatz, M. Brauer, M. Carnes, M.J. Nathan, and C.E. Ford. 2017. 'Your comments are meaner than your score': Score calibration talk influence intra- and inter-panel variability during scientific grant peer review. *Research Evaluation* 26 (1): 1–14.

Porter, A.L., and F.A. Rossini. 1985. Peer review of interdisciplinary research proposals. *Science, Technology, & Human Values* 10 (3): 33–38.

Porter, R. 2005. What do grant reviewers really want, anyway? *Journal of Research Administration* 36 (2): 5–13,13.

Ringlemann, M. 1913. Recherches sur les moteurs animes: Travail de l'homme. *Annales de l'Institut National Agronomique* 12 (1): 1–40.

Rinia, E.J., T.N. van Leeuwen, H.G. van Vuren, and A.F.J. van Raan. 1998. Comparative analysis of a set of bibliometric indicators and central peer review criteria: Evaluation of condensed matter physics in the Netherlands. *Research Policy* 27 (1): 95–107.

Roumbanis, L. 2016. Academic judgments under uncertainty: A study of collective anchoring effects in Swedish Research Council panel groups. *Social Studies of Science* 47: 1–22.

Roy, R. 1985. Funding science: The real defects of peer review and an alternative to it. *Science, Technology, & Human Values* 10 (3): 73–81.

Salter, A.J., and B.R. Martin. 2001. The economic benefits of publicly funded basic research: A critical review. *Research policy* 30 (3): 509–532.

Samuel, G.N., and G.E. Derrick. 2015. Societal impact evaluation: Exploring evaluator perceptions of the characterization of impact under the REF2014. *Research Evaluation* 24 (3): 229–241.

Sandstrom, U., U. Heyman, and P. Van den Besselaar. 2014. The complex relationahip between competitive funding and performance. In *Context counts: Pathways to master big and little data – STI*, ed. E. Noyons, 523–533. Leiden: CWTS. https://doi.org/10.13140/2.1.5036.6728.

Schmid, A.A. 2004. *Conflict and cooperation: Institutional and behavioural economics*. Malden, MA: Blackwell.

Schwartz, B., A. Ward, J. Monterosso, S. Lyubomirsky, K. White, and D.R. Lehman. 2002. Maximizing versus satisficing: Happiness is a matter of choice. *Journal of Personality and Social Psychology* 83 (5): 1178.

Simms, A., and T. Nichols. 2014. Social loafing: A review of the literature. *Journal of Management Policy and Practice* 15 (1): 58.

Simon, H.A. 1957. *Models of man*. New York: Wiley.

———. 1972. Theories of bounded rationality. *Decision and Organization* 1 (1): 161–176.

Simon, H.A., and A.C. Stedry. 1968. Psychology and economics. In *Handbook of social psychology*, ed. G. Lindzey and E. Aronson. Reading, MA: Addision-Wesley.

Sinclair, C., and P. Foley. 2009. Skin cancer prevention in Australia. *British Journal of Dermatology* 161 (s3): 116–123.

Sivertsen, G., and J. Schneider. 2012. Evaluering av den bibliometriske forskningsindikator.

Smith, R. 2001. Measuring the social impact of research—Difficult but necessary. *British Medical Journal* 323: 528. https://doi.org/10.1136/bmj.323.7312.528.

Smith, S., V. Ward, and A. House. 2011. 'Impact' in the proposals for the UK's Research Excellence Framework: Shifting the boundaries of academic autonomy. *Research Policy* 40 (10): 1369–1379.

Solomon, M. 2006. Groupthink versus the wisdom of crowds: The social epistemology of deliberation and dissent. *The Southern Journal of Philosophy* 44 (S1): 28–42.

Sorkin, R.D., S. Luan, and J. Itzkowitz. 2001. *Rational models of social conformity and social loafing. Subjective probability, utility and decision making conference.* Amsterdam: Netherlands.

Spaapen, J., and L. Van Drooge. 2011. Introducing 'productive interactions' in social impact assessment. *Research Evaluation* 20 (3): 211–218.

Stern, N. 2016. *Building on success and learning from experience: An independent review of the Research Excellence Framework.* Department for Business, Energy & Industrial Strategy.

Sunstein, C.R., and R. Hastie. 2015. *Wiser: Getting beyond groupthink to make groups smarter.* Boston, MA: Harvard Business Review Press.

Taylor, J. 2011. The assessment of research quality in UK universities: Peer review or metrics? *British Journal of Management* 22 (2): 202–217.

Technopolis. 2010. REF research impact pilot exercise lessons-learned project: Feedback on pilot submissions.

Thaler Richard, H., and R. Sunstein Cass. 2008. *Nudge: Improving decisions about health, wealth, and happiness.* New Haven, CT: Yale University Press.

Travis, G.D.L., and H.M. Collins. 1991. New light on old boys: Cognitive and institutional particularism in the peer review system. *Science, Technology, & Human Values* 16 (3): 322–341.

van Arensbergen, P. 2014. *Talent proof. Selection processes in research funding and careers.* Den Haag: Rathenau Instituut.

van Arensbergen, P., I. van der Weijden, and P. van den Besselaar. 2014. The selection of talent as a group process. A literature review on the social dynamics of decision making in grant panels. *Research Evaluation* 23 (4): 298–311.

van den Besselaar, P., and L. Leydesdorff. 2009. Past performance, peer review and project selection: A case study in the social and behavioral sciences. *Research Evaluation* 18 (4): 273–288.

Van der Meulen, Barend, and Arie Rip. 2000. Evaluation of societal quality of public sector research in the Netherlands. *Research Evaluation* 9 (1): 11–25.

Vedung, E. 1997. *Public policy and program evaluation.* New Brunswick and London: Transaction Publishers.

Viner, N., P. Powell, and R. Green. 2004. Institutionalized biases in the award of research grants: A preliminary analysis revisiting the principle of accumulative advantage. *Research Policy* 33 (3): 443–454.

von Schomberg, R. 2013. A vision of responsible innovation. In *Responsible innovation*, ed. R. Owen, M. Heintz, and J. Bessant. London: John Wiley.

VSNU, KNAW, and NWO. 2015. *Standard evaluation protocol 2015–2021: Protocol for research assessments in the Netherlands.* The Netherlands: Koninklijke Nederlandse Akademie van Wetenschappen.

Watermeyer, R. 2015. Lost in the 'third space': The impact of public engagement in higher education on academic identity, research practice and career progression. *European Journal of Higher Education* 5 (3): 331–347.

———. 2016. Impact in the REF: Issues and obstacles. *Studies in Higher Education* 41 (2): 199–214.

Watermeyer, R., and A. Hedgecoe. 2016. Selling 'impact': Peer reviewer projections of what is needed and what counts in REF impact case studies. A retrospective analysis. *Journal of Education Policy* 31 (5): 651–665.

Williams, K., S. Harkins, and B. Latane. 1981. Identifiability as a deterrent to social loafing: Two cheering experiments. *Journal of Experimental Social Psychology* 40: 303–311.

Williams, K.D., and K.L. Sommer. 1997. Social ostracism by coworkers: Does rejection lead to loafing or compensation? *Personality and Social Psychology Bulletin* 23 (7): 693–706.

Willmott, H. 2011. Journal list fetishism and the perversion of scholarship: Reactivity and the ABS list. *Organization* 18 (4): 429–442.

Wilsdon, J. 2016. *The metric tide: Independent review of the role of metrics in research assessment and management.* London: SAGE.

Wilson, T.D. 2005. Evolution in information behavior modelling: Wilson's model. In *Theories of Information behavior*, ed. K.E. Fisher, S. Erdelez, and L. McKechnie. Medford, NJ: Information Today.

Wooding, S., S. Hanney, M. Buxton, and J. Grant. 2005. Payback arising from research funding: Evaluation of the Arthritis Research Campaign. *Rheumatology* 44 (9): 1145–1156.

Wooding, S., S. Hanney, A. Pollitt, M. Buxton, and J. Grant. 2011. Project retrosight: Understanding the returns from cardiovascular and stroke research: the policy report. *Rand Health Quarterly* 1 (1): 16.

www.ref.ac.uk. 2014. Consistency across UOAs: REF2014. http://www.ref.ac.uk/2014/results/analysis/consistencyacrossuoas/. Accessed 20 Sep 2016.

Index[1]

[1]Note: Page number followed by 'n' refer to notes.

© The Author(s) 2018
G. Derrick, *The Evaluators' Eye*,
https://doi.org/10.1007/978-3-319-63627-6

Printed by Printforce, the Netherlands